A TALE OF
TWO COUNTRIES

*How the Great Demographic
Imbalance is Pulling Canada Apart*

RICHARD SAILLANT

Foreword by Donald J. Savoie

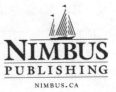

NIMBUS
PUBLISHING

NIMBUS.CA

Nimbus Publishing Limited
3731 Mackintosh St, Halifax, NS, B3K 5A5
(902) 455-4286
nimbus.ca

Printed and bound in Canada

NB1244

Cover photo: iStock Photography
Design: John van der Woude, JVDW Designs

Library and Archives Canada Cataloguing in Publication

Saillant, Richard, author
A tale of two countries : how the great demographic imbalance is pulling Canada apart / written by Richard Saillant ; foreword by Donald J. Savoie.

ISBN 978-1-77108-447-5 (paperback)

1. Canada—Population. 2. Age distribution (Demography)—Canada. 3. Population aging—Canada. I. Savoie, Donald J., 1947-, writer of foreword II. Title.

HB3529.S23 2016   304.60971   C2016-903737-1

Canada ❦ Canada Council   Conseil des arts
for the Arts   du Canada

Nimbus Publishing acknowledges the financial support for its publishing activities from the Government of Canada through the Canada Book Fund (CBF) and the Canada Council for the Arts, and from the Province of Nova Scotia. We are pleased to work in partnership with the Province of Nova Scotia to develop and promote our creative industries for the benefit of all Nova Scotians.

For Eli and Johanna

CONTENTS

LIST OF TABLES & CHARTS

I know you feel reluctant to make recommendations that our data cannot support. With this I am in complete accord. Nevertheless it is methodologically impossible to make a recommendation completely supported by data; in that case you would have a description. In other words recommendations always involve an element of interpretation—you are always somewhat out on a limb. Now I believe that the recommendations we are making really are a minimum. If we water it down any further it will be unassailable but also meaningless. As our study develops we may amend some conclusions. There is nothing wrong with this. If one waits until one can say everything before saying anything, one will wind up saying nothing.

—Henry Kissinger to C. Darwin Stolzenbach,
February 7, 1952[1]

FOREWORD

Richard Saillant has an important message for all Canadians that should resonate in every region. This book invites us to reflect on what will be one of the country's most demanding challenges for the next two decades.

As he did so well in his first book, Richard Saillant goes about his research in a detached, clinical fashion. He always speaks truth to power and to citizens in his work. Canadians who believe in evidence-based policy advice will find comfort in this book. Every argument is based on solid evidence and data that are available to everyone. He has, however, assembled the evidence in a highly accessible fashion to enable Canadians to appreciate and debate the challenges that lie ahead. An aging population—a phenomenon that will affect the entire country but eastern provinces most—the impact on both economic growth and the provision of public services, and the difficult fiscal situation confronting all governments add up to a powerful brew that all politicians will have to address both at the national and provincial levels.

There are things the reader should know about Richard Saillant: He is a deeply committed Canadian, an author of integrity who takes great pride in writing without fear or favour. He, unlike many social scientists, deliberately stays away from consulting contracts. I recall a media outlet offering him an honorarium to participate in a planned event. He accepted the invitation but declined the honorarium. He explained that he was already being paid and saw no need to be paid more to help citizens better understand complex public policy issues.

I invite the reader to reflect on the findings of this book and on what they mean for our country. Richard Saillant raises fundamental questions about what it means to be Canadian, how the federation has evolved since the Rowell-Sirois report, and how we go forward. This is a very timely book for the country.

—Donald J. Savoie
Canada Research Chair in Public Administration
and Governance, Université de Moncton

PREFACE

This book is an outgrowth of a previous one, *Over the Cliff? Acting Now to Avoid New Brunswick's Bankruptcy*. My New Brunswick readers will recognize certain extracts as well as the book's broad thrust, which is deeply anchored in demographics. I do hope, however, that they will gain a better understanding of why I have been arguing that our province is in a much tighter spot fiscally and economically than most of the rest of the country.

It is all too easy to blame people for their own fate and to attribute a special virtue to those who fare well, even when their fortune is due to chance. A key aim of the book is to demonstrate that much of what is happening to Canada's poorer, faster-aging provinces has little to do with the presupposed character flaws of their residents. The current residents of the Maritimes or Newfoundland and Labrador cannot be held responsible for how the baby boom unfolded, nor should they be blamed for the forces that have shaped their region's economic geography since Confederation. But they will have to live with the consequences. It may be tempting for many to rush to the conclusion that those living in less fortunate provinces should stop complaining and simply pull themselves up by their bootstraps. That remedy is no doubt needed, but it will not stop the devastation resulting from the twin forces of economic and demographic gravity that I discuss in this book. Let us hope the upcoming celebration of Canada's 150th anniversary provides an opportunity to reflect on these forces that have shaped and will continue to shape our destiny as a country.

I owe a debt of gratitude to many people.

I was proud to lead the rebranding of our institute in 2015 by renaming it in honour of its founder, Donald J. Savoie. Donald is known to many as one of this country's most accomplished scholars of public administration. I know him first and foremost as a proud Maritimer. In politics as much as in almost everything else in life, where you stand depends on where you sit. Donald is the single most important voice in academia who tells the Maritime story. Every region needs a Donald Savoie to tell its story to all Canadians in a powerful and honest way, because clearly the Canadian Senate has not been up to the task. I want to thank Donald again for his generosity and his support for my work.

Although writing is by nature a solitary act, what one writes is shaped by the generous contributions of others. It is impossible to list everyone who has nurtured and challenged the views I hold in this book, but I do wish to single out a few of them. Thomas Courchene, professor emeritus in economics and policy studies at Queen's University, reviewed a draft of my manuscript. It is the mark of a distinguished and generous scholar to write that a book "must be published" while not agreeing with its recommendations. Professor Courchene is such an individual. Sébastien Breau, professor of economic geography at McGill University, also generously provided detailed feedback, and so did Roger Ouellette, professor of political science at the Université de Moncton. Both are fellows at our institute. Finally, I wish to thank an anonymous reader whose comments were very useful in revising the manuscript. I remain, however, solely and fully responsible for any errors and deficiencies.

Many other people have provided an invaluable contribution to this book. Thanks to Paula Sarson, it reads better and has fewer typos. Noeline Bridge has meticulously produced a detailed and very useful index. Réjean Ouellette's excellent work has made this book available in both official languages. Céline Basque ran interference at the office so I could concentrate on my writing and forced me to clarify many of my thoughts. Valery Martial Tankou Kamela, a promising young scholar from our institute, helped me keep factual inaccuracies to what I hope are a minimum. Numerous analysts at Statistics Canada have responded to our queries with diligence and professionalism. While I am on the topic of Statistics Canada, I should note that the data from the agency in this book were current as of February 2016 but that it may revise its numbers from time to time. Finally, Whitney Moran and her team from Nimbus Publishing have given this book much of its look and feel and handled its production in a professional manner from start to finish.

On a personal note, I want to thank Kathy, Claudie, and William for their patience and for bringing love and joy to my life. This is word-for-word the way I thanked them in *Over the Cliff?* Nothing has changed, and I am grateful for that.

This book is dedicated to Eli and Johanna, two beautiful and brave children of dear friends of Kathy's and mine, who have survived serious illnesses; they, along with the staff who have treated them, have inspired me in no small part to write it.

Nothing is eternal, not even the baby boom generation. Canada's Great Demographic Imbalance, too, shall pass. My hope is that all children from coast-to-coast-to-coast who, like Eli and Johanna, need quality services from our free, universal public health-care systems will continue to access them long after the Great Demographic Imbalance is behind us.

INTRODUCTION

In twenty or thirty years, Canadian schoolchildren and immigrants may well be taught that 2011 was one of the most significant years in our country's history. Indeed, 2011 is the signpost for a phenomenon that could reshape Canada's politics and challenge our sense of what it means to be Canadian. It is the year when the first baby boomers turned sixty-five.

Of course, population aging is hardly a new topic. Canadians have been told for many decades that their country is aging. By now, most of us are familiar with what an aging population means—or at least we think we are. As Canada's population becomes older, the thinking goes, there will be proportionally fewer of us working to support us all. As a result, economic growth will slow down at the very moment that we will have to spend more to support our growing ranks of seniors. Understandably, this demographic crunch has raised concerns about the affordability of Canada's welfare state. Numerous studies have looked into this issue. Generally, however, the findings appear reassuring: a dynamic, resource-rich, and immigration-friendly country such as Canada should be able to withstand the shock of an aging population on its health-care system and social safety net. Making our way through the coming demographic crunch will not be easy, but it should not fundamentally change the face of the country.[1]

I am not so sure. Most of these studies overlook a critical point. Canada is not a unitary country like France. It does not have a single health-care system, but rather ten different ones (thirteen with the territories). To assess whether Canada can navigate its way through the demographic storm ahead, we need to look at the financial positions of provinces individually. And here the picture is not encouraging: the contrast is stark between have and have-less provinces, and it is about to get starker. There are at least a couple of reasons behind this state of affairs. First, some provinces have relatively healthy balance sheets, while others are heavily in debt. The more fundamental problem, however, is how unevenly Canada's various regions are aging.

Canada is a loose collection of settlements spread over a continental landscape. This makes a tricky task of drawing conclusions about the country based on national data. For example, if the national economy is growing at a good yet regionally unbalanced pace, does this mean Canada is doing well? If some provinces have their heads in the oven and others have their feet in the freezer, is the temperature of Canada's body just about right? Although some may argue the answer is yes, no serious analyst would claim this imbalance is inconsequential. The same applies to demographics. National trends tell only part of the story about Canada's aging population. Also of importance to the country's future is what I call the Great Demographic Imbalance: the highly uneven pace at which Canada's regions are aging. The farther east one travels, the older the population and the faster it is aging.

Canada's Great Demographic Imbalance is nothing new; it has in fact been unfolding steadily over the past half century, as we shall see. Until recently, though, it did not matter much that Canada was not aging evenly, mainly because getting older did not mean working less and thus creating less new wealth. Indeed, until the turn of this decade, the whole country was enjoying the demographic dividend that flowed from the fact all baby boomers were still of working age. This was a time when not only demography was making its peak contribution to prosperity, but also the relative economic burden of caring for dependents (the youth and senior populations) was at its lowest. The picture started to change a few years ago, when the demographic tide that lifted all provincial boats began receding. As the tide continues to ebb over the next two decades or so, it will affect the economies and public purses of older provinces much more than younger ones. And this could spell trouble for the federation. Here's why.

Canada's national unity is relatively fragile. Compared to countries such as France or the United States, Canada has a weak national identity. Canada was not born amid revolutionary fervour and such rallying cries as "Life, Liberty and the pursuit of Happiness" or "*Liberté, Égalité, Fraternité.*" Instead, our London rulers gave us "peace, order and good government." It can hardly be said either that all colonies were excited with the Confederation project.[2] With such an uninspiring start, the Fathers of Confederation had their work cut out in carving a nation from isolated British colonies with strong local loyalties spread over half a continent.

Nation-building has always been about winning the hearts and minds of citizens. In this country, it has been a long, tortuous journey to a modest destination. In the early days of our federation, nation-building took on a literal meaning: building a nation through major public works—mostly railways and canals—to unite the provinces and open the great expanses of the Prairies to settlement. Later, in the twentieth century, nation-building efforts shifted from infrastructure to social policy. As the welfare state expanded amid the growing affluence of the postwar era, social policy became central to defining Canadian identity. Those who doubt this should take a look at the results of polls and other consultations that have asked citizens what it means to be Canadian. Take, for instance, the 2004 CBC prime-time television show in which viewers were asked to vote for the greatest Canadian of all time. There was no shortage of exceptional individuals to choose from. Viewers could have opted for icons such as John A. Macdonald, Terry Fox, or Maurice Richard. Instead, they picked Tommy Douglas, the Father of medicare.[3] Universal, taxpayer-funded health-care services are a fact of life in most Western countries. Citizens in those countries may cherish their services, but nowhere do they define themselves as a nation through them as we do in Canada.[4]

The prominent role of social policy in shaping Canadian identity is also in full display in how Ottawa spends. At the time of Confederation, social policy was considered a local matter that fell under provincial jurisdiction. Until shortly before the Great Depression, Ottawa spent very little on social affairs. Today roughly one out of two federal dollars goes toward social programs, whether delivered directly by the federal government or via provinces and territories.[5]

Why did Ottawa become so involved over the years in what were initially provincial matters? Why did Pierre Trudeau argue as a scholar that spending by the federal government should be confined to areas under its jurisdiction but completely ignored his own advice as prime minister?[6] The answers to these questions are complex, but evidently Ottawa would not have become so actively involved in social policy had it not proved rewarding at the polls. As social policy took on a central importance to Canadians, federal parties competed with one another to define the "national interest," whether in health care, income assistance, or higher education. Ottawa's dedication to ensuring a minimum national standard even found its way into the Constitution in 1982, when an "equalization" principle was enshrined that commits Parliament and the federal government to ensure all provinces have sufficient revenues to provide comparable services at comparable levels of taxation.

In short, the idea that being Canadian means having access to roughly the same social services regardless of where one lives is one of Canada's few nation-building success stories. Those who remain skeptical of this and require hard numbers to be swayed may wish to take a look at the data on provincial spending. If citizens have similar aspirations across the country, one would expect that provincial governments would spend roughly the same amounts on public services.[7] The data largely confirm this. Take, for instance Alberta, Canada's richest province, and the three Maritime provinces which occupy the bottom rungs of Canada's gross domestic product (GDP) ladder. Alberta is twice as rich as New Brunswick, Nova Scotia, and Prince Edward Island, yet all four spend roughly the same amount per person on public services.

Of course, this is made possible by federal transfer payments. But that is not the entire story: residents in poorer provinces also pay larger shares of their incomes in taxes. The provincial fiscal burden is nearly two-thirds higher in the Maritimes than in Alberta.[8] In other words, rather than accept less from their provincial governments to reflect their lesser means, residents in poorer provinces are willing to pay more. None of us like to pay for things we don't want. If residents of poorer provinces are willing to shoulder a greater fiscal burden than those in richer provinces just to get similar services in return, it is only reasonable to assume it is because this is the level of services to which they have come to aspire as Canadians.

In the years ahead, the Great Demographic Imbalance could deal a mortal blow to Canada's shared experience of citizenship through social policy. As this book will show, at least this much is clear: unless major changes are brought to how wealth is redistributed across Canada, poorer provinces will not be able to maintain their much-cherished social programs—particularly their health-care systems—at comparable levels to those of richer provinces. Without further assistance, poorer, faster-aging provinces will most likely have to make decisions inconsistent with the idea that there is no second-class citizenship in this country.

Canada built its social safety net and expanded the transfer payment system that sustains it in good economic times. It is fairly easy to be generous in prosperity; however, we quite naturally tend to look to our own backyards first in more difficult times. And although it will hit poorer provinces hardest, population aging will also affect richer provinces. It is thus at a time when richer provinces will also feel the pinch of demographics that poorer provinces will be asking for more money in federal transfers.

If recent developments are any indication, richer provinces may prove in no mood to provide more help to their poorer counterparts. The federal government's ability and willingness to redistribute wealth have declined in recent years. In relation to the size of the national economy, Ottawa now takes in one-fifth less in taxes than it did at the turn of the millennium.[9] The federal government has also taken a much less redistributive stance. Equalization payments have been capped. The Canada Social Transfer (cst) and the Canada Health Transfer (cht) no longer provide more money to poorer provinces; money is now allocated on a per capita basis. This shift obviously benefits faster-growing provinces west of the Ottawa River. Tellingly, the province that gained the most from changing the cst and the cht to a per capita basis—Alberta—is also Canada's richest.

For some, it may be tempting to blame the Harper government for having loosened the "tax-and-spend" ties they believe bind us as a country. It may be equally tempting to conclude the Harper years were simply a digression and things will go back to what they were before, now that Canadians have voted out his Conservative party. But when it comes to shifting more money from richer to poorer provinces, all major federal parties have so far remained coy, including Justin Trudeau's Liberals. During the 2015 election campaign, none of the major parties meaningfully broached the topic of dealing with the effects of the Great Demographic Imbalance. The only party that firmly committed to factoring age in allocating federal transfers such as the CHT was the one that did not stand a chance of winning the election: the Green Party. This was no oversight on the part of the three major parties. Like the rest of us, their leaders read the news—they are well aware that Canada is not aging evenly. But they are also acutely aware that a strong and growing majority of voters live in younger, slower-aging provinces west of the Ottawa River.

Canada's Great Demographic Imbalance will further strengthen the position of these provinces in the years ahead. It will also profoundly reshape federal–provincial relations. Canadians have become accustomed to seeing provinces decrying in unison the fiscal imbalance between them and Ottawa. The most recent episode occurred in the mid-2000s, when Ottawa was then still generating large surpluses. The argument put forward by its leading advocate, the Province of Quebec, was a familiar refrain: the money is in Ottawa and the needs are in the provinces. Such displays of provincial harmony will be unlikely in the age of the Great Demographic Imbalance. Of course, the prospect of spending more without facing the ire of voters will always be attractive to provincial governments. But as it becomes clear that the provinces have vastly different interests, it will become increasingly difficult for them to agree on what to ask for—other than more money for infrastructure. Poorer provinces will argue they have greater needs and lesser means and they should get more than richer provinces. This will not sit well with the latter, who will balk at the idea of footing a larger bill without getting more in return.

In short, the scene is set for a frontal collision between what will increasingly look like two distinct Canadas. On one side, there is a poorer, older Eastern Canada that will struggle to stay afloat amid the demographic storm. Unless it receives much more help from Ottawa, this Canada may well be stuck between the financial abyss and the politically suicidal prospect of scaling back social programs to the point of turning their residents into second-class citizens. On the other side, we find a younger, more dynamic Canada that can better afford to keep things as they are for itself but with little appetite for bailing out the older Canada.

Whether these two Canadas can go on leading parallel lives is doubtful. Canada is an economic union; its residents are free to move as they see fit in search of good jobs and richer social programs at lower levels of taxes. We could reach a point where people will leave parts of the older Canada in droves, starting with the most mobile in our society—those who earn more and are better educated. Once this starts, some provinces may be engulfed in a vicious circle of fiscal, economic, and social failure.

"History," as Winston Churchill once put it (and many others before and after him), is "one damned thing after another." Just as the threat of Quebec secessionism appeared to recede, Canada must now face the Great Demographic Imbalance. This book makes no prediction as to how the country will respond to this new challenge. While the book does offer recommendations for addressing the consequences of this imbalance, its main aim is to set the scene for this new chapter in our country's history. How the chapter ends will be written by Canadians and their political leaders.

Part I

CANADA'S GREAT DEMOGRAPHIC IMBALANCE AND ITS ECONOMIC CONSEQUENCES

Chapter 1

CANADA'S GREAT DEMOGRAPHIC IMBALANCE

nlike forces that can disrupt our lives almost instantly, such as technology, demography operates gradually. Its impact, however, can be just as powerful. We rarely pause to note that we lose a few minutes of sunlight every day after the summer solstice, yet this is how we go from the heat waves of summer to the blizzards of winter. Canada's Great Demographic Imbalance is the result of such gradual yet transformational change.

Today the effects of this imbalance are clearly visible. With the exception of British Columbia,[1] Canada becomes younger the farther west one travels. The Prairies are now eight years younger than Atlantic Canada. In the Prairies, one in eight residents is a senior; in Atlantic Canada, this ratio is close to one in five. This is an enormous gap, and it is about to get bigger. Yet, fifteen years ago, there were barely any age differences among provinces. If demography is supposed to operate gradually, how could such wide gaps open up so fast?

The answer is simple. The Great Demographic Imbalance may only be catching our attention now, but it has been with us for quite some time—since the end of the baby boom nearly half a century ago, in fact. For most of that time, this imbalance progressed in silence, just like an undiagnosed cancer. Indeed, until recently, few people had noticed and even fewer appeared to care about the fact that Canadian provinces were aging at vastly different speeds. There are at least two reasons for this indifference. First, today's oldest provinces, the four Atlantic provinces and Quebec, started off from a lower base: they were significantly younger than the rest of Canada when the baby boom ended.[2] Their faster aging was thus of little immediate concern when they were still younger or only slightly older than the rest of the country. Second, until the turn of the current decade, Canada's population aging did not matter much as the whole country was still enjoying the demographic dividend that came with all baby boomers being of working age.

The benign days of population aging are now behind us. And while it will affect the entire country in the years ahead, population aging will impact eastern provinces most, exerting severe pressures on their already strained public purses and dragging down their economic growth further than in the rest of the country.

Unlocking the Secrets of Aging

To understand why Canada is aging unevenly, we must first look at the phenomenon of population aging itself. For us as individuals, aging is a simple process: we become a year older every year for as long as we are alive. For society, things are much less straightforward. Whether a region or country ages or becomes younger and just how fast it does so depends on three things: births (natality), deaths (mortality), and the number of people entering versus leaving (net migration).

Naturally, births are a source of rejuvenation. When a region or country's birth rate grows, its population ages more slowly. If the increase is large enough, it may even become younger. Birth rates, in turn, depend on the number of children women typically have over their reproductive lives (fertility rates) and the share of women of child-bearing age in the overall population.[3]

In a developed country such as Canada, where the vast majority of people die at a relatively advanced age, the impact of mortality is similar to natality: when the mortality rate increases, population ages more slowly. Canada's mortality rate depends mainly on two factors working in opposite directions. The first is life expectancy. Thanks to medical progress and changes to their life habits and environment, Canadians live longer and longer. Over the last decade alone, life expectancy gains have led to a decline of nearly 20% in the age-adjusted mortality rate.[4] On the other hand, the fact that fewer people die each year as life expectancy improves, fuels growth in the ranks of seniors. And this takes us to the second factor driving mortality rates, which is the share of the overall population in high mortality age groups. Over the last decade, Canada's crude mortality rate (i.e., unadjusted for age) has remained relatively stable as life expectancy gains have offset growth in high mortality age groups.

The last variable that plays into population aging is migration, both international and interprovincial. The immediate impact of migration depends on the circumstances of host populations. Migrants tend to be young adults, with women of child-bearing age. If the host country or region is older than the migrants it welcomes, migration will slow population aging. And even if they are slightly older than their host population when they arrive, migrants usually end up slowing population aging through their favourable impact on birth rates.

Whether and how fast a country or region ages depends on how the various factors above stack up. Over the last century, the clear trend has been for Canada's population to grow older with time. In 1901 the median Canadian was close to 23 years old. Today she is slightly over 40.[5] The only major exception to this trend was during the baby boom (mid-1940s to mid-1960s), when Canada became younger.[6] This was a rare occasion when annual births had the upper hand on life expectancy in determining whether Canada's population would grow older or become younger.[7]

Why Some Regions Age Faster than Others

The above framework applies to any province, region, or country. Therefore, to understand why some parts of Canada are older and aging faster than others, we have to look at how natality, mortality, and migration have evolved historically in each region.

Table 1.1 shows the progression of two key indicators of population aging: median age and the share of seniors (age sixty-five and above) for Canada and provinces. The table reveals a clear dichotomy between the first two postwar decades and those that followed. As we saw earlier, during the baby boom years Canada was not aging; it was actually getting younger. There was also no marked east-west pattern in how fast the country was doing so: the Maritimes, for instance, saw its median age decline just as fast as the Prairies. Finally, Eastern Canada (Atlantic Canada and Quebec) was younger at the start of

Table 1.1: Median Age and Percentage of Seniors, Canada and Provinces

Source: Statistics Canada, data provided to author, and CANSIM, table 051-0001.

	1946		1966		1986		1996		2006		2015	
	Median age	%65+	Median age	%65+	Median age	%65+	Median age	%65+	Median age	%65+	Median age	%65+
Newfoundland and Labrador*	n/a	n/a	19.3	5.9	27.9	8.7	34.1	10.7	41.3	13.5	45.0	18.4
Prince Edward Island	26.5	9.8	24.0	10.8	30.6	12.6	34.7	12.9	40.3	14.6	43.7	18.6
Nova Scotia	26.5	8.2	24.7	8.9	31.0	11.8	35.7	12.9	41.2	14.6	44.4	18.9
New Brunswick	24.4	7.2	22.2	8.2	30.4	11.0	35.4	12.5	41.1	14.3	44.8	19.0
Quebec	24.6	5.5	23.9	6.1	31.8	9.8	36.1	12.0	40.5	13.9	41.9	17.6
Ontario	30.4	8.3	27.2	8.2	31.9	10.7	35.0	12.2	38.4	13.0	40.6	16.0
Manitoba	28.6	7.3	26.7	9.2	31.1	12.4	34.5	13.6	37.6	13.6	37.7	14.8
Saskatchewan	26.4	6.5	25.6	9.3	30.0	12.6	34.2	14.5	37.9	14.9	37.0	14.6
Alberta	27.2	6.3	24.5	7.1	29.0	8.0	33.3	9.8	35.5	10.3	36.2	11.6
British Columbia	31.3	8.9	28.2	9.5	32.8	11.9	35.4	12.5	40.1	14.1	42.0	17.5
Canada	**27.7**	**7.2**	**25.4**	**7.7**	**31.4**	**10.5**	**35.2**	**12.1**	**38.9**	**13.2**	**40.5**	**16.1**

*Newfoundland joined Canada in 1949. The province was renamed Newfoundland and Labrador in 2001.

the boom, and its age gap with the rest of the country was more or less the same twenty years later.

All of this changed in the 1960s, when Canada's population aging dynamics started looking like they do today, with the country aging fast and eastern provinces aging fastest. However, as eastern provinces were much younger at the end of the baby boom, they took a long time to catch up with the Canadian median age. Quebec and the Maritimes only did so in the 1980s and the 1990s, while Newfoundland remained younger until the turn of the millennium. (Newfoundland was renamed Newfoundland and Labrador in 2001. In this book, I use Newfoundland when referring to the province exclusively prior to that date.) But once they caught up with their western peers, eastern provinces continued to pull ahead. Today Atlantic Canada is more than four years older than the rest of the country. The gap between Quebec and the rest of the country is more modest, at around two years.[8]

Conversely, all provinces west of the Ottawa River aged more slowly than their eastern counterparts. While it was two years older in 1966, Ontario is now the same age as Canada.[9] The Prairies, which were about the same age as Canada fifty years ago, are now almost five years younger than the rest of the country. And while British Columbia was the oldest province in the country in 1966, it now has the same median age as Quebec. This stands in stark contrast with Newfoundland and Labrador, which, with a median age gain of more than twenty-five years, went from being the youngest to the oldest province in the federation.

The other key variable in table 1.1 is the share of seniors. This indicator evolved along a broadly similar pattern as median age, but with a twist. Here too provinces east of the Ottawa River have seen significantly faster growth since the end of the baby boom. Today Atlantic Canada's share of seniors is two-thirds larger than Alberta's. The twist is that while eastern provinces were younger at the end of the baby boom (their median age was lower), there was no discernible east-west pattern in the share of seniors. Although Quebec and Newfoundland's shares were smaller, those of the Maritimes were not.

Why was Eastern Canada younger than the rest of the country fifty years ago? How could some provinces be significantly younger than others, yet have higher shares of seniors? Why did Eastern Canada, and the Atlantic provinces in particular, age so much faster over the last half century? To answer these questions, we begin our investigation with the all-important two decades that followed World War Two, the baby boom years.

The baby boom deserves special attention. It may have ended fifty years ago, but its effects remain very much with us. Without it, Canada would still be aging but it would be much younger. And although a regional demographic imbalance would still exist, its consequences would not be as dramatic. The Great Demographic Imbalance matters to Canada because the aging of the baby boom generation is having a much deeper impact on some regions than on others.

The Baby Boom Years: Defying Canada's Laws of Demographic Gravity

In 1967 Canada celebrated its first century in style by showcasing itself to the world in Montreal, then the country's metropolis. At Expo 67, Canada was portrayed as a young, dynamic, and promising country. It certainly was young; at the time, the median Canadian was merely twenty-five years old. And with so many young workers about to enter the labour market, Canada could look to prosperous times ahead. Add to this the fact that the country had relatively few seniors to care for, and the setting was perfect for a new charismatic leader to run for office on the promise of a "just society."

When Pierre Trudeau was elected in 1968, Canada was coming out of two decades during which it had grown younger. At the end of World War Two, the country's median age was twenty-seven. The two-year drop in the median age in the two decades following the war may not seem like much, but it actually was enormous. This period was marked by rapid progress in many areas, including life expectancy. Improvements on this front alone were such that in most other periods of our history, Canada would have grown significantly older. Furthermore, immigration was not the powerful rejuvenator it is today as immigrants were then, in general, older than other Canadians. There was thus only one force that could make the country younger: babies.

We live in a world in which hyperbole comes easy. As a consequence, words tend to lose their power to shock. But the spectacular explosion in births that Canada witnessed over the two decades after World War Two truly deserves to be called a "baby boom." Indeed, this phenomenon was so stupefying both in its scale and ramifications that nothing less could aptly describe it. By comparison, the much-publicized recent uptick in birth levels in Canada that some have labelled a new baby boom is a mere blip.[10]

Chart 1.1 shows the magnitude of Canada's baby boom. At its height in the late 1950s, close to half a million babies were born every year, roughly 100,000 above today's level. To put this number in perspective, Canada's population in the mid-1940s was about a third of what it is today. In order for births to have a similar impact as the baby boom on Canada's age structure, Canadian women would need to deliver well in excess of 1 *million* babies annually rather than the 375,000 they are having today.

A number of reasons explain the baby boom. The postwar era witnessed exceptionally strong and steady economic growth, which made people secure in thinking they could afford larger families. At the peak of the boom, in the late 1950s, Canada's fertility rate—the number of children a woman typically has over her reproductive life[11]—was hovering around 4.0.[12] Today, this figure stands at around 1.6.[13] The

Chart 1.1: Births in Canada 1934–2014
Source: Statistics Canada, Vital Statistics, vol. 2, 1972; and CANSIM, tables 051-0001 and 051-0004.

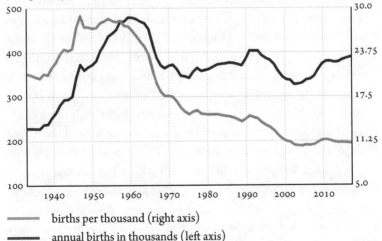

········ births per thousand (right axis)

▬▬▬ annual births in thousands (left axis)

postwar years were also a time of heavy immigration. As we saw earlier, immigration has a positive impact on birth rates. From 1946 to 1965, Canada welcomed on average about 125,000 immigrants every year—appreciably more than today in relation to the country's population.[14] Finally, the baby boom took place right before the social revolution of the 1960s that led more women to pursue higher education and join the workforce, postponing childbirth and having fewer children. This revolution is the main reason the baby boom ended. It was brought about by a number of interrelated developments including the general progress of education, the rise of values of self-realization (closely linked to the feminist movement), growing freedom from traditional forces of authority (particularly religion), as well as widespread adoption of more effective contraception methods (such as the birth control pill).[15]

So how did Canada's various regions experience the baby boom? Did it have a similar impact across the country? The short answer is no. Generally, the baby boom was strongest in the eastern provinces, with Newfoundland leading the country. As table 1.2 illustrates, provinces east of the Ottawa River had higher average birth rates than their western counterparts, except for Alberta.

Of the two drivers of birth rates—fertility rates and the share of women of child-bearing age—fertility rates played a bigger role in explaining why the baby boom was stronger in some provinces than in others. A key factor behind regional differences at the time was the level of urbanization, with women typically having more children in rural than in urban areas. Ontario and British Columbia, the most urban provinces, had the lowest fertility rates, and Atlantic Canada, led by Newfoundland, had the highest. Differences between French and English-speaking Canada constituted another key factor. French Canadian women had more babies than their English-speaking counterparts during most of the baby boom, extending a trend that dated back to the late nineteenth century.[16] This is why Quebec had an above-average fertility rate during most of the baby boom, despite ranking among the country's most urbanized provinces. Quebec's fertility rate remained above the Canadian average until the late 1950s, when *la revanche des berceaux* (the "revenge of the cradles") gave way to the Quiet Revolution. Similarly, the French-English difference also

Table 1.2: Birth Rates (annual births per thousand of population)
Source: Statistics Canada, *Canada Year Book 1959* and *Canada Year Book 1973*.

	1941–45	1946–50	1951–55	1956–60	1961–65
Newfoundland	29.8	36.2	34.1	34.6	32.1
Prince Edward Island	23.7	30.5	27.2	26.6	25.7
Nova Scotia	25.2	28.9	27.5	26.9	24.7
New Brunswick	28.2	34.0	31.0	29.0	25.8
Quebec	28.4	30.4	30.0	28.6	24.0
Ontario	19.9	24.6	26.1	26.4	23.5
Manitoba	21.8	25.9	26.4	25.6	23.4
Saskatchewan	21.7	26.3	27.5	26.9	24.4
Alberta	23.7	28.4	30.6	30.6	28.3
British Columbia	19.8	24.0	25.1	25.7	21.5
Canada	**23.5**	**27.4**	**28.0**	**27.6**	**24.1**

explains, at least in part, why New Brunswick, with its large Acadian minority, had higher rates than its neighbour Nova Scotia.[17]

However, fertility rates do not explain all regional differences. Next to Newfoundland, the Maritimes had the highest fertility rate in the country, yet only one Maritime province, New Brunswick, made the top four of provinces with the largest baby booms. This is because the Maritimes had a lower share of women of child-bearing age. A look at their migration records will explain the reasons.

The Decisive Role of Migration During the Baby Boom

The baby boom gave the country a very powerful demographic boost: a total of 8.4 million Canadians were born during that period, or roughly two-thirds of Canada's population when the war ended. It was not, however, the only major force shaping the country's demographic landscape at the time. From 1946 to 1965, Canada welcomed 2.5 million immigrants, historically a very large number in relation to the country's population.[18] These strong immigration flows had a significant impact on birth rates: without them, there would not have been much of a baby boom. It is not a coincidence that the Western countries that experienced a baby boom all had high immigration.

Indeed, contrary to popular perceptions, the baby boom was not a universal phenomenon in the Western world. Aside from Canada, only three other countries experienced a similar development: the United States, Australia, and New Zealand. Canada's boom was the loudest of all four.[19]

While immigration was key to Canada's overall postwar demographic explosion, its impact on provincial fortunes differed greatly. Newcomers to Canada did not settle evenly across the land. Rather, they mostly headed for Ontario and British Columbia. Quebec also managed to draw significant numbers of immigrants but remained a distant third, proportionately speaking. Atlantic Canada, for its part, trailed far behind the rest of the country.[20]

The effects of immigration were magnified by interprovincial migration. Here, the reality during the baby boom was much the same as it is today: the East was losing people to the West.[21] It's worth noting that domestic migration, by its very nature, has twice the impact of immigration on differences in provincial demographic fortunes. When an immigrant lands in Canada, she increases the population of the country and her host province by one. When a person moves from one province to another, she lowers the population of the province she departs by one *and* increases the population of her host province by the same number. And when a province loses a resident to another province or country, odds are that it will also have lost the migrant's children, grandchildren, and so on.

Migration is the reason why Eastern Canada lost some demographic weight during the baby boom, despite its significantly higher birth rates. It also explains why there was no major east-west difference among provinces in how fast their shares of senior citizens grew. Had all provinces witnessed similar migration patterns, Eastern Canada, with its stronger baby boom, would have seen its share of seniors grow slower than the rest. Yet, because of its poorer migration record, its share of senior citizens did not grow appreciably slower.[22]

After the Boom: Normalcy Returns with a Vengeance

The baby boom was a unique phenomenon. While it lasted, it almost entirely suspended Canada's laws of demographic gravity. Before the boom, Canada's population was on a secular aging trend thanks mostly to sustained improvements in life expectancy. The baby boom did not only halt this process, it temporarily reversed it. Before the boom, Canada's population centre of gravity had been shifting west rapidly. The baby boom considerably dampened this shift.

Normalcy returned with the end of the baby boom. Canada started aging again. Its westward population shift accelerated sharply, not only because eastern provinces did not attract as many migrants, but also because it went from having more to fewer babies than their western counterparts. As a result, eastern provinces began to rapidly lose demographic weight within the country and to age faster. These two trends continue largely unabated to this day.[23]

Obviously, the baby boom ended because Canadian women were having fewer babies. Although not sudden, the decline in Canada's fertility rate was steep. It's worth noting that this rate was far from stable during the baby boom itself: When the boom began, in the mid-1940s, Canada's fertility rate stood at 3.0 babies per woman. It then peaked at 3.9 in 1959, and by 1966 it was down to 3.2.[24] The baby boom did not end because Canada's fertility rate had dropped to that level but rather because the decline did not stop there—far from it. By 1971 Canada's fertility rate was down to 2.1, a nearly 50% drop relative to its peak in 1959. From then on, it continued to decline steadily but much more slowly. It stabilized at 1.6 in 1983, a level in line with today's rate.

The timing and magnitude of the decline differed considerably from province to province. The four Atlantic provinces exited the baby boom with the highest fertility rates in the country. While rates had started declining fast there too, they remained above the Canadian average for another decade or so, likely because the societal changes behind declining fertility rates took longer to unfold in rural areas. But once these changes reached maturity in Atlantic Canada, rates continued to decline faster there than in the rest of the country. Newfoundland and Labrador went from having the highest fertility rate during the baby boom to the lowest of all Canadian provinces today. And while their drop was less spectacular, the Maritimes also went from significantly above- to below-average rates. For its part, Quebec, a more urban province undergoing its Quiet Revolution in the 1960s, witnessed an earlier and more sudden drop. While its fertility rate was above-average for most of the baby boom, by the end of it, Quebec already had the low-est rate of all provinces. Quebec remained in the bottom rungs until the turn of the millennium. By the middle of the last decade, however, its rate had climbed to above the Canadian average.

It is beyond the scope of this book to examine in detail the driv-ers of fertility rates and how they interact to shape differences among Canada's provinces. There is extensive literature on this topic.[25] I will simply note that, though it played a key role during the baby boom, the level of urbanization has lost much of its explanatory power over time, to such an extent that other factors now shed more light on dif-ferences among provinces. These include the evolution of attitudes regarding family, income levels and distribution, educational attain-ment, labour market conditions, social policies facilitating labour force participation, and the importance of Aboriginal people in the overall population. The Prairie provinces, which have high incomes and a greater concentration of Aboriginal citizens, have by far the highest fertility rates among Canadian provinces, a position they have maintained since the late 1970s. And Quebec, with its heavily subsidized daycare facilities and other pro-family policies, now also has an above-average rate, as we just saw.

The post–baby boom era also witnessed Eastern Canada fall pro-gressively behind the rest of the country on the other driver of annual births: the number of women of child-bearing age. Unsurprisingly, as they are now older, all provinces east of the Ottawa River have lower shares of women of child-bearing age. And here also, Newfoundland and Labrador is the province with the smallest share.[26]

In sum, annual births, which have slowed considerably the secular westward shift in Canada's demographic centre of gravity during the baby boom, have since done exactly the opposite—they have been pull-ing provinces further and further apart. Newfoundland and Labrador, which had the highest birth rate during the baby boom, now has the lowest in Canada. The Prairies, whose performance was comparable to the Canadian average during the baby boom, now has the highest birth rates, around one-fifth on average above Canada's.[27]

Migration (International and Interprovincial)

Ever since the American Revolution pushed Loyalists north, migration has almost always been the main force driving differences in the demographic fortunes of Canada's regions. The contrast between the Maritimes and the rest of Canada clearly illustrates this. Prior to Confederation, the Maritimes and the Canadas (the colonies of Upper and Lower Canada, which were united in 1841 to form the Province of Canada) were all growing fast, drawing large numbers of immigrants. From 1803 to 1861, the Maritimes' population grew by a fivefold factor, and that of the Canadas grew eightfold. Since then, the population of the Maritimes has only tripled, while that of the rest of Canada has grown tenfold.[28] A much poorer migration record driven by a weaker economy explains the bulk of this stunning difference in population growth since Confederation.

Migration is the main reason why Eastern Canada is losing demographic weight within the federation. Half a century ago, the population of Quebec and Atlantic Canada was 50% higher than that of the four westernmost provinces. By the late 2000s, the latter had become more populous than the former.[29] Comparing Newfoundland and Labrador to Alberta reveals just how critical the role of migration is. From 1971 to 2014, Newfoundland and Labrador lost nearly 122,000 people—one-fifth of its population—to the rest of the country. If we subtract the number of people it gained from net immigration (immigration less emigration), the province's loss remains a colossal 103,000. This very poor migration record helps explain why Newfoundland and Labrador lost population over that period—the only province to do so. By contrast, Alberta welcomed 1.3 million new residents, representing half of its population gain since 1971.[30] And that's not considering the significant impact this million-plus influx of people has had on the province's annual births.

So why are some regions so good at attracting and retaining migrants, while others mostly fail at this task? Two main factors shape provincial migration outcomes: economic growth and large cities. When a region is lacking in both, outcomes are poor.

The Maritimes provide a clear illustration of this. Numerous analysts have justifiably dwelled on the link between the Maritimes' chronic underperformance and the fact that its urban system is less mature. The region has no big metropolitan centre to speak of; Halifax ranks only as a large medium-size city by Canadian standards. Moreover, the region is more than twice as rural as Canada (45% compared to 19% for Canada as a whole).[31] Still, though a modest affair, the drawing power of Halifax has allowed Nova Scotia to attract more immigrants than its neighbour, New Brunswick. The rub, though, is that even when they succeed in drawing immigrants, smaller, poorer provinces are at a disadvantage when it comes to keeping them. Many immigrants who arrive in those provinces do not stay long. They move elsewhere in the country, thereby further deteriorating the already bleak interprovincial migration records of the provinces they leave. According to a recent study, more than one in two immigrants who arrive in Atlantic Canada eventually leave for other provinces. For Ontario, it is less than one in ten.[32]

When looking at migratory patterns, it is essential to draw a distinction between domestic and international migrants. As a rule, interprovincial migration patterns closely mirror regional economic trends. From the mid-2000s until recently, Ontario's economy had been lacklustre relative to much of the rest of the country. This showed up in interprovincial migration numbers: a net total of around 125,000 Ontarians moved to other provinces from 2004–05 to 2013–14, the largest deficit of all provinces. At the opposite end of the spectrum, Alberta drew more people from across the country than any other province.[33]

A similar economic logic is at play with immigration patterns, but it is far less pronounced. That's because immigrants have a clear propensity to settle in Canada's largest cities, particularly Toronto, Vancouver, and to a lesser extent, Montreal. All three cities have large concentrations of residents born in various parts of the world, which makes the integration of immigrants easier. (Toronto has one of the largest shares of foreign-born residents of all major cities in the world.) This propensity explains why Ontario has managed to welcome more than 1 million immigrants since 2004–05, although its economy was reeling. Indeed, from 2004–05 to 2013–14 the province has managed to attract 44% of Canada's immigrants—more than its share of the country's population—even though its economy grew more than a third slower than the rest of the country.[34]

Table 1.3: Components of Population Growth, 1971–2014
Source: Statistics Canada, CANSIM, tables 051-0001 and 051-0004.

	Population 1971	Natural increase	Net immigration	Net interprovincial migration	Population 2014	Population growth 1971–2014* (%)
Newfoundland and Labrador	530,854	144,841	19,271	-121,944	529,069	-0.3
Prince Edward Island	112,591	25,233	17,053	1,057	146,142	29.8
Nova Scotia	797,294	142,884	74,587	-26,063	942,387	18.2
New Brunswick	642,471	141,657	36,743	-32,285	754,578	17.4
Quebec	6,137,305	1,588,999	1,313,244	-582,470	8,214,885	33.9
Ontario	7,849,027	2,604,163	3,736,685	-15,552	13,677,687	74.3
Manitoba	998,876	296,562	269,450	-220,415	1,280,242	28.2
Saskatchewan	932,038	285,821	132,255	-196,386	1,122,283	20.4
Alberta	1,665,717	1,134,695	663,474	648,810	4,120,897	147.4
British Columbia	2,240,470	733,076	1,202,492	567,694	4,638,415	107.0
Canada	21,962,032	7,162,418	7,474,355	0	35,543,658	61.8

*Population gains over the 1971 to 2014 period do not equal the sum of gains from natural increase, net immigration, and net interprovincial migration. Statistics Canada refers to this discrepancy as the "residual deviation."

Ontario's economy would have expanded even less were it not for this steady flow of immigrants joining its workforce. And this brings us to a critical point about the relationship between migration and growth. For small provinces without large metropolitan centres, migration patterns are mainly driven by economic opportunities. For provinces with large metropolitan centres, the relationship actually goes in both directions. Even though stronger economic growth does attract more migrants, immigration also drives economic growth. This is not to say that smaller provinces lacking large cities should not actively work to better attract and retain immigrants. It simply means they should not expect the same results as provinces that are growing faster and/or have large metropolitan centres (more on this in chapter 7 and the annex to this book).

Looking Ahead

Now that we have insight into the dynamics fuelling Canada's Great Demographic Imbalance, we can turn our attention to what the future likely holds. Since 1974 Statistics Canada has periodically been producing population projections for Canada, including provinces and territories. The latest exercise was carried out in 2014 and covers the 2013–38 period. Statistics Canada's projections are based on the long-standing and widely used "component" approach: it looks at individual sources of population growth (fertility, life expectancy, net immigration, interprovincial migration) and formulates "relevant and plausible" assumptions for each of them. These various assumptions yield a large number of scenarios, but the agency focuses on what it calls its low-, medium-, and high-growth scenarios.[35] I use the medium-growth scenario as the baseline, as its assumptions best reflect historical trends (the low- and high-growth scenarios do not meaningfully alter my conclusions).

The results speak for themselves. In 2013 Quebec and Atlantic Canada had roughly the same population as Canada's four westernmost provinces. By 2038 the latter will have 30% more residents than the former. And while Newfoundland and Labrador is projected to lose more than one-eighth of its population, Alberta's could grow by more than half.

Just as importantly, Canada's regions will continue to age at vastly different speeds. As we saw earlier, barely fifteen years ago there was very little difference in the age structures of provinces east and west of the Ottawa River. Today, the median Prairie resident is eight years younger than his Atlantic Canadian counterpart. By 2038 this age gap will exceed ten years. While the median Prairie resident will gain 3.5 years (going from 36.5 to 40), the median Atlantic Canadian will age nearly twice as fast, from 43.9 in 2013 to 50.3 in 2038. As for the median Ontarian, Quebecer, and British Columbian, they will gain around 4 years, reaching around 45 in 2038.

These growing age differences among provinces will translate in vastly different shares of seniors. Today, one in eight Prairie residents is aged sixty-five and above. By 2038 the ratio will be around one in five. In Atlantic Canada, this share will shift from nearly one in five to close to one in three. In other words, in less than a quarter century from now, the Prairies will have more or less the same share of seniors that Atlantic Canada currently has, while the latter's share will have grown by more than two-thirds.

As for Quebec, Ontario, and British Columbia, their shares of senior citizens will grow from one in six today to one in four. It's worth noting that although the three provinces will see their median age and share of seniors follow a similar path, their underlying aging dynamics will differ. For instance, Quebec is projected to post a significantly higher fertility rate than British Columbia but a poorer migration record. This, as we shall see in the next chapter, will have major economic consequences, with British Columbia's economy projected to grow 50% faster than Quebec's over the 2013–38 period.

In short, according to Statistics Canada's projections, the Great Demographic Imbalance will only worsen with time. There is no reprieve in sight, at least not for a quarter century. And, as I have argued earlier, we have now entered an era where this regional imbalance actually matters.

A Note on Prince Edward Island

Readers familiar with the Maritimes will no doubt find something odd about the population projections for Prince Edward Island in

Table 1.4: Baseline Population Projection, 2013–38

Source: Statistics Canada, CANSIM, table 052-0005; and data provided to author.

	2013			2038		
	Pop ('000)	Median age	%65+	Pop ('000)	Median age	%65+
Newfoundland and Labrador	526.7	44.2	17.1	455.6	53.3	34.5
Prince Edward Island	145.2	43.1	17.3	178.3	47.7	27.9
Nova Scotia	940.8	43.8	17.7	933.9	49.6	30.9
New Brunswick	756.1	43.9	17.6	752.5	49.8	31.3
Quebec	8,155.3	41.6	16.6	9,405.3	45.2	25.1
Ontario	13,538	40.3	15.2	16,548.8	44.3	24.7
Manitoba	1,265	37.7	14.4	1,623.1	40.6	20.6
Saskatchewan	1,108.3	37.1	14.4	1,315.2	41.1	21.4
Alberta	4,025.1	36.0	11.2	6,224.8	39.7	18.5
British Columbia	4,582	41.4	16.4	5,918.8	44.9	25.1
Canada	35,158.3	40.2	15.3	43,490.1	43.9	24.0

table 1.4. Historically, the birthplace of Confederation has largely followed the same path as its two sister Maritime provinces, New Brunswick and Nova Scotia. Yet, according to Statistics Canada, the island province should part ways with them spectacularly in the years ahead. Indeed, while population growth in Nova Scotia and New Brunswick should grind to a halt, Prince Edward Island is set to see its ranks explode by a whopping 23% from 2013 to 2038. Such a gain would exceed Quebec's by a wide margin (+15%) and would even be slightly larger than Ontario's (+22%).

If something seems wrong with this picture, it is because something is indeed wrong. Prince Edward Island's population may well grow faster than the rest of the Maritimes in the decades ahead, but its performance will almost certainly not put the province in the same league as Central Canada. The annex to this book explains why. In doing so, it emphasizes the importance of investigating outliers when making projections based on historical trends. Incidentally, it also serves as a cautionary tale about how seemingly noble public policy intentions can be perverted to produce questionable—if not unethical—results.

This book makes a number of projections about economic growth and public spending over the next quarter century or so. These show that Prince Edward Island should do better than its two sister Maritime provinces on virtually all counts. Readers should take these results with a grain of salt and assume that the island province's performance will in fact be more in line with Nova Scotia and New Brunswick than the numbers suggest.

Summing Up

Population aging is far from a recent phenomenon. It has been with us for over a century as medical advances and other improvements to our way of life have led to sustained increases in life expectancy. This phenomenon was temporarily reversed during the postwar baby boom, when the country's population actually became younger; however, it resumed with a vengeance over the last half century as birth rates dropped and immigration slowed.

The effects of Canada's population aging are far from uniform across the country. With the exception of British Columbia, the farther east one travels across Canada's regions, the older the population becomes and the faster it is aging. The provinces with proportionally more baby boomers—those that have been less successful at producing babies as well as attracting and retaining migrants over the last half century—will be aging and seeing their shares of seniors swell fastest.

The negative impact of the Great Demographic Imbalance on the economic prosperity and public purses of poorer, older provinces will only grow worse with time. As we will see in this book, barring major changes to the way their governments do business and dramatic increases in federal transfer payments, the pressures on the balance sheets of these provinces, all of which are already strained, will eventually prove unbearable.

Chapter 2
GROWING APART

Twenty-five years is an eternity in economic history. A quarter century ago, the world was just starting to dismantle the Iron Curtain. The idea that nations east and west of the curtain and from the Third World would join a race to integrate global value chains linked together by seamless data flows and dramatically cheaper shipping remained the province of futurists. And while Deng Xiaoping had opened China to greater trade and private initiative, the country was still an economic backwater. Several years would go by before the emergence of broad swathes of the Third World led by China would fuel the massive commodity boom that turned Newfoundland and Labrador and Saskatchewan into "have" provinces.

The world will remain a fast-changing place over the next quarter century. Climate change will remind us with even more frequent and destructive weather events that we are pushing our luck with our addiction to fossil fuels. Books on "climate terrorism" will likely migrate from the science fiction to the current affairs tabs of online bookstores. On a less grim note, progress in areas such as 3D printing, nanotechnology, and information technology will transform our lives, from how we manage our health to how we manufacture cars and drive them more safely. Returning to the heart of this book, we can predict with confidence that Canada's economy will grow more slowly than it did over the past quarter or half century. We can also predict that, after decades of converging in terms of growth and prosperity, Canadian provinces will start growing apart again. And of course, it is the older, faster-aging eastern provinces—Atlantic Canada in particular—that will be on the wrong side of the widening prosperity gap.

Regional Disparities: The Never-Ending Quest for Convergence

Mainstream economic theory has always had a troubled relationship with geography. Simply put, the very existence of sustained prosperity gaps in a country where goods, people, and money can move freely does not square neatly with the neoclassical school, which dominates economic thinking. In the view of neoclassical economists, if market forces were allowed to operate freely—that is, if politicians did not get in the way with policies that keep people in less productive regions—provinces would eventually converge economically. Workers would earn roughly the same salaries, and capital would earn similar returns across regions.[1]

The six decades between Confederation and the Great Depression provided a good testing ground for this theory. Back then, the dominant doctrine in Canada and many other parts of the world was *laissez-faire*. In such an environment of benign neglect, conditions were ripe for the neoclassical prediction of convergence to pan out. But regional economies did not converge over that period—quite the contrary.[2] Certainly, neoclassical economists never claimed regional prosperity gaps would disappear overnight if market forces were left to prevail. Still, if such a long period of *laissez-faire* was not enough to make a serious dent in disparities, then this theory is of little comfort to those who live in Canada's less prosperous regions. After all, as the British economist Lord Maynard Keynes famously put it, "in the long run, we are all dead."[3]

In any case, politicians were in no mood after World War Two to wait and see if the neoclassical prediction of convergence would become a reality. Obsessed with not returning to the days of the Great Depression, they embraced a new paradigm, heavily influenced by the teachings of Keynes himself. This new paradigm called for a much more activist role for government in various areas, including in economic and social affairs. The postwar years were also marked by robust and sustained growth, producing an era the French economist Jean Fourastié labelled *Les Trente Glorieuses* ("The Glorious Thirty").[4] In this new age of plenty the welfare state flourished, and concerns about social justice and regional balance escalated on Ottawa's agenda.

As noted earlier, in the 1968 election, the newly minted Liberal leader, Pierre Trudeau, promised Canadians a "just society." Trudeau also campaigned hard on the increasingly salient issue of national unity, claiming that only a strong, interventionist Ottawa could prevent the destruction of Canada. To be sure, much of his focus was on Quebec, where the secessionist movement was on the rise. But Trudeau's concerns were broader: he also passionately argued that regional disparities in economic development were just as much a threat to national unity as French-English relations.[5]

To view Trudeau's position on regional disparities as an attempt to belittle Quebec's burgeoning secessionist movement by framing it as simply one among many threats to Canada's unity would be to misread the context in which he made his comments. Trudeau was not the first politician to express concern about Canada's highly uneven pace of regional development, nor was he the first prime minister to act on this file. By the time he was elected, several initiatives were already in place to deal with regional disparities. Canada's Equalization program, which addressed the gnawing gaps in fiscal capacities among provinces, was adopted in 1957. In 1960 the federal budget announced targeted fiscal measures to entice firms to locate in slow-growth regions. Shortly thereafter, Parliament passed the Agricultural Rehabilitation and Development Act, which aimed to boost rural economies. This was the federal government's first among what eventually became an alphabet soup of regional development programs.[6]

Notwithstanding the prediction of neoclassical economists, something very interesting happened once politicians meaningfully interfered with market forces: *regional economies began to converge.* Indeed, one of the most striking (and comforting) developments of the last half century is the considerable narrowing of prosperity gaps among Canadian regions. On virtually every single indicator of production, income, and productivity, regional differences are smaller today than they were fifty or sixty years ago.[7]

What happened? Surely this did not occur simply because politicians started meddling with market forces? The answer is both yes and no. At the outset, it is worth recalling that even though governments took a much greater role in the lives of Canadians, market forces remained alive and well. Capital was free (for the most part) to seek the best returns wherever they could be found across the country. Similarly, workers had the option of voting with their feet, and many did; there is a reason why Alberta's population tripled over the past fifty years while Newfoundland and Labrador's stagnated.[8] That said, migration may have been key to keeping the engines of Canada's faster-growing economies humming along, but it was not the main reason for the narrowing of regional differences in prosperity. Rather, the most important driver of convergence of production (GDP) and income per person over the last half century was the general progress of education (or human capital, in the jargon of economists). While they were much less educated fifty years ago, residents in poorer regions have largely caught up with their peers in richer ones. As they did so, prosperity and productivity levels in poorer provinces grew much closer to the national average.[9]

Evidently, little of the progress in poorer provinces would have happened had governments not invested heavily in education, including in a much more universal and accessible post-secondary education system. And in poorer provinces, these investments were made possible in no small part by large Equalization and other transfer payments from Ottawa. These heavy investments—much more than the alphabet soup of regional development initiatives concocted by Ottawa and the provinces over the years—are the main reason why politicians interfering with market forces sparked a regional convergence process.

Regional Disparities: Returning to the Fore

The issue of regional disparities has lost much of its salience in recent decades, both as a field of study and as a topic of public policy debates. This is hardly surprising given the actual amount of convergence that has taken place and the falling into disrepute of activist governments in the post–Thatcher and Reagan era. Few politicians nowadays have the stomach to seriously tamper with the creative destruction process that sustains national economies in an ever-changing and ferociously competitive global environment. When national politicians in Western countries do act in the name of industrial policy (another expression that has fallen into disrepute), the words "national competitiveness" are much more likely to be close behind than the loftier ideal of "regional balance." Still, whether we like it or not, odds are that regional disparities will soon again become a hot public policy topic. The reason: Canada's Great Demographic Imbalance.

There are many ways to measure regional disparities. One of them is to look at productivity indicators, for instance the wealth created per worker or per hour worked (labour productivity). It is a welcome development that labour productivity in have-less regions has caught up to a significant extent with the rest of the country. But labour productivity is only one part of the picture when it comes to regional disparities. In order to understand where regional economies are headed, we also have to consider the other half of the growth equation, which is how many workers each region will employ in the coming years. We saw in the previous chapter that the provinces most affected by population aging are those with the largest concentrations of baby boomers. Those are the provinces that have had less success in producing babies as well as in attracting and retaining migrants over the years. They are also the very provinces that will see their number of workers grow much more slowly than the rest of the country, if not witness outright decline.

All of Canada will have to grapple with dimmer growth prospects in the years ahead, but the Great Demographic Imbalance means that older, faster-aging provinces will have lower and faster-declining shares of their respective populations in the labour force (i.e., people employed or actively looking for work). As a result, their economies will grow more slowly. Regional disparities should widen again. But before we consider in greater detail what lies ahead, we first need to examine the past to fully appreciate just how differently Canada's various regions will be affected by population aging.

Looking Back

Canada's economy has slowed appreciably in recent years. From 2003 to 2013, it grew by 1.9% annually, around one-third below the pace of the previous twenty years. It may be tempting to blame the financial crisis and the sharp, though short-lived recession Canada underwent in the late 2000s for this counter-performance. Yet, business cycles are nothing new. Canada experienced a more prolonged setback in the early 1990s and still managed to turn in a 2.5% annual GDP gain from 1983 to 1993. And while the economy experienced uninterrupted growth between 1993 and 2003, the average annual gain over that period was 3.4%. Clearly, something more than cyclical factors contributed to the slower growth of the 2003–13 period.

That "something" was the end of a phenomenon that contributed more than anything else to the country's growth and prosperity over the last half century. From the late 1960s to the late 2000s, Canada's economy was boosted by a sustained, spectacular increase in its labour force. This phenomenon was unique in that it bore little relationship to the growth of the country's population. From 1965 to 2008, Canada's population grew by 64%; yet, its labour force grew nearly two and a half times faster, by 153%.[10]

Such dramatic labour force growth was bound to have an equally dramatic impact on Canada's economy. An economy grows when existing workers produce more wealth (labour productivity growth), or when the number of workers increases (labour force growth).[11] Table 2.1 breaks down the respective contributions of labour force and labour productivity growth to economic growth over the three decades from 1983 to 2013. From 1983 to 2008, labour force growth accounted for three-fifths of Canada's robust 2.8% average annual growth. From 2008 to 2013, it accounted for only four-tenths of a much smaller average annual GDP gain of 1.4%. The contribution of labour force growth to Canada's economic growth was nearly three times smaller from 2008 to 2013 than over the previous quarter century.

Two main phenomena were behind the spectacular labour force growth that Canada experienced until recently. One is a central focus of this book, and both will be familiar: the aging of the baby boom generation and the rise of female workers.

The Aging of the Baby Boomers: A Declining Demographic Dividend

Nowadays the aging of baby boomers is viewed as a public policy challenge because it means proportionally fewer and fewer workers supporting public programs for a growing population of seniors. This was not always so. For a long time, it actually meant the opposite. From the mid-1960s to the mid-1980s, Canada's labour force

Table 2.1: Components of Growth, Canada and Provinces
Source: Statistics Canada, CANSIM, tables 282-0018 and 384-0038.

	Real GDP (%)				Hours worked (%)				GDP/Hours worked (%)			
	1983–93	1993–2003	2003–08	2008–13	1983–93	1993–2003	2003–08	2008–13	1983–93	1993–2003	2003–08	2008–13
Newfoundland and Labrador	1.8	4.4	3.1	-0.3	0.2	1.0	1.6	1.8	1.6	3.3	1.5	-2.0
Prince Edward Island	1.8	3.2	2.1	1.5	0.6	2.0	0.6	1.3	1.2	1.2	1.5	0.2
Nova Scotia	2.1	2.5	1.2	0.5	1.1	1.5	0.9	-0.3	1.0	1.1	0.3	0.8
New Brunswick	2.1	2.8	1.4	0.0	1.8	1.3	0.9	-0.4	0.3	1.5	0.5	0.4
Quebec	1.8	3.0	1.9	1.1	1.1	1.5	1.4	0.6	0.7	1.5	0.5	0.5
Ontario	2.8	3.9	1.7	1.0	1.5	2.1	1.2	0.5	1.3	1.8	0.6	0.5
Manitoba	1.8	2.5	3.0	2.0	0.7	1.0	1.3	0.4	1.1	1.5	1.8	1.6
Saskatchewan	2.0	2.2	2.9	2.3	0.3	0.1	2.2	1.7	1.7	2.1	0.8	0.6
Alberta	3.1	3.8	3.9	2.9	1.4	2.9	3.7	1.6	1.7	0.9	0.2	1.3
British Columbia	3.3	2.7	3.4	1.6	3.2	1.4	2.7	-0.1	0.1	1.3	0.7	1.6
Canada	2.5	3.4	2.4	1.4	1.5	1.8	1.7	0.6	1.0	1.6	0.6	0.8

swelled as baby boomers progressively reached working age (fifteen to sixty-four). Then, from the mid-1980s to the late 2000s, the country was fully enjoying the "demographic dividend" that flowed from all baby boomers being of working age. This was not only a period when demography was making its peak contribution to economic prosperity, but also when the relative economic burden of caring for dependents (typically defined as individuals aged zero to fourteen and sixty-five and over) was at its lowest.

As mentioned, the year 2011 can be viewed as a watershed since this is when the first baby boomers reached the age of sixty-five, thus exiting the working-age population. In reality, however, as the average retirement age at the turn of the decade was approximately sixty-three,[12] the exit of baby boomers from the labour force started earlier. This exit will continue over the next twenty years or so, dragging down economic growth and affecting older, faster-aging provinces much more than others.

The Rise of Female Workers

We just saw that the baby boom generation made its fullest contribution to Canada's prosperity from the mid-1980s to the late 2000s, when all of its members were of working age. However, the actual contribution of the aging of baby boomers to labour force growth—and therefore to economic growth—stopped in the 1980s, when the youngest among them joined the workforce.[13] Yet, Canada's strong labour force growth did not stop then—far from it. That's mainly because another key labour market phenomenon was still in full bloom: the sustained, rapid increase in women's participation in the labour force. From the mid-1970s up to the turn of the century, their participation grew at a pace not witnessed before or since.[14] This development, though critically important to Canada's economic growth over that period, was only one aspect of an ongoing, century-long transformation in women's relationship to paid work. The rise of women in the labour force—and the resulting shift in their social and economic position—was succinctly summarized in 2000 by then-MIT economics professor D. L. Costa:

In the first few decades of the twentieth century, the "factory girl" set
the stage for the unmarried "office girl." The unmarried office girl paved
the way for the entry of married women into the labor force in the late
1950s, even though this entry was primarily in dead-end jobs in the
clerical sector. In turn, the married women in the labor force paved the
way for the rise of the modern career woman, doing work that requires
a lengthy period of training and that offers genuine opportunities for
promotion. As late as 1970, only 14 percent of all doctoral degrees
were awarded to women, only 8 percent of all students enrolled in law
schools were women, only 8 percent of all medical school graduates
were women. By the end of the 1990s, women earned 40 percent of all
doctoral degrees and represented over 40 percent of all graduates from
medical and law schools.[15]

Professor Costa's statistics are for the United States, but the same
pattern applies to Canada. Moreover, her statistics are already out-
dated. Both in Canada and the United States, women currently outnumber—or are on the verge of outnumbering—men in medical and
law schools.[16] As well, more women than men are enrolled in doctoral
programs in the United States, and in Canada, women are about to
become the majority. More generally, 57% of full-time university students in Canada are women.[17] In brief, although there is still progress
to be made—particularly in pay equity and female presence in the
nation's corner offices, corporate boardrooms, and legislative assem-
blies—women's participation in the labour market has vastly increased.

Much of this progress is in full display in labour force statistics.
Since the mid-1970s, the labour force participation rate of Canadian
women aged twenty-five to sixty-four increased spectacularly, from
49% to 76%.[18] The wide gap separating men from women was narrowed by nearly 80%, from forty-three percentage points in 1976
to nine in 2008. This progress was fastest in the fourteen years from
1976 to 1990. From the early 1990s onward, growth in female labour
force participation has been more modest and has slowed gradually.
The process of convergence with men has stalled since the turn of the
decade.

The labour force explosion produced by the baby boom generation and the rise of female workers boosted all of Canada's regional

economies. It played, however, a much more important role in older, faster-aging provinces. Take, for example, the Maritimes. From 1978 to 2008, the region's population grew 9%, from 1.67 to 1.82 million. Had the region's age structure and participation rate remained the same, this population gain would have translated into 62,000 more people in the labour force by 2008. Yet, the actual gain was much more significant: 296,000. In other words, nearly four-fifths of the Maritimes' labour force growth was accounted for not by population growth, but by changes in its participation rate driven mostly by the rise of female workers and the aging of the baby boom generation. By contrast, these two forces accounted for less than two-fifths of Canada's labour force growth (2.6 million of a total labour force gain of 7 million).[19]

By the late 2000s, the growth dividend of these forces had turned into a liability. As women are no longer catching up with men in labour force participation, Canada's participation rate is not growing anymore; in fact, it is declining as baby boomers are exiting the workforce. From 1978 to 2008, changes in Canada's participation rate added 88,000 new people to its labour force each year. Since 2008, they have *subtracted* more than 42,000 annually. This largely explains why labour force growth slowed from an average of 232,000 from 1978 to 2008 to about 167,000 since the turn of the decade. But at least Canada's labour force is still growing strong. The story is entirely different, however, in older regions such as the Maritimes. From 1978 to 2008, the Maritimes added on average 10,000 workers each year. Since the turn of the decade, it has been losing 1,000 annually.

More generally, the Great Demographic Imbalance is having a highly uneven impact on labour forces across the country. After having progressed at a healthy clip of 1.7% annually from 1998 to 2008, Central Canada's labour force since grew by a much more modest 0.8%. Meanwhile, the Prairies' labour force growth only declined by about one-quarter, from 2.2% to 1.7%. The Great Demographic Imbalance has contributed to cutting labour force growth by more than half in Central Canada, while in the Prairies, growth remains roughly in line with where Central Canada stood before 2008.[20]

In short, the labour market, long the main engine of growth across Canada, is slowing. In younger, slower-aging provinces, it is still going strong; in some older, faster-aging provinces, the transmission has actually shifted into reverse.

Productivity Growth

So what can we expect in the years ahead? What is the new normal for Canada's economic growth in the age of the Great Demographic Imbalance? Just as importantly, how does this new normal differ from region to region?

So far, we have examined only one aspect of the growth equation: how an aging population is reshaping labour supply. To fully answer the above questions, we must also turn our attention to productivity growth, the other driver of long-term economic growth prospects.

In common parlance, the term *productivity* refers to *physical productivity*, or the efficiency with which a given task is carried out. The faster it can be performed, the more productive we are. In economic terms, it refers to the value created by a given unit of input. The more value we can create in a given amount of time, the more productive we are. In turn, this greater value can come from producing more, selling at a higher price, or both.

The most commonly used measure of productivity is labour productivity. This term refers to the average value created per hour worked and is usually expressed as real GDP per hour worked. Canada's low productivity relative to the United States, the world's most productive major economy, has been a secular concern of policy-makers. In 2013 GDP per hour worked stood roughly 25% below that in the United States.[21] Within Canada itself, the gap separating the more from the less productive provinces is even wider. In 2013 GDP per hour worked was twice as high in Alberta as in Prince Edward Island (seventy versus thirty-five dollars).[22]

Despite its name, labour productivity depends on many factors beyond labour. One is luck. From the turn of the millennium until recently, the run-up in the price of oil and other commodities generated a major windfall for many resource-rich provinces. As the value of the resources they extract shot up, labour productivity most often did as well (with the notable exception of Alberta's oil sands[23]). This windfall is why, until recently, oil-rich Newfoundland and Labrador was witnessing the fastest increase in productivity growth of all provinces (see table 2.1). Not only did the province's economic base shift to include a much greater share of high-value commodities (first and foremost, oil), the latter's average prices rose considerably, thus further increasing the value of the province's output and its labour productivity. However, since oil prices began declining from their peak in the late 2000s, Newfoundland and Labrador has been registering the worst productivity performance of all provinces. Luck cuts both ways, particularly when it comes to natural resources.

Industrial setbacks can also lead to labour productivity growth. Major negative shocks often lead to the failure of less efficient or marginal operators. This usually results in a smaller but more efficient industry. Although jobs are lost, production losses are typically smaller and/or of relatively short duration; as a result, average output per worker goes up. This was the case, for instance, in the forest products industry across Canada for most of the past decade.[24] So long as employment losses in industries going through consolidation are more than compensated by gains in fast-growing, well-paying industries, this process of industrial restructuring is a good thing. It is through this creative destruction that an economy grows and remains competitive, perpetually renewing itself by shifting workers from one industry to another in reaction to changing market circumstances. However, in more rural, resource-based regions, a drop in employment in a given industry will often result in a loss of economic vitality, forcing people to accept lower-paying employment locally or to migrate to find better-paying jobs, often outside their home province. In short, in smaller, resource-based provinces, creative destruction, *though inevitable*, can often destroy as much as it creates. Productivity growth and economic health should not always be held as synonymous: *why* labour productivity grows is just as important as *how fast* it does.

Another source of labour productivity improvement is investment, in both physical and human capital. Accumulation of physical capital improves productivity through two main channels: capital deepening (improvements resulting from workers having more equipment to work with) and embodied technological change (improvements flowing from the fact that new, state-of-the-art equipment is more productive). As for human capital, it accumulates when workers improve their productive knowledge. An economy's stock of human capital is a key determinant of its innovation potential. Innovation, in turn, is a source of economic growth. Innovation often brings to mind white-coated scientists in a laboratory working on a new invention. This is only a small part of the innovation spectrum. In fact, Canada benefits much more from broader forms of innovation: refinements to existing technologies and processes or the adoption of technologies and processes that already exist but are new to Canadian firms (more on this in the next chapter).

It is easy to discuss generalities about the fundamental determinants of productivity growth; predicting how it will evolve over time is much trickier. Productivity statistics can be quite fickle, fluctuating considerably over short and even relatively long periods. This is the case particularly for resource-dependent economies, whose productivity numbers tend to change dramatically with commodity prices. In larger, more diversified economies, productivity trends normally reflect a broader array of factors; yet, this does not mean they are immune from large swings. Take Central Canada, the country's largest and most diversified economic region. From 1993 to 2003, Central Canada's labour productivity grew by a robust 1.7% annually. Back then, the region's exports of manufactured and other products were strong, buoyed notably by a very robust United States economy and a low Canadian dollar. As these forces turned from tailwind to headwind over the following ten years, labour productivity growth dropped dramatically, to an average of 0.5% annually.

The Business Sector

So far, we have looked at productivity statistics from an economy-wide perspective, including the public sector. This chapter seeks to ascertain the economic prospects of provinces, and thus their ability to support public spending through their own revenues. A province's ability to generate own source revenues depends on two things: how large its tax base is and how much it can (and wants to) tax it. In turn, the size of a government's tax base depends first and foremost on the size of its business sector. Therefore, in assessing the ability of a province to generate own source revenues, we must zero in on the business sector.

·I noted earlier that poorer provinces have been converging with the rest of the country on key indicators of standards of living over the past half century or so. This process has stopped in recent years. If we exclude Newfoundland and Labrador, business sector productivity grew slowest in the Maritimes, Canada's poorest region. From 2005 to 2015, the region's business sector productivity grew 0.2% annually, three times slower than the Canadian average. Compounding the impact of this bleak productivity record is an equally bleak job growth performance. From 2005 to 2015, Canada's business sector added a total of 1.3 million jobs, an increase of 10.1%. Proportionally speaking, the Maritimes added nearly ten times fewer jobs. The region's business sector added 7,300 jobs, for a gain of 1.2%. Since the turn of the decade, employment in the region is no longer growing.

As a result of this poor performance, the Maritimes' business sector is shrinking and falling further behind the rest of the country. In 2005, the business sector accounted for 67.3% of the region's economy. By 2015, this proportion was down to 63.6%. For Canada as a whole, it stood at around 75%, while in the prosperous Prairies, it was around 80%. In short, the Maritimes' economy is showing increasing signs of distress. This is a disturbing state of affairs as we are entering an era where the pressures to expand the public sector to care for an aging population will only worsen and will be sharpest in older, faster aging provinces. And the money to fund extra public spending will have to come from the local business sector—or Ottawa.[25]

Projections for Productivity Growth

So what can be said about the productivity growth prospects of Canada and its various regions? How will provincial governments differ in their ability to fund their programs through productivity growth?

As noted earlier, a province's tax base depends not only on how fast productivity is growing in the business sector, but also on the size of said sector. Therefore, if one assumes that productivity will grow at the same pace across Canada, the regions that have proportionally larger business sectors (e.g., the Prairies) will see their tax bases grow faster than those with smaller sectors (e.g., the Maritimes). The projections below make no such assumption, but they do take into account the fact that the size of the business sector differs considerably throughout the country. To reflect this situation, the labour productivity projections are applied to the entire economy, including the public sector (total economy labour productivity). In doing so, it is assumed that labour productivity growth in the non-business sector—which essentially covers public services—will remain flat. Although productivity growth in this sector is notoriously slow (it is at times negative, as we will see in chapter 5), there are two other more important reasons for this assumption.

The first relates to how productivity is measured in the public sector. In the business sector, market prices are available to determine the value of output, and thus, productivity. In the public sector, where most services are heavily if not entirely subsidized, price information cannot be used as a proxy for output value. Productivity is instead measured using the amounts spent producing the services. This means, for instance, that a real wage increase will show up in the public sector as a productivity gain regardless of whether workers have become more productive.

The second reason relates to the ultimate purpose of this chapter: to assess the economic growth prospects of provinces and, as a consequence, their ability to sustain future public spending pressures through own source revenues. Given how productivity is measured in the public sector, it makes no sense to assume positive productivity growth. In most provinces—and in poorer ones in particular—spending more means borrowing more. Assuming positive productivity growth in the public sector is thus tantamount to claiming that when a province adds to its debt to spend more to cover costs such as wage increases and other current consumption items, it enhances its ability to spend more in the future. In the real world, it usually works the other way around, as we all know.

With these precisions, let's turn to economy-wide (total) labour productivity projections. As noted earlier, predicting future productivity growth is a risky venture. Some have speculated that population aging will exert an upward pressure on productivity as labour scarcity pushes wages up, thus providing businesses with greater incentives to invest in labour-saving technology. Some of this will no doubt happen, but population aging will also increase demand in numerous labour-intensive service industries that have notoriously low productivity growth, such as elderly care. The two phenomena are likely to cancel each other out, at least to some extent. In fact, available empirical evidence suggests that population aging actually tends to mildly depress rather than increase labour productivity growth.[26]

In any event, the reality is that productivity growth depends on a much broader set of variables. These range from technological change,[27] human capital accumulation, changes in demand for Canadian products, other shocks affecting the competitiveness of firms (such as energy costs and exchange rates), and so on. While prospects for productivity growth are uncertain, on balance, there are no reasons to expect things to change dramatically. This is why my productivity growth projections are based on the common approach of extrapolating from past trends. I settle on fifteen years as the appropriate length for the reference period. This strikes a good balance between focusing on relevant recent trends affecting productivity while still covering a period long enough to capture the effects of business cycles. This period extends over a decade of robust expansion (1998–2007) and more tepid growth afterwards. Just as importantly, it covers two sub-periods of comparable duration when commodity prices were low (1998–2005) and then generally high (2005–2013). Finally, opting for a fifteen-year horizon does away with much of the volatility inherent in productivity statistics.[28]

Labour productivity in the Canadian business sector grew on average by 1.2% annually from 1998 to 2013, while for Canadian provinces it ranged between 0.5% (Alberta) and 1.7% (Newfoundland and Labrador).[29] These are the rates we use in our projections, except for Newfoundland and Labrador for which I assume a growth rate one-third lower. We saw earlier that Newfoundland and Labrador's labour productivity was boosted by a shift in its economic structure from relatively low value-added products to high-value commodities (first and foremost, oil). As this shift has already occurred, its positive impact is embodied in economic data. Furthermore, Newfoundland and Labrador's labour productivity is now the worst in the country as oil prices have come down sharply from their high of $145 per barrel in 2008.[30] The next chapter illustrates that with the shale revolution and other developments in the oil industry, the long-term price out-look appears moderate, which means it is unlikely the province could witness the kind of productivity growth experienced on average over the past fifteen years.

Combining business and non-business sector productivity growth produces an economy-wide growth rate for labour productivity of 0.9% for Canada as a whole. This is in line with the growth rate for the past thirty years. To reflect the uncertain nature of this projection, the low and high scenarios are 25% below and above this rate; they are respectively set at 0.7% and 1.1%.

Projections for Labour Input Growth

We now turn to the other main force shaping the economic pros-pects of Canada's various regions: the likely evolution of labour input growth, that is, the number of hours worked. There are four elements to consider.

The first relates to the projected size and age distribution of the pop-ulation. I use Statistics Canada's scenarios described in chapter 1 (low, medium, high). The second relates to how the average number of hours worked per worker will evolve. This number has declined slightly in recent decades, and now stands at about thirty-three hours per week.[31] I assume it will remain at that level until the end of the projection hori-zon, 2013–38. The third factor is unemployment rates. Canada's unem-ployment rate has decreased considerably over time as its population has aged. The average unemployment rate declined from 9.4% in the 1980s to 7.0% in the first decade of this millennium. I assume that with greater labour scarcity in the years ahead, the unemployment rate will continue its downward trajectory, decreasing by 0.05 percentage points annually. Canada's unemployment rate will reach 5.8% by 2038 in this scenario. The final factor relates to labour force participation rates. My projections are based on the following assumptions:

- Female participation. Women will modestly further catch up with men; women's participation rate has declined since the turn of the decade, and the gap with men's rate has held steady at about 9%. As women have now caught up and surpassed men in educational attainment—a key determinant of labour market participation—the prospects for a further narrowing of this gap depend on other variables such as more progressive daycare and other social and workplace policies that further facilitate workforce participation. I assume progress in this area will narrow the gap by a further two percentage points from now until 2038, at a pace of 0.1 percentage points annually until 2033.

• *Youth participation.* The youth participation rate for ages fifteen to twenty-four will remain unchanged. This rate has remained relatively constant over the past decade, at around 64% for Canada as a whole. Part-time employment rose modestly, while full-time employment declined, which reflects at least partly the fact that a greater share of young people attend college or university and tend to do so for longer. I assume these trends will continue in the years ahead.

• *Male participation.* The men's participation rate for the age group twenty-five to sixty-four, which currently hovers around 86%, will grow modestly. Male labour force participation increased slightly over the past three decades, although it dipped significantly during the recession and the austerity years of the mid-1990s. I assume this rate will grow further by a percentage point from now to 2038, at a pace of 0.05 percentage points until 2033. As the evolution of women's rate is pegged to that of men, this increase in men's participation rate is reflected in that of women's.

• *Older individuals' participation.* The participation rate of individuals aged sixty-five to sixty-nine, which is currently around 26%, will grow by half from now to 2038. This reflects the fact that people remain healthy longer and that further policy changes will make it easier for older workers to remain in the labour force longer. The participation rate for those aged seventy and over will remain the same, at around 7%. While more and more people aged seventy to seventy-four will no doubt remain in the labour force, I assume this trend will be offset by the significant growth of the population aged seventy-five and over with the aging of the baby boomers.

Economic Growth in the Age of the Great Demographic Imbalance

As table 2.2 shows, Canada's economy will grow appreciably slower than in previous decades. Over the twenty-five-year period ending in 2008, when all baby boomers were of working age and women were still catching up with men in terms of labour force participation, the Canadian economy grew on average by 2.8% annually.[32] From 2013 to 2038, it is projected to expand by a more modest 1.7% or two-fifths slower in the baseline scenario.

However, focusing on the national outlook hides much of the story, which will unfold at the regional level. Between 1983 and 2008, *all* of Canada's regional economies grew at a robust rate. The country's fastest-growing region, the Prairies, grew at around 3.1% annually, while the slowest growing, the Maritimes, posted a still robust 2.2% average annual gain. Moreover, these differences almost entirely disappear if we consider growth in GDP per capita. On this metric, not only did the Maritimes fare almost as well as the Prairies, they in fact outperformed the rest of the country by a comfortable margin.[33] Rather than growing further apart, the Maritimes were pulling closer to the Canadian average. Oil-rich Newfoundland and Labrador did even better, making its way from the bottom rungs to the top three of Canada's GDP per capita ladder.

The Great Demographic Imbalance will change all of this. Over the next two decades, the gaps will widen between rich and poor, young and old, east and west. While population aging will depress growth across the country, its impact will range from moderate in the Prairies to devastating in Atlantic Canada. In the baseline scenario, the Prairies are expected to post a healthy 2.1% annual gain in GDP over the 2013–38 period. By contrast, growth in Atlantic Canada will grind to a halt (around 0.1% annually). As for Quebec, Ontario, and British Columbia, their economies are projected to grow 1.1%, 1.4%, and 1.7% respectively, a decline of around 50% relative to the quarter century from 1983 to 2008. Comparing Quebec and British Columbia is instructive. As we saw in chapter 1, both provinces are expected to age at the same pace from 2013 to 2038—at least when only considering the two provinces' median age and share of seniors—yet economic growth in British Columbia is expected to be 50% stronger than in Quebec. This is because their underlying aging dynamics will differ. British Columbia, with its stronger migration outlook, will see proportionally more people joining its labour force than Quebec.

Given that faster population growth is the main reason why some regions will grow faster than others, disparities in real GDP per capita among provinces are projected to be much smaller than for real GDP. But two critical points remain. First, after having narrowed for over half a century, regional disparities will widen again.[34] More importantly, it is the older, faster-aging provinces that will grow slowest. By 2038 the Prairies' economy will be around 70% larger than it is today. The region will thus have a much larger tax base to support its seniors, who will account for just below one-fifth of the population. By contrast, in 2038 Atlantic Canada's economy will be only 3% larger than it is today, while its share of seniors will grow from 19% to 31%. In short, the provinces that need economic growth the most to meet rapidly escalating health and elderly care bills are the ones that will grow slowest. These are the very provinces whose public finances are already among the most strained.

It's worth pointing out in closing that these projections do not take into account the future course of fiscal transfers, which I discuss in chapters 6 and 7. Under current federal programs, most notably elderly benefits (Old Age Security, Guaranteed Income Supplement, Spousal Allowance) and—to a lesser extent—Equalization[35], population aging should translate into more federal money going to poorer, faster-aging provinces. This should somewhat improve economic conditions in those provinces, but one should not expect an improvement that would put them on a growth path anywhere near their own past performance or the future performance of their slower-aging counterparts.

Table 2.2: Growth Projections, Canada and Provinces, 2013–38

Source: Author's calculations based on Statistics Canada, CANSIM, tables 051-0001, 052-0005, 282-0002, 383-0029, and 384-0038.

	Low Growth (%)				Medium Growth (%)				High Growth (%)			
	Hours worked	Labour productivity	Real GDP	Real GDP per capita	Hours worked	Labour productivity	Real GDP	Real GDP per capita	Hours worked	Labour productivity	Real GDP	Real GDP per capita
Newfoundland and Labrador	-1.3	0.7	-0.6	0.1	-1.2	0.9	-0.3	0.3	-1.0	1.1	0.0	0.4
Prince Edward Island	0.3	0.2	0.5	0.0	0.6	0.3	0.9	0.1	0.9	0.3	1.3	0.1
Nova Scotia	-0.5	0.4	-0.1	0.1	-0.3	0.5	0.2	0.2	-0.3	0.6	0.3	0.3
New Brunswick	-0.5	0.4	0.0	0.2	-0.3	0.6	0.3	0.3	-0.2	0.7	0.6	0.3
Quebec	0.1	0.5	0.6	0.3	0.4	0.7	1.1	0.5	0.7	0.9	1.5	0.6
Ontario	0.3	0.5	0.8	0.4	0.7	0.7	1.4	0.5	1.0	0.8	1.9	0.7
Manitoba	1.0	0.9	1.9	1.4	1.2	1.2	2.4	1.4	1.5	1.5	3.1	1.7
Saskatchewan	0.6	0.6	1.1	0.8	0.8	0.7	1.6	0.9	1.1	0.9	2.1	1.0
Alberta	1.4	0.3	1.7	0.3	1.8	0.4	2.2	0.4	2.1	0.5	2.6	0.4
British Columbia	0.4	0.5	1.0	0.5	0.9	0.7	1.7	0.6	1.4	0.9	2.3	0.8
Canada	0.4	0.7	1.1	0.7	0.8	0.9	1.7	0.8	1.1	1.1	2.3	1.0

Note: Scenarios are formulated using Statistics Canada's low, baseline, and high population growth scenarios outlined in chapter 1, as well as the low, baseline, and high labour productivity growth scenarios and labour market assumptions outlined earlier in this chapter.

Summing Up

From the mid-1960s until a few years ago, Canada's economy surfed on a rising tide of labour force growth, fuelled by the baby boom generation and the steady, largely successful march of women toward equal participation in the workforce. Although this tide lifted all provincial boats, it played a particularly important role in Atlantic Canada.

This tide is now receding, dragging down economic growth. It will affect older, faster-aging provinces much more than the rest of the country. As a result, after having narrowed over the past half century, the prosperity gap between Canada's have and have-less provinces will widen. It is thus in a context of much slower growth that older, faster-aging, and heavily indebted provinces will face much greater pressures to spend more on public services.

Chapter 3

AND NOW FOR THE "WHAT IF" SCENARIOS...

The first two chapters outline projections about Canada's population aging and economic growth dynamics. It may be tempting
to dismiss these projections as simply that, projections. After
all, how can we be so sure about what the future holds? Who
would have thought merely two decades ago that provinces such as
Newfoundland and Labrador as well as Saskatchewan, both limp-
ing under the crippling weight of debt and outmigration, would stop
receiving Equalization payments? And aren't things changing right
before our eyes with oil now trading at much lower prices than just a
few years ago? Isn't this rebalancing economic growth across the country and thus dampening the progress of Canada's Great Demographic
Imbalance?

The short answer is no. While no one can predict the future, there
are nevertheless strong reasons to put a great deal of stock in the central
conclusion of this book: eastern and western provinces will continue
to pull apart demographically and economically in the years ahead.

The Weight of History

Let's start with demographics. There are three related reasons why
Canada's Great Demographic Imbalance will remain with us for at
least the next quarter century. All three have to do with how history
weighs heavily on demography. We saw in chapter 1 how a region's
population level and age structure are products of past events—births,
deaths, and migratory gains or losses that have occurred over time.

These past events shape future outcomes.

Birth rates are the first reason why the Great Demographic Imbalance is not going away anytime soon. In addition to seeing more young workers entering their labour forces today, provinces that have welcomed more migrants and had more babies over the past few decades are in a much better position to have more babies in the future. That is because past births and migration gains have kept them younger, with greater shares of women of child-bearing age. Conversely, provinces that are aging faster do so because they have had fewer babies and attracted fewer migrants in the past. As a result, they are left with faster-growing ranks of seniors and fewer women of child-bearing age. It took nearly a half century of lower births and poorer migration outcomes in eastern provinces for the age gap between them and their western counterparts to open up as wide as it is today.[1] The age gap between Alberta and the Maritimes is not likely to shrink just because the oil sands are having a few or even several bad years. In fact, it will most likely continue to expand regardless.

The 2006 to 2009 period is highly instructive in this regard. In those years, Alberta's economy declined on average by 0.8% annually, while the Maritimes posted an annual gain of 0.7%. Unsurprisingly, Alberta's economic setback had a negative impact on its migration record. From a level of 46,000 in 2005–06, net interprovincial migration into Alberta declined steadily, and even turned negative in 2009–10 (-4,000). For their part, the Maritimes saw a steady improvement, from an annual deficit of 8,000 in 2006–07 to a surplus of 1,000 in 2009–10. Yet, despite all this, Alberta's median age only grew by 0.2 year from 2006 to 2009, while it grew six times faster in the Maritimes. This, in turn, is in no small part because Alberta had proportionally many more babies than the Maritimes: while its population in 2006 was less than two times larger than the Maritimes, Alberta produced three times more babies from 2006–07 to 2009–10.[2]

A second, similar reason why east and west will continue to diverge demographically is that migratory patterns tend to be self-reinforcing. Over time, sustained migratory inflows contribute to building the critical mass that makes drawing new migrants easier. This means that migrants, whether interprovincial or international, are not likely to head to Moncton or Charlottetown just because one or a few western provinces are not faring as well as in the past. Rather, they are more likely to concentrate in places that have already welcomed more migrants and are more dynamic economically—Vancouver and Toronto in particular. In short, if the Prairies run out of favour with migrants—not a foregone conclusion, as we will see later in this chapter—this is much more likely to benefit Ontario and British Columbia than provinces east of the Ottawa River. There is more than a century of migratory history supporting such a prediction.

The third reason why the Great Demographic Imbalance will remain with us in the decades ahead has to do with the limitations of deliberate policies to boost fertility rates (natalist policies). If the weight of history clearly favours provinces west of the Ottawa River, then this leaves Eastern Canada with raising fertility rates as the only way to bring population aging in line with Western Canada. We saw in chapter 1 that since the mid-2000s, Quebec's fertility rate stands above the Canadian average, a situation not seen since the end of the baby boom. Some have credited Quebec's natalist policies for having contributed to this outcome.[3] Yet, just because Quebec has an above-average fertility rate does not mean it is better at making babies than Canada as a whole. Quebec's fertility rate may be higher than Canada's, but its birth rate is not since the province has a lower share of women of child-bearing age—a product of a history of lower birth rates and poorer migration outcomes.[4] As for Atlantic Canada, its share of women of child-bearing age is significantly lower than Quebec's. This means that in order to emulate Quebec's success in having more babies, it would have to bring its fertility rate much higher than Quebec's. Given the region's average fertility rate is the lowest in Canada next to British Columbia, this would be no small feat.

Furthermore, at the risk of pointing out the obvious, having more babies does not produce immediate results in terms of growth and prosperity. Quebec's recent fertility uptick will only start paying economic dividends in ten to fifteen years from now, when those born since the mid-2000s start entering the labour force. In other words, rather than helping it out over the next little while, Quebec's recent fertility gain means it will have to support a larger population of dependents with proportionally fewer and fewer workers. For another fifteen years or so, Quebec, like the rest of Eastern Canada, can rely only on migration to boost its working-age population. And for reasons already discussed and on which the book later expands, it is unrealistic to assume Eastern Canada will perform better than the rest of the country in drawing migrants from Canada and abroad. In fact, migration can be expected to continue exacerbating the consequences of the Great Demographic Imbalance in the years ahead. As we saw earlier, it notably explains why British Columbia's economy is projected to grow 50% faster than Quebec's, even though both provinces will age at roughly the same pace.

Why Canada's Regional Economies Will Grow Apart

Just as there are many reasons to conclude the Great Demographic Imbalance will not go away anytime soon, there are equally strong reasons to believe Canada's regions will continue to diverge economically, pulling have and have less, east and west, further apart.

The first reason is obvious yet of critical importance: the much dimmer growth prospects of eastern provinces flow directly from the Great Demographic Imbalance. For decades, these provinces have produced fewer babies and attracted and retained fewer migrants than their western counterparts. As a result, they are left with proportionally more baby boomers exiting the labour force and with fewer new workers coming in. A few years of solid economic growth in eastern provinces will not meaningfully alter this reality. For eastern provinces to witness labour force growth in line with their western counterparts over the long term, they will need to consistently outperform them on economic growth by a very wide margin. Such an outcome would run counter to more than a century of history.

Having said this, hope springs eternal. There will always be observers to argue that older, faster-aging provinces can turn things around, even when facing a formidable force that has been gathering strength for over fifty years, such as the Great Demographic Imbalance. When not simply taking a leap of faith, those who make such claims usually wager on innovation or natural resources development—or both.[5] Unfortunately, neither is likely to reverse the economic effects of the Great Demographic Imbalance.

Innovation an Unlikely Panacea

Innovation is touted by many as the cure-all for local economic development. Often when a politician wants to portray himself as a visionary leader with a plan for the economy, he will don a white laboratory coat and fancy protective eyewear to pay a visit to one of the many firms or research labs that have received one form of government support or another. Typically, his speech will be filled with data showing how little local businesses invest in research and development (R&D) and conclude that this is what ails the economy. Rather than ask himself why this is so, he will most likely simply state that his plan will leverage private sector resources to change this state of affairs and—if he feels bold or delusional enough—turn the community or province into the next Silicon Valley. Because no one wants to be seen opposing these sorts of "motherhood and apple pie" statements, critics will usually remain silent. They will rarely point out the obvious, which is that Canadian governments have been pouring enormous amounts of money into R&D funding over the last two decades, yet Canada in general—and provinces outside Central Canada in particular—remains in the bottom rungs in the developed world when it comes to business sector R&D.

The purpose here is not to put government efforts to promote R&D on trial. There is a very strong rationale for public investments in knowledge creation, particularly in basic or fundamental science. The point is simply that politicians in older, faster-aging provinces without major metropolitan centres should not mistake their wishes for reality: the odds of closing the prosperity gap with the rest of the country through innovation are next to nothing.

To explain why this is so, let's start with a definition. The term *innovation* refers to *the process through which new knowledge is put to the test of markets.* An equivalent definition that is more common in the economic literature refers to innovation as *the changes in the goods and services we consume or in the way they are produced.*[6] An example of a change in goods or services is the smart phone launched by Research in Motion more than fifteen years ago, while an example of a new way of producing goods would be Henry Ford's introduction of the mass-production technique almost a century ago. These are two instances of major innovations that have had a great impact on our economy and society. Such innovations are usually called *radical*; they are also relatively rare. The vast majority of innovations are incremental in nature and consist in refinements to existing goods and services or production processes.

There are several other important points about innovation. The first is that invention and innovation are not one and the same. Key to the definition of innovation is the notion of commercialization, or putting things to the test of markets. A glove with six fingers may be an invention, but it would likely not have much success as an innovation. Commercialization is how invention is turned into innovation. It is how economic value is extracted from knowledge.

The second observation is that innovation is an ongoing process; it does not end when a new idea or product is brought into the marketplace. The adoption of an innovation by users, which usually leads to further changes to the original product, is also part of the innovation process. The economic literature makes a distinction between when an innovation is first commercialized (world-first innovation) and the process through which it is diffused throughout society (innovation adoption).

Great rewards can accrue to world-first innovators, particularly when their innovations cannot be easily replicated by competitors. The same applies to regions. Regions that are hotbeds of world-first innovative activity tend to grow faster, showing greater resiliency and higher average wages than others. That said, however large the local rewards of world-first innovation, they pale in comparison to the broader societal benefits of innovation adoption. The global impact of the smart phone is much larger now that over 50% of adults around the world own one compared to when it was first launched.[7] Similarly, the Internet plays a much bigger role in global commerce today than it did when Netscape introduced it to the masses two decades ago. Technology diffusion (innovation adoption) is the main conduit through which society at large benefits from innovation.

As is the case for all processes involving change, innovation creates winners and losers—the third key point. As demand shifts toward new products or technologies, those who fail to adapt often end up losing market shares or wages, as their products or skills become obsolete. The same applies to regions. Ultimately, innovation lifts all regional boats: the standards of living we enjoy across the developed world today are built on numerous innovations, from electricity to the internal combustion engine, mass manufacturing, computers, and the Internet. But innovation can also have severe long-term regional implications.

The Maritimes is a clear case in point. As we saw earlier, prior to Confederation the Maritimes was a very fast-growing place. From 1803 to 1861, the region's population grew by a fivefold factor. The Maritimes had many banks and one of the world's largest merchant fleets supporting a thriving maritime trade with Great Britain, New England, and the British West Indies. The region's situation started to change shortly after Confederation. The "sea and sail" era, which had made the region's prosperity, drew to an end. Steam replaced sail as the dominant propulsion technology, and iron replaced wood in the construction of vessels. Shipbuilding fell into decline. Railways quickly opened up the North American continent, turning the focus of trade increasingly inland. Later, in the early twentieth century, the advent of a third innovation, mass manufacturing, further concentrated economic activity in Central Canada. Consolidation is inherent to the logic of mass manufacturing. To ensure its efficiency, mass manufacturing requires economies of scale. The Laurentian lowland region, with its larger population and greater proximity to fast-expanding United States and Western Canadian markets, was best positioned to become Canada's mass-manufacturing heartland, and so it did. As this happened, it set in motion a virtuous cycle of industrialization and population growth. The Maritimes, for its part, was left at the periphery, its economy depending mostly on natural resources and its population growing much slower than in Central Canada.[8] While Maritimers ultimately benefited from steamships, railways, and mass manufacturing, the region's population growth and prosperity have been lagging behind the rest of the country since. History, it turns out, matters to regional economic development just as much, if not more, than it does to demography.

A fourth key point is that the relationship between innovation and economic geography is a two-way street. Just as innovation has historically shaped Canada's economic geography, the latter is now also shaping the country's innovation performance. World-first innovation does not occur randomly across the country. Rather, it is disproportionately concentrated in large urban regions, particularly the Quebec City–Windsor Corridor. This is nothing new, nor is it unique to Canada. The propensity of world-first innovative activity to cluster in large urban areas has been a defining feature of the economic landscape since the early days of industrialization. The reasons for this clustering have not changed much either: now just as then, firms and entrepreneurs are on a quest for location-specific *external economies*, that is, sources of competitive advantage that can only be tapped by locating in specific areas. Examples of such external economies include large pools of well-trained workers; dense and responsive networks of suppliers; easy access to sophisticated capital providers; shared specialized infrastructure (which nowadays includes knowledge assets such as world-class universities and research laboratories); and access to "sticky" knowledge (expertise and know-how that can only be effectively transmitted through face-to-face interactions). Places that thrive on world-first innovation, such as Silicon Valley, Route 128 around Boston, or North Carolina's Research Triangle, do so precisely because they offer rich innovation "ecosystems."

To be sure, there will always be individual successes in the technological field outside large urban areas. This, however, does not mean it is reasonable to assume that peripheral economies can bank on such successes to dramatically reverse more than a century of economic history and turn themselves into "have" regions. Providing a subsidy to a research lab in a small city, though important to knowledge creation, will often not do much to build the critical mass needed to develop a rich innovation ecosystem. Leaders in smaller, poorer regions may dream of making their provinces self-reliant through innovation-led growth, but the historical record shows just how much the odds are stacked against them. There is little in the history of regional development in Canada that suggests predominantly rural, resource-dependent regions can be turned into world-first innovation powerhouses. Atlantic Canada's largest city, Halifax, ranks as medium-size by Canadian standards. Even though the outlook for innovation-led growth is better there than anywhere else in the region, there are few reasons to believe the city will outperform larger centres across Canada and turn Atlantic Canada into a hotbed of innovation. In fact, while indicators of world-first innovation are better in Nova Scotia than in all other Atlantic provinces, they clearly lag behind the rest of the country by a wide margin.[9]

None of the foregoing points diminish in any way the importance of innovation to all of Canada's regional economies. Innovation is key to the competitiveness of firms and communities across Canada. The type of innovation that matters most to all regions, however, is not world-first innovation but rather innovation adoption. Canada is a small country that produces only a small fraction of the world's knowledge. Relatively few Canadian firms are world-first innovators, but all of them must be good innovation adopters to grow their productivity and maintain their competitiveness. World-first innovation may be the holy grail of innovation policy in Ottawa and in provincial capitals alike, but innovation adoption explains why firms in the Maritimes are not lagging much behind the rest of the country on productivity indicators. Yet, as all firms across the country must be good innovation adopters to secure their future, it is unrealistic to assume that innovation adoption can provide slower-growing regions with a competitive edge over the rest of the country. As such, innovation adoption cannot be relied upon to bridge the growth gap caused by the Great Demographic Imbalance.

Natural Resources and the Future of Regional Economic Development
In the fall of 2014, David Alward's Progressive Conservative Party sought re-election with a slogan asking New Brunswickers to "Say Yes!" to natural resource development. With such a rallying cry, the Progressive Conservatives ostensibly aimed to drive a wedge between them and their main rival, Brian Gallant's Liberals, who had called for a moratorium on all hydraulic fracturing activity in the province. As part of their campaign, the Tories frequently compared New Brunswick to Saskatchewan, a former have-less province that chose, according to them, to "say yes" to resource development.[10] All New Brunswickers had to do to stumble upon prosperity was say yes too.

If only reaching "have" status were so simple. New Brunswick chose to say yes to developing its natural resources a long time ago. Just like Saskatchewan, New Brunswick was built on its natural riches, and these continue to sustain its economy today. The rub, though, is that New Brunswick's natural resource base pales in comparison to that of Saskatchewan. While Saskatchewan's population is only one-third larger than New Brunswick's, its geographic area is nine times greater. The western province contains 40% of the nation's arable land, a precious asset at a time when the emerging world is consuming ever-larger quantities of agricultural products (and with climate change, the province could even see its land surface under cultivation expand as the growing season lengthens[11]). Saskatchewan also sits on the world's largest potash deposits, an essential and much sought-after product to improve agricultural yields throughout the globe. And last but not least, Saskatchewan is the nation's second largest oil and gas producer.

New Brunswick, too, has natural riches, including potash and shale gas deposits. But the reality is that Saskatchewan's natural resource economy is more than fifteen times larger than New Brunswick's. In fact, in 2012 Saskatchewan's natural resources GDP was almost as large as New Brunswick's entire GDP.[12] And that's excluding the size-able contributions of support and downstream manufacturing indus-tries to Saskatchewan's natural resources–fuelled prosperity.

In the end, the Liberals won the 2014 election and imposed a moratorium on hydraulic fracturing shortly thereafter, effectively stalling the development of New Brunswick's shale gas industry in its tracks. But Gallant's decision to say no to shale gas (for now, at least) does not mean, as the PC's slogan implied, that he has foregone New Brunswick's opportunity to turn itself into an economic powerhouse like Saskatchewan; the opportunity simply was not there to begin with. According to available estimates, a mature shale gas industry in New Brunswick could contribute around $1.5 billion in annual GDP, doubling the province's natural resource sector GDP.[13] While a sub-stantial sum, this is still a far cry from Saskatchewan's $24-plus billion natural resources heft (data for 2012).[14]

What applies to New Brunswick applies to other Maritime prov-inces and perhaps even Quebec: natural resources are not likely to work wonders as they did in Saskatchewan. This is in part because their nat-ural resource base in relation to their population is not large enough to have the same economic impact as in Saskatchewan. There is, however, another critical development playing against them: in the years ahead, natural resources are unlikely to generate the same impressive growth in economic rents as they did in the recent past. And rents—the excess of revenues over production costs—are critical as they are the well from which governments can fill up their coffers with royalties and go from have-less to have status. To understand why rents are not likely to follow the same impressive trajectory as in the recent past, a quick detour into the economics of natural resources—in particular the so-called *commodity supercyle theory*—is necessary.

The End of the Commodity Boom

Natural resources have always been critical to Canada's economy. Yet, not so long ago, Canadians were told that to succeed in the twenty-first century, they had to pivot from being a nation of hewers of wood and drawers of water to one of global innovators. This pessimism about the future of natural resources was understandable. Over the last quarter of the previous century, commodity prices were in secular decline. While overall inflation ran on average at 4.8% annually, commodity prices only grew by 2.5%. This means that a basket of commodities worth $100 in 1975 was worth less than $60 in constant dollars twenty-five years later.[15]

The situation changed dramatically toward the turn of the millennium. From 2002 to 2011, commodity prices more than doubled in value (+145%). With such an escalation, commodities returned as the main growth engine of the Canadian economy. This showed clearly in economic statistics, with Newfoundland and Labrador and western provinces growing twice as fast as Central Canada. Interestingly, as commodities regained their lustre, the mantra of turning Canada into an innovation powerhouse receded, giving way to a new ambition of making Canada a global energy superpower.

Experts generally agree the commodity price boom is now over. From 2011 to mid-2014, the prices of commodities produced in Canada have declined mildly. Recently, they have fallen much more due mainly to a very sharp drop in oil prices. Some of the softness in global oil markets is related to demand conditions, with China decelerating from double-digit annual gains to under 7%. There is another, more fundamental reason though: high commodity prices carry the seeds of their own demise. As prices rise and remain high over an extended period, supply eventually expands as new projects are brought online. Many of these projects require heavy upfront investments but have comparatively low operating costs. Once such new projects are developed, they will typically continue operating, even if they are no longer profitable. In fact, in the hope of recovering more of their sunk costs, producers may even be enticed to ramp up production.[16] If this makes sense for producers individually, the overall effect on their industry is to lower prices further. This is part of the logic underlying the commodity supercycle theory, according to which an episode of rapid price increases, such as the one the world has witnessed over the past decade, is usually followed by one of lower prices that lasts until supply and demand are brought into balance again.

That commodity prices tend to follow decades-long supercycles is documented.[17] Yet, there will always be observers to argue that this time is different and that commodity prices will keep rising. And, until recently, this was a popular view among analysts of the oil and gas industry. Indeed, merely a few years ago, many assumed the world was entering a new era of oil scarcity as declining conventional supplies were rapidly eaten up by the emerging world's ever-increasing appetite to fuel its massive growth. From its low of $11 a barrel in 1999, the oil price shot up as high as $145 in 2008. Economists were fretting about the severe consequences of ever-increasing prices, as epitomized by books such as *The End of Growth* by noted Canadian economist Jeff Rubin. In North America, the pressure on conventional supplies also extended to natural gas: as recently as 2005, Alan Greenspan, then chairman of the Federal Reserve Board, was warning Congress that America was running out of natural gas and that rising prices threatened economic growth.[18] There was widespread concern the continent would have to start importing vast amounts of natural gas. The Canaport LNG import terminal in Saint John, New Brunswick, is an eloquent reminder of this very recent yet bygone era.

It turns out, however, that even for the oil and gas industry, the idea that higher prices carry with them the seeds of their own demise has value. Just as for other commodities, sustained higher prices triggered an adjustment process from both supply and demand. On the demand side, more expensive oil translated notably into more

fuel-efficient vehicles. On the supply side, Big Oil pushed explora-
tion and drilling further into politically and geographically difficult
terrain, including kilometres deep into ocean floors in remote offshore locations. Most importantly, though, high prices accelerated
the development of unconventional sources of supplies, such as the
extraction of bitumen from sands and of oil and gas trapped in shale
formations.

Canada owes much of its emergence as an energy superpower to
the development of Alberta's vast oil sands deposits. But the global
game changer is shale, not oil sands. Indeed, the ability to extract oil
and gas economically from shale through hydraulic fracturing and
directional drilling is changing the paradigm for the industry. It is
reshaping the world's energy landscape so rapidly that it is called a
revolution—the shale revolution. The renewed abundance unleashed
by the shale revolution has rebalanced oil and gas markets to an extent
that was thought impossible just a few years ago. Its impact is clearly
visible in the North American gas industry, where shale production
has brought prices down considerably, stabilizing them at around
two-thirds below their level of ten years ago. In the global oil industry,
too, the impact of the shale revolution has manifested, having played
a key role in the dramatic price decline of late 2014.

The shale revolution will not stabilize the oil industry to the same
extent it did for the North American natural gas market. Oil is much
easier to trade across continents than natural gas, which makes it subject to numerous global supply and demand shocks, including the
uncertain path of Asian demand and volatility in the Middle East. But
it remains that the shale revolution is also radically transforming the
oil industry. Contrary to deep-sea drilling and oil sands development,
shale oil production is highly scalable and does not involve enormous
upfront investments. As a result, shale producers are well-positioned
to replace the Saudis as "swing producers," ramping up or scaling
down drilling activity with changes in oil prices. As *The Economist*
put it in December 2014: "a shale-oil well can be drilled in as little
as a week, at a cost of $1.5m. The shale firms know where the shale
deposits are and it is pretty easy to hire new rigs; the only question
is how many wells to drill. The whole business becomes a bit more
like manufacturing drinks: whenever the world is thirsty, you crank

up the bottling plant."[19] The fact that shale output can be brought online quickly and easily makes any move from Saudi Arabia or other Organization of Petroleum Exporting Countries (OPEC) members to lower supply in the hope of propping up prices less effective and more costly—and thus less likely.

Shale and other "tight oil"[20] resources are abundant. While individual estimates vary considerably, the consensus is that there is ample room for the United States to grow its output. Canada, too, has considerable room to grow its production. And while conditions in the near term may not be right for large-scale production outside North America, many other countries with vast deposits are taking active steps to exploit their resources.[21]

The shale revolution could well mean we have entered an era of moderation in oil prices. Even OPEC was forecasting in 2015, in its most optimistic scenario, that oil should only sell for around $76US per barrel by 2025.[22] In fact, while it is projecting global demand to continue growing, OPEC is not expecting oil prices to go much beyond $80US in real terms over the next quarter century—50% below the peak reached in 2008.[23]

It is unclear how this new era of moderation could affect Canadian oil production. Oil sands production will likely grow more slowly than previously anticipated. Still, it is relatively safe to assume that Canada's oil output will continue to grow at a robust clip in the years ahead. As conventional supplies continue to dwindle, more and more oil will have to come from offshore and unconventional sources to meet global demand. While the world will eventually have to wean itself from its addiction to fossil fuels, this will not occur overnight.

It remains, however, that the shale revolution and the end of the commodity supercycle are changing the outlook for provincial governments in terms of the revenues they will draw from oil production. Canada is a high-cost producer. In a world of lower prices, low-cost jurisdictions (e.g., Saudi Arabia) will continue to reap large resource rents, but high-cost jurisdictions, much less so. As long as Canadian oil production remains at the higher end of the spectrum, the prospects for large resource rents, as the country witnessed in recent years, remain bleak.

In short, oil and gas will likely continue to contribute to economic growth in producing provinces in the years ahead. But resource rents per barrel of oil could well end up in the same direction as natural gas: down, way down. The lesson here is that even if some older, faster-aging provinces, such as Quebec, New Brunswick, and Nova Scotia, were to decide to exploit their hydrocarbons (Quebec has known shale gas and oil deposits, while New Brunswick and Nova Scotia have shale gas), they should not expect the same kind of royalties that oil-producing provinces have reaped until recently.

Summing Up

Clearly, Canada's Great Demographic Imbalance and its economic consequences are not going away anytime soon. This is to a large extent because of the critical weight of history: an imbalance that has built up over fifty years cannot realistically be undone in a few or even several years. History also weighs heavily insofar as time's passage has only served to strengthen the very forces that fuelled this imbalance. The provinces that had more babies and welcomed the most migrants are now those best positioned to have still more babies and receive more migrants. As their cities have grown, they are more likely to produce world-first innovation. Innovation will in turn remain critical to Canada's economic performance, but, as noted, it is not a cure-all, particularly for smaller provinces without major metropolitan centres. As for natural resources, they will most likely remain an important source of growth in the years ahead. However, with the exception of Newfoundland and Labrador, they are likely to favour western provinces most. Furthermore, even if one or more eastern provinces were to succeed in becoming natural resource powerhouses, there are strong reasons to suspect natural resources would not fill up their coffers as they did until recently for Canada's resource-rich, easternmost province.

Part II

PUBLIC SPENDING IN THE AGE OF THE GREAT DEMOGRAPHIC IMBALANCE

Chapter 4

GRASSHOPPERS, FROGS, AND LOUIS VUITTON: WHY PROVINCIAL PUBLIC SPENDING IS SO HARD TO ROLL BACK

Many financial crises have punctuated the course of globalization over the past quarter century, from the Mexican peso crisis (1994), to the Asian financial crisis (1997), and the dot-com bust (2001). Compared to these, the global financial crisis of 2007–08 was of an entirely different order. The end of the last decade will go down in history as the time when Wall Street and other global finance capitals nearly took down the world economy. To use an earthquake analogy, this was the "Big One."

The root causes of the 2007 and 2008 global financial crisis were many and long in the making. The event that triggered it, however, was the implosion of the United States subprime mortgage market. For several years prior to the crisis, mortgage lenders had extended record amounts in loans to borrowers with poor credit and a high risk of default. These loans were subsequently repackaged into complex securities deemed safe by credit rating agencies although they turned out to be anything but. When subprime borrowers started to default on their mortgages amid collapsing home prices, panic struck financial markets. The dominoes fell quickly afterwards: credit flows nearly froze up, stock markets nose-dived, and the global economy fell into the deepest recession since the Great Depression, earning the label "Great Recession" along the way.

While the crisis was a severe trauma, in the end, the global economy avoided spiralling into depression thanks to a coordinated effort by governments around the world. After having hailed for decades the virtues of deregulation and free markets, global economic leaders embraced government intervention on a colossal scale to avoid the abyss. Central banks pumped massive amounts of liquidity into the economy while governments borrowed heavily to finance unprecedented stimulus spending packages. The United States federal government, for instance, nearly doubled its debt in only five years.[1] "We're All Keynesians Now" declared the *Wall Street Journal* on January 18, 2008, recognizing the dire need for massive stimulus spending to revive the economy amid a crisis threatening a global collapse.[2]

In Canada, the recession was felt less sharply than almost anywhere else due to a conservative domestic banking industry and a still-strong commodity sector. Nevertheless, while the effects of the crisis were less severe, here, too, our leaders were consumed with the global crisis and its aftermath. After a slow start in responding to rapidly deteriorating conditions, Canadian governments multiplied efforts to revive domestic growth. The media reflected the climate of economic anxiety and political frenzy with countless reports on topics such as shovel-ready infrastructure projects and the bailouts of GM and Chrysler. Amid all this turmoil, very few Canadians noticed another phenomenon was kicking in, one of even greater significance whose effects were immediate and will continue to be felt long after the tail of the Great Recession has stopped wagging the global economy: the exit of the first baby boomers from the labour force.

As chapter 2 illustrates, since the mid-1960s Canada's economy had been surfing on an exceptionally strong tide of labour force growth fuelled by baby boomers progressively reaching working age and by the steady march of women toward equal participation in the workforce. By the time the global crisis hit in 2008, the combined effect of these forces had turned from tailwind to headwind. As this happened, Canada's economic growth potential was *immediately* set on a lower path. The tepid global recovery that followed the Great Recession receives much blame for Canada's subpar average economic growth since the turn of the decade. The reality, however, is that Canada's average growth from 2008 to 2014, at 1.6% annually, is strikingly consistent with the new normal for growth outlined in chapter 2. We should get accustomed to this lower-growth regime.[3]

It is a truly fascinating paradox that a gradual process like demographic change can have such sudden consequences. Unfortunately, this paradox is not just of academic interest: it has vast implications on our society. We have a propensity to think in a linear manner: it is hard for most of us to imagine a world where tomorrow can be drastically different from yesterday. We also tend to have a myopic outlook: we are much better at dealing with immediate threats than with problems that will affect us down the road. This is why as a society we are ill-equipped to deal with phenomena that progress silently until they suddenly erupt into major crises with destructive consequences, such as climate change. The same applies to fiscal challenges in general and those that are induced by demography in particular. In fact, it is no exaggeration to say that one of the great peacetime challenges of democracies is to deal with major misalignments in the timing of fiscal revenues and spending.

Recent Canadian experience illustrates just how hard it is for democracies to save when times are good in order to deal with a coming disruption. Canadians have long known their society was aging and that this would have important implications for economic growth and public spending. From the mid-1990s until 2008, Canada enjoyed nearly uninterrupted robust growth. After having wrestled down its large chronic deficits by the late 1990s, Ottawa started producing surpluses again as the economy picked up steam. This was an ideal time for governments to act like ants rather than grasshoppers, but little of this happened. Rather than using this opportunity to bring the debt down sharply, federal politicians were busy divvying up a growing "fiscal dividend." After several years of restraint, public spending returned with a vengeance. From 1992–93 to 1999–2000, federal program spending (including transfers to provinces) declined by 3%. From 1999–2000 until 2008–09 (just before the government borrowed heavily to stimulate the economy) public spending grew by 79%. A similar although less pronounced development occurred on the other side of the ledger with fiscal revenues. From 1992–93 to 1999–2000, the federal fiscal burden (revenues as a percentage of GDP) was mostly stable, hovering around 17.5%. By 2008–09, it was down by almost one-fifth, to 14.4% of GDP. From 1999–2000 to 2008–09, the federal government piled on more than $450 billion in cumulative new program spending and took in close to $200 billion less in taxes than would otherwise have been the case had it not lowered the fiscal burden. Meanwhile, net debt was brought down by a more modest $65 billion, to $525 billion in 2008–09 (it shot back up to $582 billion in 2009–10).[4]

What happened at the provincial level provides further proof of just how hard it is for societies to deal with poor timing between revenues and spending. Although the Great Demographic Imbalance provided much greater incentives to older, faster-aging provinces to save when the times were still good, the data suggest there was no clear pattern in the evolution of public spending between older and younger provinces. Provincial spending followed a similar path across the country, slowing considerably in the 1990s and growing sharply over the next decade. The same happened with revenues: provincial fiscal burdens (own source revenues as a percentage of GDP) held more or less steady across the country throughout the 1990s and then declined—albeit less sharply than at the federal level—over the following ten years.[5]

This should not come as a surprise. Until 2008 *all* provinces were witnessing relatively robust growth. Furthermore, as we saw in chapter 1, differences in the age structures of provinces were less pronounced in the mid-1990s and even in the mid-2000s than they are today. With most provinces on a reasonable fiscal footing and elections never far away, it was just as difficult for politicians in faster-aging as in slower-aging provinces to convince voters they needed to generate large surpluses to face a coming demographic crunch.

This crunch is now with us. The rub, though, is that its impact on public spending is gradual. It does not produce a sudden break with the past as it did for economic growth. Rather, the pressures on public spending are mounting slowly but surely, with the worst still to come. Provinces, particularly older, faster-aging ones, are like the proverbial laboratory frogs in waters that gradually warm up until they unwittingly boil to death.

The next chapter examines how unevenly the waters are heating up across the country, but first a simple, yet fundamental question needs addressing: why is slowing public spending sustainably so challenging? Why can't cash-strapped provinces simply cut spending drastically, as the federal government did in the 1990s?

Public Spending and the Luxury Good Paradox

Economists can be frustrating to listen to. Many of them speak in complex jargon. Some hedge their bets so heavily that we could be forgiven for wishing they had only one hand, which would render moot their "on one hand/on the other hand" arguments. And perhaps even more frustrating, economists often contradict one another. Sometimes these differences of opinion simply reflect the state of the discipline with its inherent contradictions and uncertainties. More often, though, it is because the economist's profession is unregulated. Doctors are not allowed to invent their own medicine, and accountants are forbidden from creating their own accounting rules; however, many self-proclaimed economists do not hesitate to play with both facts and theories to advance their interests.

Another reason why listening to economists can be frustrating is that they sometimes use words in ways that differ from common usage. A good example is the concept of luxury good. Few Canadians, save perhaps diehard right-wing ideologues, would call public spending on welfare, health care, and education a luxury. Yet, to an economist, the term *luxury good* is simply one for which demand grows more than proportionally as income rises. And on this score, the historical record makes it easy to see why an economist would regard public spending as a luxury good: over the past fifty years, as developed countries grew in prosperity, they have continued to spend growing shares of their rising incomes on government programs. Public spending in the rich world has grown from less than 30% of GDP half a century ago to about 45% today.[6]

If government programs are luxury goods, one would assume that trimming provincial public spending should not be too difficult when times grow tough. Things are not that simple, unfortunately. While governments tend to spend more as societies gain in prosperity, most citizens do not regard much of what they are spending on as luxuries. With greater prosperity comes the ability to dedicate a growing share of income to building a fairer, safer, greener society with healthier and better-educated citizens. What was considered unaffordable by some in previous eras—for instance, the abolition of slavery prior to the advent of mechanization, or publicly funded, universal health care in the nineteenth century—later becomes a hard-won gain, a sign of progress and civilization.

In other words, once hard-won gains are made in areas such as health care, education, or social assistance, public spending becomes hard to roll back. This is not just because those who draw benefits from public spending—including public sector workers—will fight tooth and nail to keep them. It is also because social policy has come to play a critical role in defining ourselves as a society. This is most evident in health care. In polls conducted from 1997 to 2012, Environics, a polling and market research firm, found that among more than a dozen symbols of national identity (including the Canadian Charter of Rights and Freedoms, the Canadian flag, hockey, the Queen), Canada's health-care system consistently topped the list as the one most likely to be considered "very important" by the largest number of Canadians. This perspective is unique to Canada. The British, for instance, may be proud of their National Health Service, but they do not tell pollsters this is what best defines them as a nation.

While it may have reached iconic status, health care is not the only area of social policy that has played a role in defining Canadians' collective sense of self. Indeed, social policy as a whole has been so important to nation-building efforts that the principle Canadians should have similar services regardless of where they live was enshrined in our Constitution more than thirty years ago.[7]

The idea there should be no second-class citizens when it comes to social programs is not an anachronistic aspiration existing only in our Constitution. There is, in fact, plenty of evidence that it continues to find its way deep into the hearts and minds—and wallets—of Canadians. Table 4.1 illustrates this. It compares provincial spending per person and as a share of GDP for the years 2003–04 and 2013–14. The table looks only at program spending (it excludes debt-servicing charges) so as to focus on how much governments spend to deliver services to their citizens.[8]

A key point from table 4.1 is that spending is strikingly similar across the country despite large differences in prosperity among provinces. Six of the ten provinces are within $700 of the average of Canadian provinces of $10,600 per person. Spending per person is roughly the same in Prince Edward Island as in Alberta, although the latter is twice as rich as the former. Ontario and British Columbia are outliers, spending significantly less than the average of Canadian provinces. This, however, does not mean they offer fewer or less generous services than the rest of the country. A much more plausible explanation is that, as large provinces with much of their populations concentrated in major urban centres, they benefit from significant economies of scale in the provision of their services. Such a conclusion seems all

Table 4.1: Provincial Program Expenditures, 2003–04 and 2013–14
Sources: Finance Canada, *Fiscal Reference Tables*; Nova Scotia Public Accounts;
   Statistics Canada, CANSIM, tables 051-0001 and 384-0038.

	Per capita			Expenditures as % of GDP	
	2003–04 expenditures	2013–14 expenditures	Growth rate 2003–04 to 2013–14 (%)	2003–04	2013–14
Newfoundland and Labrador	8,007	13,305	5.2	22.6	20.1
Prince Edward Island	7,201	11,149	4.5	26.0	28.0
Nova Scotia	5,636	9,909	5.8	17.7	24.2
New Brunswick	6,841	10,057	3.9	22.2	23.9
Quebec*	6,768	10,342	4.3	19.6	23.3
Ontario	5,752	8,545	4.0	13.8	16.7
Manitoba	7,109	10,997	4.5	21.5	22.5
Saskatchewan	6,882	11,978	5.7	18.3	15.9
Alberta	6,749	10,966	5.0	12.3	12.8
British Columbia	6,816	8,929	2.7	18.8	18.1
Canada**	**6,776**	**10,618**	**4.6**	**19.3**	**20.5**

*Due to accounting reforms, data from 2003–04 not directly comparable with 2013–14.
**Average of Canadian provinces (not a weighted average).

the more reasonable given that Quebec, the country's second largest province, spends slightly less than the average of Canadian provinces, despite having more "generous" social programs than the rest of the country.[9] Finally, oil-rich Newfoundland and Labrador is also an out-lier, spending considerably more than the rest of the country. This reflects both its greater means (until recently, at least) and its small, fast-aging population dispersed over a large territory.

The fact that poorer provinces spend as much, if not more, than some of their richer counterparts has led a few commentators to argue that poorer provinces are using Equalization and other federal transfers to build welfare states that richer provinces cannot afford. This, they claim, provides proof that we live in a dysfunctional system where poorer provinces drive BMWs while richer provinces have to make do with Hyundais. While they may be provocative, such arguments tell us more about the ideological biases of their advocates than about reality. I am not aware of a comprehensive and objective analysis comparing the "generosity" of social programs among provinces. Available evidence strongly suggests, however, that those interested in shopping for better social programs should not look to a have-less region such as the Maritimes.[10]

A more plausible explanation as to why provinces spend roughly the same amounts despite their highly uneven means is that—save perhaps for Quebecers to some extent—Canadians have come to expect similar services regardless of where they live. Some will argue it is easy for residents in poorer provinces to uphold such aspirations when the money to meet them comes from Ottawa. Such a claim, however, would be economical with the truth. While Equalization and other federal transfers do help poorer provinces in providing ser-vices reasonably comparable to the Canadian average, the fact remains they tax their citizens much more than their richer counterparts. For instance, the provincial fiscal burden (own source revenues as a share of GDP) is 60% higher in Prince Edward Island than in Alberta.[11] None of us like to pay for things we do not want. If residents in poorer provinces are willing to shoulder heavier fiscal burdens than those in their richer counterparts only to get similar services in return, we can only reasonably assume it is because this is the level of services to which they have come to aspire as Canadians. In short, public spending at the national level may be a luxury good—growing faster than the economy—but when we compare provinces, public spending looks much more like a basic necessity, with poorer provinces dedicating greater shares of their incomes to it. And, of course, spending on basic necessities is much harder to roll back than spending on luxury goods. The fact that provinces cannot easily download their responsibilities to other jurisdictions, as Ottawa did in the 1990s, only adds to this difficulty.

If history is any guide, cash-strapped provincial governments are likely to look elsewhere first to lower spending before attempting to transform the way they do business in areas such as health care, education, and other social programs. And one of the first instincts of most governments looking to ease their fiscal loads in tough times is to examine their assets—Crown corporations in particular—to find ways to monetize them and/or eliminate the subsidies needed to operate them. This is what the federal government did in the late 1980s and 1990s when it sold icons such as Air Canada, CN, and Petro-Canada and moved out of operating ports, airports, civil air navigation, and the St. Lawrence Seaway. Ottawa had much more success at the time in divesting itself of these assets—fuelling less protest and controversy—than in reforming social programs such as Unemployment Insurance.

The odds today are slim that provinces will be successful in taking a page from the federal government's book. Some provinces have had success in privatizing their Crown corporations—Potash Corporation of Saskatchewan and BC Rail, for instance—but these privatizations occurred in the same areas where the federal government found success, namely transportation and natural resources. The remaining provincial Crown corporations are in industries that have, for the most part, resisted privatization: electric utilities and liquor monopolies.

There are many pitfalls—both economic and political—of privatizing electric utilities. Past attempts have met with mixed results. While Nova Scotia managed to privatize its public utility at the turn of the century, New Brunswick's botched attempt to sell NB Power to Hydro-Québec in the late 2000s is an eloquent reminder of how politically explosive such files can be. And the fact Halifax tops the list of cities with the highest residential electricity rates in Canada does not help the case of those who push for privatization.[12]

As for government liquor monopolies, the outlook for their privatization or dismantling appears more promising. However, the importance of these assets to governments pales in comparison to utilities. Contrary to public perceptions, liquor monopolies are not the cash cows or crown jewels many mistake them for. Rather, they are akin to more or less efficient tax collectors. Carried out properly, their privatization or dismantling may in some instances lead to additional revenues for governments but would not meaningfully alter their long-term fiscal position.[13]

Provincial governments obviously have many assets beyond Crown corporations, including infrastructure and natural resources. Raising revenues from existing infrastructure can be viewed as a form of taxation.[14] Further on, I revisit the broader issue of the ability of provincial governments—particularly in older, faster-aging provinces—to raise their fiscal burdens in a sustainable manner. As for natural resources, devising royalty regimes that are fair to both the owners of the resources (the public) and those that exploit them is a complex process involving considerable trial and error. On the whole, there are no reasons to expect provincial governments will be in a better position to draw more revenues from their natural resources than they did in the recent past. If anything, as chapter 3 shows, the outlook is bleak for generating more royalty revenues in an era of lower commodity prices.

In short, while there are opportunities for governments to improve their public finances by drawing more from their assets, the scope of such efforts is limited. The inescapable reality is that provincial governments spend around three-quarters of their program dollars in three areas involving hard-won social gains that have come to play a key role in defining us as a nation: health care, education, and income support and other social services. It is in these shark-infested waters that politicians, particularly in older, faster-aging provinces, will have to swim in search of savings.

Summing Up

The first part of this book delineates how the Great Demographic Imbalance is affecting older, faster-aging provinces most, crippling their economic growth—and thus the growth in their tax bases—precisely at the time when their shares of seniors is climbing fast. In this context, leaving aside for the moment the possibility of Ottawa coming to the rescue with significant assistance, the fiscal sustainability of older, faster-aging provinces is inextricably tied to their ability to considerably moderate public spending growth.

This chapter explored just how formidable such a challenge will prove. Democratic societies are ill-equipped to deal with major mismatches in the timing of fiscal revenues and spending needs. It is extremely difficult for politicians who must get elected every four years to convince voters to generate large surpluses now to meet a challenge in a more distant future. Although the pressures of population aging on spending act slowly, almost imperceptibly, we must pay heed as they will be felt most acutely in some of the areas we cherish the most, particularly health care. The next chapter describes just how difficult moderating public spending sustainably will prove for provincial governments in the years ahead.

Chapter 5

PUBLIC SPENDING: A BALKAN MAP

The Great Demographic Imbalance will be with us for at least the next quarter century, and it is producing a perfect storm for Canada's older, faster-aging provinces. As discussed, population aging will affect economic growth in all regions in the years ahead, but its impact will be regionally uneven, ranging from relatively modest in the Prairies to devastating in Atlantic Canada. Similarly, population aging will exert pressures on the public purses of all provinces, but these will be felt to widely varying degrees across the country.

This chapter examines the impact of the Great Demographic Imbalance on public spending in more detail. It exposes a portrait of a broken landscape. Provincial governments may have so far proven able to provide roughly similar services, but this will not be the case in the future. Barring a major change in how Ottawa redistributes wealth, the collection of social programs that provinces offer will increasingly resemble a Balkan map, with all the inherent fragmentation, dysfunction, and tension.

Health Care

There is a tendency to refer to Canada's single largest industry, health care, as a national "system." In reality, as health care is under provincial jurisdiction, Canada has ten public health-care "systems," if we exclude the territories. These systems have many things in common, some of which are mandated by the Canada Health Act, the federal legislation that sets the conditions provinces must meet to receive federal funding.[1] For instance, the act requires that public health-care insurance be available to all and that medically necessary services be provided free of charge. Provincial health systems also share commonalities not required by federal legislation. For example, the act does not preclude publicly funded, for-profit hospitals, yet virtually all hospital services in Canada are provided by non-profit institutions. Moreover, most physicians are independent, private sector practitioners rather than salaried professionals. No statute requires this practice; it simply reflects the bargain governments and physicians concluded when public health insurance was put in place half a century ago.[2] But provincial health systems also differ in important ways, particularly for publicly funded services, as well as how prescription drugs are paid for. Such differences, which can be quite significant, are the main reason why we cannot speak of Canada as having a single public health-care system.

There are many myths about health care in Canada. Perhaps the most misguided is that Canada's health-care "system" is the best in the world. There is very little in international studies supporting this conclusion. In fact, while Canada ranks among the world's top five spenders on health care, its outcomes are generally rated as middling, falling far short of the money invested.[3] As is too often the case, Canadians tend to compare themselves almost exclusively to their southern neighbours, whose health-care "system" is among the worst performers in both access and value-for-money. Indeed, the American health-care industry is fundamentally different from Canada's and is therefore not a good comparator for international benchmark studies. We should hold ourselves to a higher standard than the United States when it comes to health care.

Another myth reflecting our obsession with the United States relates to what we Canadians hold dearest about our health-care "system": its fairness. Our politicians like to boast that when we need care, we are not asked for a credit card. By international standards, we in fact tend to do so more than most other countries. The private sector accounts for three out of ten dollars spent on health care in Canada. In 2013 private sector health-care spending was the fifth highest among thirty-four industrialized countries.[4] This is because public health care in Canada is deep but narrow:[5] if what you need is deemed "medically necessary" and thus covered by your provincial health plan, it is provided free of charge by the public system. If not, then you will need to get it from the marketplace, just like in the United States. And among the items generally considered not medically necessary by provincial health plans are critical ones, such as eye care, non-surgical dentistry, and pharmaceuticals consumed outside the walls of a hospital. Contrary to popular perception, Canadians are not equal when it comes to health care.

Another belief Canadians seem to hold dear is that hospital services should not only be publicly funded, but also delivered by non-profit entities. Canadians have long accepted that physician services are provided by private sector practitioners, but when it comes to hospitals, the profit motive is suspect. Yet, in many countries, such as France and Australia—whose health systems are regularly ranked higher than ours in international studies—publicly funded services are often delivered by for-profit hospitals.

That said, whatever the strengths and weaknesses, real or perceived, of Canada's health-care system, one fact of critical importance to this chapter remains: provincial governments have an effective monopoly over many essential services. This means Canadians are severely restricted in their ability to spend their own money on what matters most to them: their health. In return for this monopoly, Canadians, particularly as they become older, expect public health care to deliver high-quality services in a timely manner. This is not just a political imperative for governments; it is also becoming a legal issue. In 2005 the Supreme Court of Canada found that Quebec's prohibition on private medical insurance violated the Quebec Charter of Human Rights and Freedoms in light of unreasonable wait times for accessing services.[6] Several lawsuits have also recently been launched across the country, arguing that long wait times and the inability to jump the queue violated the right to life, liberty, and security of the person provisions of the Canadian Charter of Rights and Freedoms.[7]

Provincial governments across the country thus face tremendous pressures to maintain free, unrationed, and high-quality services. In such a context, it is not surprising that health-care spending has historically grown very quickly, at a pace far outstripping growth in tax revenues and the economy. Numerous reform proposals have been formulated over the years to improve public health care and address escalating costs, whether from the ranks of academe, practitioners' circles, or the countless commissions assembled by politicians eager to control costs but not to suffer the political consequences of cutting back services or asking patients or taxpayers to contribute more.[8] Yet, the fundamentals of Canada's health-care system have not changed much since its inception more than fifty years ago. This speaks volumes about the political near-impossibility of discussing health-care reform in Canada. It also further underscores the importance of taking seriously the impact of an aging population on health-care spending, especially in older, faster-aging provinces.

Population Aging and Health-Care Spending

Data from the Canadian Institute for Health Information (CIHI) show just how sensitive health-care spending is to population aging (see chart 5.1). With the exception of the first year of a child's life,

Chart 5.1: Provincial Health-Care Spending Per Person by Age Category, Canada*, 2012

Source: CIHI, National Health Expenditure Trends, 1975 to 2014.

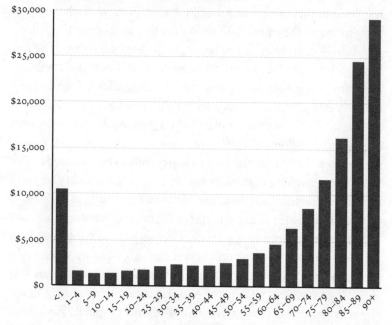

*Weighted average for provinces and territories.

public spending on health care tends to increase as people grow older. From the age of one until sixty, spending progresses in a more or less linear fashion. It then increases exponentially, from $4,600 for individuals aged sixty to sixty-four to $29,200 for individuals who are more than ninety (data for 2012).[9]

The effects of Canada's Great Demographic Imbalance on health-care spending are already visible. Chart 5.2 shows the evolution of real (inflation-adjusted) provincial health spending per person over the 2002–12 period. It breaks down spending growth into two components: aging-induced and other sources of cost escalation.[10] Unsurprisingly, aging-related spending growth was strongest in Atlantic and Central Canada. The Prairies, meanwhile, were the least affected.

**Chart 5.2: Real Provincial Health-Care Spending
Per Person, Annual Growth, 2002–2012**

Source: Statistics Canada, CANSIM, table 051-0001; and CIHI, *National Health Expenditure Trends, 1975 to 2015.* Author's calculations.

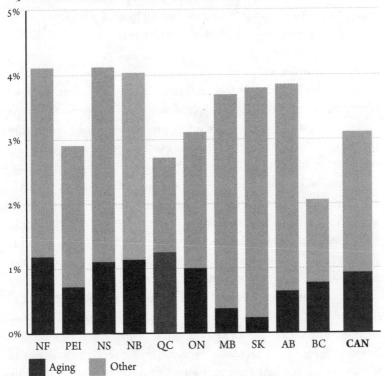

The impact of aging on health-care spending may seem modest so far, but in some older, faster-aging provinces, the situation is already serious. What is even more worrisome is that we have only seen the tip of the iceberg. The first baby boomers reached the age of sixty-five in 2011. Average health-care expenditures for people aged sixty-five to seventy-four are well below what is spent on individuals aged seventy-five and above. Aging should therefore further accelerate health spending toward the beginning of the next decade as the first baby boomers turn seventy-five. And this will affect older, faster-aging provinces most.

If demographics were the only pressure on health-care spending, the situation could be managed, perhaps even in some poorer, faster-aging provinces. But this is clearly not the case. Notwithstanding its importance, aging is still not the main driver of health-care spending in any Canadian province, as chart 5.2 shows. Rather, the main driver has been compensation growth. Another major cost driver is technological change in general, and drugs in particular. This chapter returns to the impact of Canada's Great Demographic Imbalance, but we first need to consider the above two factors for a better sense of the outlook for health-care spending in Canada.

Compensation Growth

As is the case for most service industries, wages and other forms of labour compensation (such as physician fees) represent the lion's share of health-care costs. Developing projections about health-care spending is thus, to a large extent, an exercise in assessing the likely trajectory of labour costs (compensation) growth.

Hospitals account for roughly half of provincial health-care spending. About 60% of hospital spending goes to wages and salaries. From 2002 to 2012, provincial spending per capita grew at a robust clip of 5% annually, resulting in a total increase of 63%.[11] The bulk of this extra spending went to labour costs. Some of it was used to hire new staff to meet growing demand for services and to improve care quality. For instance, the number of regulated nurses per thousand of population grew by close to 0.9% annually, for a total increase of slightly more than 7% from 2005 to 2013.[12] Most of the new money, however, went to pay increases. Hospital employees, the majority of whom are nurses, saw their real wages grow around 1.7% annually over the 2005–13 period, nearly twice as fast as real economy-wide earnings growth.[13]

Similarly, physician compensation, which represents one-fifth of public spending on health care, has grown sharply. Between 2002–03 and 2012–13, total clinical payments have nearly doubled (+97%).[14] Here, too, part of this extra spending went to hiring new people to the system. From 2003 to 2013, the number of physicians grew by 30%.[15] In turn, this inflow of new physicians translated into more medical visits, consultations, and procedures. But this only explains a relatively small part of the increase in clinical payments. The bulk of it is explained by the amounts paid per service performed, a rough proxy for wage growth.[16] In fact, from the late 1990s until recently, the average earnings of Canadian physicians grew at one of the fastest rates in the history of medicare.[17]

How can one explain this explosion in the earnings of health professionals? It is tempting to blame powerful special interests such as public sector unions and medical associations. Seeing the results of their bargaining with governments and health authorities, there are certainly no reasons to believe they failed to effectively represent their members' interests. Yet, many elements suggest this is far from the only factor behind the increase. For instance, no other major part of the heavily unionized public sector has witnessed such strong growth as hospital employees—teachers' pay, as we will see, grew more or less in line with economy-wide earnings. (See the section on education at page 95.)

Another explanation is plain economics—a matter of supply and demand. An aging population pushed up demand for health services precisely at a time when an aging workforce was starting to weigh on the supply of health workers. As a result, prices—wages and physician fees—shot up. Competition among provinces to attract qualified personnel also further fuelled this growth. Interestingly, Quebec is one of the only provinces where hospital employee wages did not grow appreciably faster than economy-wide earnings over the last decade. Quebec is an instructive outlier because, as a result of its distinct language and culture, it needs to worry less about losing its health-care professionals to other provinces. For instance, despite paying lower and slower-growing salaries in recent years, Quebec has managed to maintain a stable and higher-than-average number of nurses per 100,000 inhabitants.

However, supply and demand also tell only part of the story. As governments have an effective monopoly over the delivery of many services, health care is far from a perfectly competitive sector where supply and demand operate seamlessly. Relative to many of their key service providers (such as nurses and physicians), governments and health authorities usually are in a local monopsony position, being essentially the only purchasers of services provided by a large number of sellers. This position gives them considerable market power.

During the 1990s, in particular the six years from 1991 to 1997, governments across Canada did exercise their market power. This period is atypical in the modern history of health care in Canada. It is marked by what we could call the "Great Deceleration," that is, a considerable slowdown in health-care and other spending, including three years when real provincial spending per person actually went down (1993–95).[18] During those years, provincial governments across the country were grappling with major deficits, and the Chrétien-Martin program review in Ottawa implemented major spending cuts almost everywhere, including federal transfers. Indeed, provincial governments accused the federal government of downloading its deficit problem to them.

However, the Great Deceleration is not only instructive in showing that halting spending growth for a significant period of time is possible. It is equally instructive for what happened after—spending catching up with a vengeance. Indeed, as chart 5.3 shows, spending growth over the 1997–2010 period was the fastest in the nearly four decades of spending data compiled by the CIHI.[19] Part of the gap in growth rates before and after the Great Deceleration can be explained by population aging. However, the much more important development is that, after several years of restraint, federal and provincial governments across the country decided reinvestment was needed to improve access and quality of care—and win elections. With its budget back in the black and with growing surpluses, Ottawa re-engaged, doubling the Canada Health and Social Transfer (CHST) and its successors, the CHT and CST, within a decade.[20]

Many will recall that then prime minister Martin cranked up the hyperbole when his minority government announced in 2004 its health care "Fix for a Generation," a plan that included only ten years of funding. Still, with a total of $41 billion in new money, this plan

Chart 5.3: Real Provincial Health-Care Spending Per Person, Canada*, 1975–2012, 2000=100

Source: CIHI, *National Health Expenditure Trends, 1975 to 2014*; Statistics Canada, CANSIM, table 326-0021. Author's calculations.

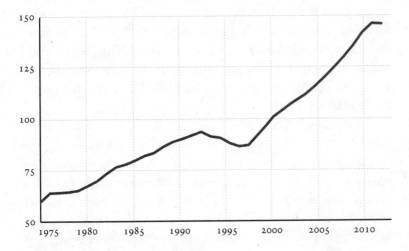

*Weighted average for provinces and territories.

paved the way for an annual increase of 6% in federal health transfers. A steady and generous flow of cash, as well as strong political incentives to spend most of it on health care, were thus likely as important as the simple logic of supply and demand in explaining the great explosion in health spending from 1997 to 2010. Most of that money, it bears repeating, did not end up in service improvements but in higher pay for service providers.

Technology (Including Drugs)
Another important driver of public health-care spending is technological change, a term used broadly here in order to encapsulate not only new capital equipment and new drugs that improve diagnostics and/or treatments, but also new ways of doing things, such as shifting from inpatient to outpatient care. Technological change is thus embedded in the main spending components of the health-care sector, from hospitals and residential care facilities to physician fees, capital spending, and drug costs.

Technological change has the potential to increase or lower costs. A clear example of its potential to bring costs down is cataract removal surgery. New technology has made this procedure safer and much quicker; however, in order to realize savings from these efficiency gains, the fee-for-service schedule paid by provinces must be amended accordingly. Failing to do so leads to specialists increasing their billing considerably without necessarily working longer hours and to stories such as the one cited in the media in which a New Brunswick ophthalmologist would have billed the province $1.7 million in one year.[21]

The inability to amend fee-for-service schedules to adjust to technological change speaks to the inertia built into the fee-setting process in Canada. In theory, this process involves negotiations between provincial governments and medical associations. In practice, however, governments have historically limited their involvement to setting the overall envelope for physician compensation. As Canadian health economists Hugh M. Grant and Jeremiah Hurley note, medical associations typically allocate fees "through a 'bear pit' session among representatives of different specialty groups with the procedure 'explicitly viewed by physicians as an income allocation process.'"[22] Grant and Hurley further note that

[m]odification to relative fees is a politically sensitive issue for both governments and medical associations. By ceding responsibility to medical associations, governments avoid further confrontation with a profession intent on retaining some autonomy over the fee-setting process, while the medical association faces the difficult task of balancing the interests of a membership increasingly fragmented along specialty lines. For these reasons, there is a reluctance to radically alter the fee structure. "Revisions to internal weights of the schedule are politically difficult and dangerous for the profession, as they tend to undermine and fragment the united front. And provincial governments have neither the interest nor the expertise to take on the political risks of a struggle with physicians over the internal structure of the schedule."[23]

While technological change has the potential to generate significant savings, until now it has usually meant extra costs, particularly for drugs. New drugs can be viewed as technological change to the extent they allow for improvements in existing therapies or new therapies, and thus new ways to treat patients. Over the last three decades, drugs have been the fastest-growing component of health-care spending. The share of drugs in provincial health spending has more than doubled, from 3.4% to 7.4%.[24]

Interestingly, Canadians' spending on drugs has stalled and even declined slightly in recent years, which is remarkable given Canada's aging population. The reason for this decline, however, is not that they consume less drugs. Rather, it is because they caught a break as a slew of cheaper generic products flooded the marketplace with the expiry of patents for many drugs used to treat common conditions, such as high blood pressure, high cholesterol, heartburn, and depression.

But according to Canadian health policy expert Steve Morgan, this situation is just a temporary reprieve. Drug spending will soon start escalating again, for at least two reasons. First, the wave of patent expiration for blockbuster drugs is receding—we cannot expect similar relief from the "genericization" of drug spending in the years ahead. Secondly, the pharmaceutical industry has found a new lucrative business model focused on developing speciality drugs used to treat fewer patients and whose cost per patient is much higher than for blockbuster drugs.[25] Among those specialty or designer drugs are promising but expensive new drugs to treat cancer. While the prospect of dramatic progress in treating various cancers is exciting, it remains that cancer is much more prevalent in older people and that governments will be under strong pressure to cover these costly drugs. The coming wave of designer drugs should give sobering pause to techno-optimists who believe technology could bring health-care costs down in the future.

Provincial Health-Care Spending Under the Status Quo

So where does the above discussion leave us in assessing the future course of provincial spending on health care in Canada? This section looks at population aging and other historical trends to project how spending could evolve in the years ahead. This is an exercise in making projections based on the status quo; given the near-impossibility of discussing fundamental reforms to Canada's health-care system, it is an important exercise.

To build the projections, I follow a two-step approach using Statistics Canada's most recent population projections for the 2013–38 period as well as CIHI data on historical health-care spending. My projections start in 2013 because reliable data on health-care spending by provinces at the time of writing was available only up to 2012.

The first step is to formulate scenarios about the likely impact of aging on health-care spending. For this purpose, I use CIHI data on provincial spending per capita by age category for 2012 and calculate the impact of aging based on the age distributions resulting from Statistics Canada's three main population scenarios outlined in chapter 1 (low, medium, and high growth).[26]

The second step is to formulate assumptions about non-aging-related spending. We have seen that health-care spending can fluctuate considerably over time, with periods of great moderation followed by sharp recoveries. For instance, aging-adjusted real per capita spending growth stood at a low of 0.9% from 1992 to 2002, followed by a much more robust expansion of 2.2% annually from 2002 to 2012. This makes selecting the appropriate reference periods for the scenarios particularly critical.

A good approach for this type of projection is to use a period of the same length as the projection horizon—the 1987–2012 period. The key advantage of such an approach is that the reference period is likely to capture the broad range of events that typically occur over the projection horizon and have a significant impact on health spending. As real non-aging-related spending grew by 1.6% annually over the quarter century from 1987 to 2012, this is the number to use as the average growth rate for the baseline scenario. I do not assume, however, that this growth rate will be constant over the entire projection horizon (2013–38). Rather, I assume that real average annual growth will be contained to 1.0% for the first decade (2013–23) and that it will subsequently increase to 2.0% for the remaining fifteen years, producing an overall growth rate of 1.6%. As we have seen, in the short run, governments can exercise considerable control over spending, particularly when it comes to compensation, which represents the lion's share of health-care costs. Provinces managed to keep non-aging-related real health spending growth during the ten years from 1992 to 2002 to around half the pace of the quarter century from 1987 to 2012.

The current climate, with all provinces facing fiscal challenges of one form or another, is particularly propitious for similar restraint as during the 1990s. In fact, moderation in health-care spending is already upon us. After more than a decade of robust compensation growth across most of the country, health-care professionals have seen their incomes stagnate or increase much more modestly over the past few years. If history is any guide, provincial governments should be able to maintain this moderation for a few more years. At some point, though, one or more provinces will start raising wages and fees to attract and retain health professionals to meet growing demand for health-care services. It is immaterial whether this move comes from wealthier provinces with a much greater ability to raise extra revenues or from cash-strapped, faster-aging provinces desperate to meet rapidly escalating health-care needs. What matters is that once one or more provinces start raising wages and fees, others are likely to follow suit.

It is tempting to argue this time will be different because poorer provinces are in no position to provide fast-growing compensation to their health-care professionals. But, to paraphrase eighteenth-century British writer Samuel Johnson, we should not let hope triumph over experience. Unless a national solution to the thorny issue of escalating compensation costs emerges, poorer provinces will have little choice but to follow suit if they wish to maintain their universal, publicly funded health-care systems. Numerous studies have raised the problem of escalating compensation, yet it has proven so far impossible to keep wage growth sustainably in line with economic reality. This is particularly so for physicians. Over the last three decades, the average income of Canadian physicians has increased from 300% to close to 450% of the average Canadian worker.[27] Provincial politicians did not consent to such fast-growing compensation because they believed physicians were underpaid thirty years ago. Rather, a more plausible explanation is that they felt this is what they needed to do to improve services and win elections. As noted earlier, provincial governments are under tremendous pressure to maintain high-quality and timely health-care services. In order to do so, they must compete with other jurisdictions to secure an adequate supply of health-care professionals. This competition for health-care professionals—physicians in particular—plays a significant role in fuelling escalating costs.

It's worth expanding on this point a bit more. In theory, provincial governments are free to set compensation as they see fit. After all, there is no unified health-care system in Canada, but rather one in each province (and territory). That said, just because there is no single national health-care system does not mean there is no single national market for health-care professionals. For such a market to exist, all that is needed is for health-care professionals to have the ability to work wherever they like in Canada. In a perfectly competitive market, there would be no persistent differences in earnings across the country. Real earnings would be equalized by the migration of professionals from lower to higher pay regions.

To be sure, there is no such thing as a perfectly competitive labour market. Empirical evidence suggests, however, that Canada has a reasonably well-integrated national health-care labour market, particularly outside Quebec. Consider once again the case of physicians. Studies show physicians take income differences across provinces into account when deciding where to practice. Of course, not all of them are likely to pack up and move to another province just because the pay is better. Nor, for that matter, is income the only consideration when they decide where to set up their practices—working conditions and proximity to large urban centres are two other important factors.[28] But it appears that a sufficiently large number of physicians respond to price signals to produce a single, national labour market.[29] In short, if provinces want to attract or retain the doctors they need to deliver the services their citizens want, they will need to maintain competitive wages.

This imperative is a direct consequence of health care being a provincial jurisdiction. If Canada had a single national public health-care system, the federal government would be in a much better position to exercise control over wages. Naturally, given the proximity of the United States, this control would not be perfect. The data suggest, however, that the income gap between Canadian physicians and their counterparts south of the border can grow quite wide without serious consequences. It is estimated the average earnings of physicians in the United States are between 33% and 50% higher than in Canada; yet, in some years, more doctors move north to Canada than head south to the United States.[30]

As hinted earlier, Quebec is somewhat distinct when it comes to health-care compensation trends, historically providing lower compensation to its physicians. This lower-wage regime extends not only to physicians, but also to most other health-care professionals (and public employees more generally). Quebec can afford to pay less because its distinct cultural and linguistic setting makes it less vulnerable to outmigration. Yet, recent developments suggest there are limits to how far things can go, at least in some professions. It is no coincidence that Quebec has recently been moving to increase physician wages and fees at the very time compensation growth is stalled in much of the rest of the country.[31] This suggests that, while Quebec may be in a position to maintain lower compensation for health professionals, it is doubtful it will be able to maintain much lower compensation *growth* in the future.

Having discussed the baseline scenario for non-aging-related provincial health-care spending, we can move on to the low and high spending growth scenarios. Recall that this exercise is a *status quo* projection. Its aim is to provide a likely trajectory for spending if no transformative changes are brought to Canada's health-care systems. In such a context, unless one holds high hopes that technology will save the day, it is not reasonable to contemplate a scenario where spending growth will be dramatically lower relative to long-term historical trends. We can safely assume that provincial governments, particularly in poorer provinces, will engage in frantic efforts to deliver services more efficiently within the confines of the existing model of public health care. Such exercises are likely to bear fruit, but given the preceding illustration of the dynamics of compensation growth, there are limits to how much provinces can cut down spending growth sustainably.

The projections that follow assume a low scenario where spending growth is cut down by 20% compared to the average over the 1987–2012 period. This translates into an average annual growth of

0.8% from 2013 to 2023 and 1.6% over the remainder of the projection horizon. As for the high scenario, growth is set at 20% above the 1987–2012 average. This is also a realistic scenario, particularly if compensation costs escalate as a result of a supply of health professionals that struggles to keep up with ever growing demand fuelled by population aging. Alternatively, provincial health systems could face higher costs as a result of technological change (e.g., "designer drugs" to treat cancer), particularly if they fail to capitalize on opportunities to lower costs brought about by new technologies (e.g., cataract removal surgery).

Table 5.1 illustrates the impact of the Great Demographic Imbalance in all its force. It shows the pressures exerted by population aging will be much greater in Eastern Canada—and Atlantic provinces in particular—than in the rest of the country.

Newfoundland and Labrador is the country's top health spender.[32] The province's high level of spending reflects both its greater means (until the recent collapse in oil prices, at least) and its greater needs, with its older population spread over a sparsely populated territory. In 2012 Newfoundland and Labrador spent close to 50% more on health care than the country's lowest spender, Quebec. Under the baseline scenario, Newfoundland and Labrador would continue to grow its spending much faster than the rest of Canada. By 2038 Newfoundland and Labrador would spend more than 50% or about $5,000 more than the Canadian average. It's worth noting that most of this is due to the province's faster aging since the projection assumes that non-aging-related spending will grow at the same pace across provinces.[33]

The Maritimes spend significantly less on health care than Newfoundland and Labrador—the gap stood at about $900 per person in 2012.[34] The region has also been growing its spending at a much slower pace. A quarter century ago, all four provinces spent roughly the same amounts, around $1,300 per person. Compared with the rest of the country, however, the health spending record of the Maritimes is less glowing. It went from spending around $150 less per person than the Canadian average in 1989 to around $300 more in 2012. Not all of this growth gap can be pinned to the region's faster population aging. As for the years ahead, the Maritimes is projected

Table 5.1: Provincial Real Health-Care Spending Projections, 2013–38 (constant dollars of 2012)

Source: Author's calculations based on CIHI, National Expenditure Trends, 1975 to 2015; and Statistics Canada, CANSIM, table 052-0005.

	Low scenario			Medium (baseline) scenario			High scenario		
	2013	2023	2038	2013	2023	2038	2013	2023	2038
Newfoundland and Labrador	5,210	6,763	10,947	5,219	6,893	12,403	5,248	7,028	13,374
Prince Edward Island	4,271	5,230	7,971	4,279	5,344	8,671	4,287	5,456	9,639
Nova Scotia	4,236	5,263	8,430	4,314	5,369	9,056	4,322	5,483	9,865
New Brunswick	4,162	5,209	8,398	4,169	5,317	9,029	4,177	5,429	9,832
Quebec	3,542	4,260	6,327	3,549	4,356	6,918	3,556	4,448	7,626
Ontario	3,811	4,554	6,710	3,818	4,669	7,367	3,826	4,767	8,215
Manitoba	4,479	5,055	7,151	4,488	5,181	7,842	4,496	5,290	8,784
Saskatchewan	4,341	4,875	6,884	4,349	4,988	7,535	4,357	5,093	7,401
Alberta	4,641	5,429	7,939	4,650	5,562	8,715	4,659	5,679	9,704
British Columbia	3,862	4,476	6,311	3,870	4,601	6,962	3,877	4,698	7,792

Note: Low scenario based on high population growth and low non-aging-induced spending scenario and vice versa for the high scenario.

to keep growing its spending faster than the rest of the country save Newfoundland and Labrador. By 2038 the Maritimes will be spending nearly $5,000 more per person on health care than it does today, compared to $3,500 on average for Canada as a whole.

As of 2012 Canada's three largest provinces—Ontario, Quebec, and British Columbia—spent the least on health care per capita. As noted earlier, this reflects at least in part the economies of scale inherent to the provision of health-care services. The projections suggest they will remain the lowest spenders. British Columbia will move from third to second-lowest spender, switching rankings with Ontario. Quebec will remain the lowest spender.

Finally, the Prairies spent around 15% more on health care per person than the average of Canadian provinces in 2012. Despite its slower aging, the region has been growing its spending considerably faster. At the turn of the 1990s, it spent roughly the same as Canada as a whole. The region's greater prosperity could well allow it to keep growing its spending faster than the rest of the country in the years ahead. However, assuming they succeed in containing non-aging-related spending as well as other provinces, Saskatchewan and Manitoba should witness the slowest growth in health spending in the country, while Alberta should grow its spending at a rate similar to Canada's three most populous provinces.

That said, however striking regional differences in health-care spending pressures induced by population aging may appear, the picture becomes much bleaker once ability to pay—the other critical element that determines health-care affordability—is factored in. Health-care spending as a percentage of GDP is the best indicator of a province's ability to pay for its services through its own revenues. Table 5.2 illustrates the striking impact of the Great Demographic Imbalance on provincial health-care affordability. In 2013 provincial health spending represented 7.9% of Newfoundland and Labrador's GDP. By 2038 this ratio will have more than doubled under the baseline scenario, to 17.4%. In the Maritimes, the ratio will have doubled from 10.3% of GDP to 20.5%. By contrast, spending in the Prairies will only increase from 6.3% of GDP to 9.4%. In British Columbia, spending will grow by half from 7.8% to 12.0% of GDP. In Quebec and Ontario, spending will grow by around two-thirds, to 13.7% and 12.5% of GDP respectively.[35]

Table 5.2: Provincial Real Health-Care Spending as a Percentage of GDP Projections, 2013–38

Source: Author's calculations based on CIHI, *National Expenditure Trends, 1975 to 2015*; Statistics Canada, CANSIM, table 052-0005; and baseline scenario for GDP growth outlined in table 2.2 of chapter 2.

	Low scenario (%)			Medium (baseline) scenario (%)			High scenario (%)		
	2013	2023	2038	2013	2023	2038	2013	2023	2038
Newfoundland and Labrador	7.8	9.9	15.3	7.9	10.1	17.4	7.9	10.3	18.7
Prince Edward Island	10.7	12.5	19.5	10.7	12.8	21.2	10.8	13.1	23.6
Nova Scotia	10.3	12.2	19.4	10.5	12.4	20.9	10.5	12.7	22.7
New Brunswick	9.9	11.6	18.6	9.9	11.9	20.0	9.9	12.1	21.7
Quebec	8.0	9.0	12.6	8.0	9.2	13.7	8.0	9.4	15.1
Ontario	7.4	8.2	11.4	7.5	8.4	12.5	7.5	8.6	14.0
Manitoba	9.2	8.8	10.3	9.2	9.0	11.2	9.2	9.2	12.6
Saskatchewan	5.8	5.6	7.3	5.8	5.7	8.0	5.8	5.8	7.8
Alberta	5.4	6.0	8.4	5.4	6.1	9.2	5.4	6.2	10.3
British Columbia	7.8	8.1	10.9	7.8	8.3	12.0	7.8	8.5	13.4

Note: Low scenario based on high population growth and low non-aging-induced spending scenario and vice versa for the high scenario.

What should we take away from these numbers? First, if Canada were a unitary state, population aging would likely not deal a mortal blow to health care as we know it. Under the baseline scenario, health spending as a percentage of GDP for Canada as a whole would grow from 7.4% to 12.0%. Clearly, taxes would have to increase considerably to finance growing health-care pressures, but an increase of four and a half percentage points in the fiscal burden (combined federal and provincial tax revenues as a percentage of GDP) would not bring the country into uncharted territory. As we have seen, the federal fiscal burden is down by almost 20% or three percentage points since the turn of the century, and provincial fiscal burdens (own source revenues as a percentage of GDP) are down by more than one percentage point on average.[36]

But Canada is not a unitary state, and population aging will have vastly different effects across regions. The Prairies will likely be in a position to afford the status quo in health care. Under the baseline projection, twenty-five years from now health spending as a share of GDP will be lower in the Prairies than it is in the Maritimes today. It is also relatively safe to assume British Columbia and Ontario can withstand the shock of population aging, albeit at the price of more painful tax adjustment than in the Prairies. It is much less clear Quebec can do the same. As discussed, it already pays its health professionals the lowest wages in Canada, with lingering doubts about the sustainability of the pay gap with their peers in the rest of the country. Quebec is one of North America's most heavily taxed and indebted jurisdictions. With provincial spending as a percentage of GDP already 40% higher than in Ontario, Quebec has much less room to ramp up health-care spending than its western neighbour.[37] As for Atlantic Canada, the outlook is more certain: health care as we know it is simply not sustainable without massive amounts of new funding from Ottawa (or, in the case of Newfoundland and Labrador, long-term oil prices returning to pre-2008 levels in real terms). Indeed, these provinces clearly cannot maintain the status quo on their own; the tax hikes required to finance escalating health-care costs would be prohibitive and would push residents to leave in droves. In short, the cure would kill the patient.

I insisted at the outset these projections were an exercise anchored in the status quo. Such an exercise has its merits given the near-impossibility of discussing health-care reform in Canada. Its main interest, however, is to show that unless Ottawa dramatically boosts transfers to some provinces, a balkanized "national" health-care system is all but inevitable. Again, my purpose here is not to predict how things will ultimately turn out—this will depend on the reaction of Canadians and their leaders—but rather to get a sense of how the Great Demographic Imbalance is reshuffling the deck when it comes to health-care spending pressures.

Education

Education and training is the second most important budget item of provincial governments, representing close to one-quarter of program spending. One might logically assume an aging population should allow provinces to reap savings in education, which could at least in part offset higher health-care bills. The reality is so far quite different.

The Public School Sector

Provincial governments spend approximately $60 billion annually on public schools, or around one out of every six program dollars.[38] Overall, Canada is witnessing declining enrolment as its population ages. This decline started toward the turn of the millennium, partly because the majority of the children of the baby boom generation were no longer of school-going age.[39] From 2001–02 to 2010–11—latest year for which enrolment on a full-time equivalent (FTE) basis and other key indicators were available at the time of writing—Canada lost 7% of its pupils in primary and secondary schools (K-12).[40] As was to be expected, the decline was sharpest in older, faster-aging eastern provinces. For instance, while the number of school-goers in the Prairies was stable, it declined by more than one-fifth in Newfoundland and Labrador.

However, when it comes to public schools, declining enrolment is about the only thing turning out as expected; almost everything else is counterintuitive. Take for example staffing levels. It would only be reasonable to assume provincial governments would have let go some educators as enrolment declined. Instead, most of them went on a hiring spree. Overall, the number of educators in Canada grew 8% mainly because just as Canada's student population started declining, a movement toward smaller class sizes swept most provincial capitals. The idea that smaller classes improve educational outcomes is intuitively appealing, which makes it popular with parents (and teachers' unions). However, except for kindergarten and the first one or two years of schooling, the evidence supporting the notion that smaller is better when it comes to classroom size is scant.[41] Nevertheless, in the prosperous years leading up to the financial crisis, this lack of compelling evidence was immaterial to politicians: what mattered to them was that reducing class sizes was popular with parents.

As most provinces went on a hiring spree despite declining enrolments, the student-educator ratio, a good measure of resource intensity, went down sharply. From a national average of 15.9 students per educator in 2001–02, it declined to 13.8 in 2010–11, a drop of 13%.[42] The decline was sharpest in the Maritimes, where the ratio went down one-fifth. This, however, did not happen because governments there went on a bigger hiring spree than in most of the rest of the country. Rather, the situation in the Maritimes points to the difficulties—political, geographic, linguistic, or others—in scaling down school systems as student numbers decrease.

New Brunswick provides a good case in point. The northern part of the province was struck particularly hard by rural and demographic decline, having lost approximately one-quarter of its students over the ten years from 2001–02 to 2010–11. Yet, the number of schools declined by only 13%.[43] This means significant fixed costs (school maintenance and operation, bus routes, administration, etc.) spread over a smaller number of students and smaller class sizes. Meanwhile, new schools had to be added in the southern part of the province, particularly in the fast-growing Moncton area. As a result, while New Brunswick's student ranks dropped by around 15% over the last decade, the number of schools declined by only 8%. The student-educator ratio, which was also depressed by the province's class-size reduction initiative, dropped by nearly a quarter.

While most provinces went on a hiring spree over the last decade, there were two holdouts, one at each end of the country. As table 5.3 illustrates, far from adding more people, Newfoundland and Labrador actually managed to reduce its number of educators by 11%. Still, because it lost nearly twice as many students, the province's

Table 5.3: Selected Public School Indicators
Source: Statistics Canada, catalogue 81-582-x; and CANSIM, table 478-0014.

	K-12 school enrolment			Number of educators*			Student-educator ratio			Spending per pupil** ($)		
	2001–02	2010–11	Change (%)	2001–02	2010–11	Change (%)	2001–02	2010–11	Change (%)	2001–02	2010–11	Change (%)
Newfoundland and Labrador	84,236	66,288	-21.3	6,355	5,619	-11.3	13.3	11.8	-11.0	7,222	13,034	80.5
Maritimes	299,175	253,714	-15.2	18,212	19,295	6.0	16.4	13.1	-19.9	6,776	12,671	87.0
Quebec	1,088,869	979,563	-10.0	74,925	77,338	3.2	14.5	12.7	-12.9	8,104	12,011	48.2
Ontario	2,046,333	1,953,624	-4.5	126,283	145,082	14.9	16.2	13.5	-16.9	7,557	12,738	68.6
Prairie provinces	879,257	883,385	0.5	53,358	57,839	10.8	16.7	15.3	-8.4	8,404	14,090	67.7
British Columbia	605,049	550,038	-9.1	35,930	32,694	-9.0	16.8	16.8	-0.1	8,430	11,470	36.1
Canada	5,035,949	4,708,548	-6.5	316,571	340,423	7.5	15.9	13.8	-12.9	7,887	12,727	61.4

*Full-time equivalent basis. Includes teachers, school administrators, and pedagogical support.

**Public elementary and secondary spending only for all provinces except Newfoundland and Labrador and the Maritimes, where total (public and private) expenditures are used. Given the small size of private school systems in Atlantic Canada, disaggregated data are not available (except for New Brunswick) due to confidentiality requirements.

student-educator ratio dropped more than 10% to 11.8. As for British Columbia, provincial authorities there managed to keep the student-educator ratio almost constant, as they lowered the ranks of educators by almost the same proportion as the decline in enrolment. As a result, British Columbia now has by far the highest student-educator ratio in the country. Interestingly, a recent Conference Board of Canada study concluded that British Columbia has the best K–12 outcomes of all provinces. If it were a country, the province would rank third among the Conference Board's list of sixteen comparator countries, trailing only behind Japan and Finland.[44]

Besides staffing levels, the other driver of provincial spending on public schools is wage growth. Here the news is not as discouraging financially speaking: wages in Canada's school systems did not experience the same dramatic escalation as in the health-care sector. In fact, from 2002 to 2011 real wages in primary and secondary schools grew by about 1.2% annually, a rate only slightly above that of economy-wide earnings growth. But if we add this to the extra spending triggered by the hiring spree of the last decade, we get an astonishing average annual increase in education spending of 4.7%, all of this at a time when the country's student population was declining by 0.8% on average each year.

In short, far from being a source of savings, public schools have been a major drain on most provincial budgets. In fact, it turns out that provincial governments splurged just as much on public schooling as they did on health care. From 2002 to 2011, provincial spending per person on health care grew on average by 5.6% annually. Provincial spending per pupil in public schools grew at almost exactly the same pace, 5.5%—no small feat given that health-care spending was growing at close to a record-breaking pace.

Post-Secondary Education

Provinces dedicate around 5% of their program spending budgets to post-secondary education.[45] While the K-12 population is declining in Canada, the post-secondary education system has so far defied the forces of demography. Overall, enrolment is up by one-third since the turn of the millennium. Around 2 million students were enrolled in Canadian universities and colleges in 2012–13.[46]

A number of factors contributed to this growth. Globalization and rapid technological change are continuing to depress demand at home for many less-qualified jobs and to fuel growth in many professions and trades requiring university or college training. As a result, more high school graduates attend university or college. They also tend to do so for longer—the number of graduate students in Canadian universities has nearly doubled over the last two decades.[47] Another important trend favouring university and college attendance is the generally improving socio-economic backgrounds of parents.[48] Interestingly, it is not their income as much as their level of educational attainment that matters; as parents are increasingly better educated, more and more high school graduates are attending Canada's universities and colleges. Finally, another trend behind growing enrolment is the rise in the number of international students, whose ranks have grown from 75,000 in 2002–03 to close to 200,000 in 2012–13.[49]

Predictably, enrolment is not growing evenly across the country. Over the same ten years domestic enrolment in Atlantic Canada universities and colleges was almost flat (+4%). In Quebec, enrolment growth was more significant (+14%), but still considerably below Ontario (+50%) and the four western provinces (between 36% and 41%).

Unlike the public school sector, there was no movement toward lower class sizes in universities and colleges. Also, since enrolment did not decline, not even in faster-aging regions, universities and colleges generally did not face the same challenge of having to scale down to reflect declining enrolment. Nonetheless, provincial spending on post-secondary education institutions did grow fast. Despite its relatively slow enrolment growth, oil-fuelled Newfoundland and Labrador led the country for its lavish spending on universities and colleges, growing its operating subsidies by a whopping 8.7% annually from 2003–04 to 2013–14. The Prairies, where enrolment growth was more robust, followed behind with annual growth of 7.3%. For Canada as a whole, operating subsidies grew by 5%.[50] Much of the extra spending on universities and colleges went to salaries. From the period 2000–01 to 2010–11 (last year for which data was available), the average salary of Canadian university teaching staff grew from $80,535 to $115,402.[51] Adjusted for inflation, this wage growth was twice as strong as that of the average Canadian worker.[52]

Given that enrolment grew on average by 3.0% annually, provincial spending growth on a per student basis was much lower than in the public school sector. But, here again, older, faster-aging provinces ended up growing their spending per student significantly faster than the Canadian average. While provincial spending on universities and colleges may not have grown at the same impressive pace as spending on health care or public schools, the sector was far from a source of savings. In fact, spending grew faster than Canada's ability to pay (measured by GDP growth). Here, too, the gap between spending growth and long-term ability to pay was generally widest in older, faster-aging provinces.

Will Education Save Health Care?

We can predict with near certainty that spending on education in the years ahead will not follow the same aggressive growth path as over the past decade, particularly in older, faster-aging provinces. However politically difficult the task may prove, provinces facing declining enrolment will eventually close down schools to better reflect their demographic realities. Faced with the competing priorities of caring for an aging population and that of ensuring a declining student-educator ratio, governments will most likely pick the former.

Similarly, the post-secondary education sector is not likely to witness the same wage escalation as over the last decade. As is the case in the health-care sector, wage moderation in post-secondary education is already upon us. This moderation could also prove more sustainable than in the health-care sector, given the abundance of PhD graduates looking for work in academia.

That said, perspective is important when considering whether education can "save" health care. Provincial spending on education represents about 5% of Canada's GDP. Even if severe spending moderation measures brought down this proportion to, say, 4%, this would not amount to much for older, faster-aging provinces. We saw earlier that Atlantic Canada can expect provincial spending growth on health care to escalate from around 10% of GDP to close to 20% in a quarter century from now. I am obviously not implying such a reduction in funding for education is desirable or even feasible. I am simply suggesting we should not look to education to find the kind of savings to offset much of the enormous pressures on health-care spending that older, faster-aging provinces will be facing.

Other Provincial Spending

Health care and education represent close to two-thirds of spending by provincial governments. The remaining third is spread across a broad array of programs in economic (transportation and other infrastructure, agriculture and natural resources, tourism and economic development), social (income support, social services of various types), and other sectors (environment, justice, public safety).

It is not reasonable to expect major savings in these areas to help older, faster-aging provinces to deal with rapidly escalating health-care spending pressures. While it is possible to invest less in the short term on things such as roads and highways, this will translate in the longer run into higher maintenance bills. It is not reasonable either to expect major productivity gains that could lead to sizeable savings in areas such as the administration of justice or social services (demand for the latter will in fact grow as population ages). More to the point, we cannot realistically look to these sectors to fund a major portion of future health-care spending growth.

Summing Up

Canada may be a loose, decentralized federation, but its provincial governments tend to move in lockstep when it comes to public spending. And over much of the past decade, richer and poorer provinces alike behaved more like Aesop's proverbial grasshoppers than ants, taking advantage of the robust growth of the pre-2008 period and of the federal government's largesse to boost spending unsustainably.

The days of profligacy are gone. As provinces now all face fiscal challenges of one form or another, a new era of spending moderation is upon us. If history is any guide, such moderation will be sustained for a while, but it will not last forever. As pressures build on Canada's health-care systems, calls for reinvestment will eventually be heard. Not all provinces are facing bleak financial prospects. Alberta, for example, may have been seriously affected by the dramatic drop in oil prices, but it has considerable room to grow its fiscal burden, and its economy will not be crushed by population aging; thus it will likely be able to afford to spend much more on public services. For their part, poorer, faster-aging provinces are in no position to sustainably emulate the spending patterns of their younger, richer counterparts. In a decade or so from now, the four Atlantic provinces will almost certainly no longer be able to sustain their existing health-care systems. Quebec may also eventually end up in dire straits. In other words, in most if not all provinces east of the Ottawa River, medicare as we know it could cease to exist, unless Ottawa steps in aggressively. Whether it will do so, and how it should, is the subject of the remainder of this book.

Part III

THE FEDERAL RESPONSE

Chapter 6

FEDERAL TRANSFERS: HEADING IN THE WRONG DIRECTION?

This book's central thesis is that Canada's Great Demographic Imbalance, left unchecked, will produce two classes of citizens: those who live in provinces that can afford the status quo and those who don't. There is no miracle cure for dealing with the consequences of Canada's Great Demographic Imbalance. It should be clear by now, though, that Ottawa will need to transfer more money to older, faster-aging provinces if it wishes to avoid the balkanization of Canada's welfare state.

This chapter sets the scene for a discussion of how Ottawa could best proceed in addressing the consequences of the Great Demographic Imbalance. It does not provide specific recommendations; these follow in the next chapter. Rather, the chapter takes stock of how and why Ottawa redistributes wealth across the country. To do so, it looks at history. But first, to provide some context, it starts with an overview of how much money Ottawa currently transfers from richer to poorer provinces.

Following the Loonie's Travels

The federal government is a gigantic wealth redistribution machine. In fact, if there were a single line in Ottawa's budget called "wealth redistribution," it would be among the largest, if not the largest. The reality, however, is that almost everything Ottawa does involving money results in significant redistribution among individuals and regions alike. Therefore, to get a sense of just how much money Ottawa shuffles around, we must look at how it collects and spends tax dollars.[1]

A few precisions are in order before doing so. First, the focus here is on how Ottawa transfers wealth from richer to poorer provinces rather than individual Canadians. The two are inextricably linked, however, and we need to discuss the latter in order to shed light on the former.

Second, if we are to examine how Ottawa redistributes wealth from richer to poorer provinces, these terms need to be defined. So far in this book I have generally used the expressions "poorer" and "richer" interchangeably with "older, faster-aging" and "younger, slower-aging" provinces. I have also divided the country in two halves separated by the Ottawa River. From a demographic standpoint, this perspective is mostly appropriate: although Quebec and British Columbia share similar aging dynamics (at least if we consider only median age and share of seniors), the other four western provinces are much younger and slower aging than the four Atlantic provinces.[2] The same can be said from an economic standpoint, but with a caveat about Canada's easternmost province. As the country's third richest yet oldest and fastest-aging province, Newfoundland and Labrador straddles both groups. But with respect to its future prospects, the province sits firmly with the rest of Eastern Canada. Barring a dramatic improvement in the outlook for its natural resources sector, and in particular its oil and gas industry, the province's economy is set to grow at the slowest pace in the country, if not witness outright decline. Meanwhile, its government will be facing the strongest aging-induced spending pressures. Newfoundland and Labrador may be a richer province now, but it is not in a much better position than the Maritimes with respect to its ability to meet the fiscal challenges ahead. So, unless otherwise specified, assume Newfoundland and Labrador is included along with the rest of Eastern Canada in references to poorer provinces in this chapter and the next.

Finally, it's worth noting that I make no reference to the Equalization program in defining richer and poorer provinces. As we will see later, just because a province is an Equalization recipient does not automatically mean it is poorer than the average of its counterparts.

I begin my examination of the redistributive impact of the federal government's tax-and-spend activities with taxes. Ottawa raises significantly more in taxes from residents in richer than in poorer provinces for mainly two reasons. First, more people are employed in richer than in poorer provinces. As they are younger, richer provinces have greater shares of working-age people and thus higher employment rates. More people working means higher revenues.[3] Second, taxpayers in richer provinces earn higher incomes. Since the federal tax system is generally progressive,[4] this means residents in richer provinces pay on average more in federal taxes not only in absolute terms, but also on each dollar of income.

Yet Ottawa does not spend less in poorer regions just because it collects less in taxes from their residents. Quite the contrary, residents in poorer provinces generally benefit from significantly more in federal spending than those in richer provinces. To understand why, we must turn to Ottawa's transfer payments to persons and provincial governments.

Transfers to persons are the federal government's single largest spending item, accounting for approximately 30% of its program budget. In fiscal year 2014–15, Ottawa spent $76.5 billion on these transfers. Of this amount, close to three-fifths went to elderly benefits (Old Age Security, Guaranteed Income Supplement, spousal and survivor allowances), while another quarter was spent on Employment Insurance (EI) benefits.[5] The distribution of elderly and EI benefits is heavily skewed toward poorer, older provinces. Understandably, the federal government spends more on elderly benefits in older than in younger provinces. This is not just because older provinces have more seniors; it is also that their seniors are typically poorer and therefore draw higher average benefits. In Newfoundland and Labrador, one in two recipients of Old Age Security also receives Guaranteed Income Supplement benefits; in Alberta and Ontario, this proportion is one in four.[6] The story is similar for EI. As their economies are less dynamic and more seasonal in nature, Atlantic Canadians (and Eastern Quebecers) are much more dependent on EI benefits than other Canadians. For every dollar in premiums paid, Atlantic Canadian workers get nearly two in return.[7] At the other end of the spectrum, workers in the Prairies get back only around $0.50.[8]

The second largest spending item in Ottawa's budget is transfers to provinces and territories. In 2014–15, $61.6 billion, or nearly a quarter, of Ottawa's program spending went to such transfers.[9] Here also, spending favours poorer provinces since more than a quarter of this amount goes to the Equalization program. In 2014–15, spending on Equalization stood at $16.7 billion. The remainder, approximately $45 billion, was distributed on a per capita basis in the form of payments under the CHT ($32.1 billion) and the CST ($12.6 billion).

Combined, federal transfers to persons and provinces represent approximately 55% of Ottawa's program spending budget. To fully account for how much money Ottawa transfers from richer to poorer provinces through its spending activities, we would have to examine the remaining 45%. In doing so, we would find many instances where richer provinces benefit from more in federal spending. This is notably the case in the critical area of R&D, where Ontario receives more than half of federal funds.[10] We would also find instances where there is no clear link between federal spending and provincial prosperity. For example, Manitoba and Saskatchewan get relatively large shares of the approximately $11 billion in federal funding for Aboriginal affairs.[11] This only makes sense given the share of Aboriginal residents in their respective populations is four times greater than for Canada as a whole. On balance, however, our examination would most likely show the remaining 45% of Ottawa's budget involves much less interregional redistribution than the 55% that goes to major transfers to persons and provinces.

Federal Spending and Revenues by Province

Accounting for the full redistributive impact of Ottawa's tax-and-spend activities is an extremely complex, data-heavy, and time-consuming task. By nature, it is best-suited for our nation's statistical agency. Not long ago, Statistics Canada carried out this task under its Provincial Economic Accounts (PEA) program. It stopped doing so after 2009, following cutbacks to the agency's budget. While slightly dated, the PEA's numbers do provide a rough sense of how much wealth Ottawa shuffles around the country.

Table 6.1 shows the net benefit (current federal in-province expenditures minus revenues collected in-province) that each province

Table 6.1: Net Benefit from Federal Revenues and Spending Per Person (constant 2008 dollars)

Source: Author's calculations based on Statistics Canada, catalogue 13-018-X; CANSIM, tables 051-0001 and 326-0021.

	1998			2008		
	Federal revenues from province	Federal spending in province	Net benefit (contribution)	Federal revenues from province	Federal spending in province	Net benefit (contribution)
Newfoundland and Labrador	4,032	11,812	7,780	10,420	14,540	4,119
Prince Edward Island	5,455	11,476	6,021	5,785	12,601	6,816
Nova Scotia	5,358	10,947	5,589	5,836	11,891	6,055
New Brunswick	4,921	9,566	4,645	5,093	10,359	5,266
Quebec	5,637	6,492	855	5,369	6,958	1,588
Ontario	7,792	5,662	(2,130)	7,205	6,231	(974)
Manitoba	5,497	8,253	2,756	5,584	9,947	4,363
Saskatchewan	5,684	7,746	2,062	7,175	8,508	1,333
Alberta	8,769	5,816	(2,953)	11,032	5,192	(5,840)
British Columbia	6,162	5,396	(766)	6,832	5,877	(955)

drew from the federal government's tax-and-spend activities for the years 1998 and 2008. (I present data for 2008 rather than 2009 as the latter was a recession year during which revenues were temporarily depressed while spending was inflated and partly deficit-financed. As such, all provinces benefited more from, or contributed less to, federal tax-and-spend activities than usual in that year.)

For many reasons already discussed, one should not expect a perfect relationship between a province's net benefit and its level of prosperity.[12] But overall, the relationship between the two is clear: residents in poorer provinces benefit considerably more from federal spending than they pay in taxes. Consider the contrast between Canada's poorest region, the Maritimes, and its richest province, Alberta. On average, Maritimers benefited from more than twice as much in federal spending while they contributed only half as much in revenues as Albertans did. The net benefit from Ottawa's tax-and-spend activities to the Maritimes, at nearly $6,000 per person, amounted to close to one-sixth (16%) of the region's GDP.

That Ottawa redistributes such large amounts of money from richer to poorer provinces should not come as a surprise, nor should it be a source of outrage: a core role of central governments in most federations is to redistribute wealth to achieve public policy objectives.[13] My aim in examining this issue was not to pass any moral judgment, but rather to show just how much Ottawa's tax-and-spend activities matter to the fiscal balances of provinces—and of poorer ones in particular.

Yet, however much Ottawa already matters to poorer provinces, it will have to matter even more if we are to avoid creating two classes of Canadians divided by their province of residence. The remainder of this chapter turns to history to better understand how Ottawa has come to matter this much to the public finances of all provinces. It also looks at the evolving role of Ottawa in redistributing wealth from richer to poorer provinces. Much of the focus is on fiscal federalism, that is, on how Ottawa and the provinces have interacted over the years in raising and sharing revenues from Canadian taxpayers to carry out their respective responsibilities. As we will see, few aspects of fiscal federalism are clear-cut. Debate over where the provinces' turf starts and where the federal government's ends and the extent to which they overlap is as old as the federation. The same applies to the question of who gets to tax whom and how much each needs: disputes about the vertical fiscal imbalance between Ottawa and the provinces are never far away in Canadian federalism. The issue of horizontal imbalance among provinces is also a long-standing one. Here, the debate is not about whether such an imbalance exists—it does and always did—but rather about the role the federal government should play in addressing it.

This chapter discusses all of these issues using a chronological approach. Much of the focus is on the history of the welfare state in Canada, beginning with the logical starting point: Confederation.

In the Beginning...

By definition, federalism is about the sharing of power. It is a system of government in which the sovereignty of the state is divided between a central authority and constituent units, be they Canadian provinces, American states, or German *länder*. As power is shared, there needs to be an agreement on how responsibilities are to be divided between orders of government and how each will secure the funds necessary to carry out its activities. In Canada, the division of fiscal and legislative powers is found in the British North America Act (BNA Act), the document that gave birth to the federation as a British colony (or, more formally, a British Dominion) in 1867. With a few notable exceptions, the original division of powers laid out in the BNA Act has remained much the same over the years.

Before looking into how the BNA Act shaped Canada, some context on the business of governing at the time of Confederation is in order. What did governments do back then? Where did they spend most of their money? We saw earlier that the climate at the time was one of *laissez-faire*. As a doctrine, *laissez-faire* seeks to limit government interference in public affairs to a strict minimum, leaving economic and social outcomes to the free play of market forces. While it was the prevailing doctrine, pure *laissez-faire* did not exist: to call government's role back then simply that of a night watchman would be an exaggeration. It is true that governments in North America did little to regulate the economy and counter the emerging forces of the so-called robber barons and captains of industry. But where governments did play a major role was in public works, particularly in laying down the transportation infrastructure to enable trade and commerce. The top priorities of colonial governments at the time were railways and canals—in this era of horse-drawn carts, roads were mostly for local transportation. In the couple of decades prior to Confederation, colonial governments had borrowed heavily to fund railways and canals. As a result, their finances were seriously strained, as was their credit in London financial circles. Restoring colonial credit was in fact a major motivation for Confederation.

To be sure, many other developments contributed to Confederation, key among which were the political stalemate between Canada West and Canada East (the colonies of Upper and Lower Canada were united in 1841) and the threat posed by an expansionist and militaristic America coming out of a civil war. But Canada was also made possible, if not necessary, by a confluence of economic and fiscal matters. In addition to the issue of public debts accumulated by the various colonies, there was that of markets. With the end of trade reciprocity with the United States and the loss of imperial preferences as Great Britain embraced freer trade, the colonies were in desperate need of new markets. A union of British North American colonies linked together by an intercolonial railway was seen as a concrete way not only to restore colonial credit but also to develop desperately needed new markets for local entrepreneurs.

Unlike today, colonial governments spent very little on social and other local affairs. British North America was then still an agrarian society made up primarily of self-contained rural communities. The nexus of social welfare was the family and the local community, not distant colonial governments. According to one estimate, colonial governments spent a total of only $500,000 on public welfare in 1866, a paltry 3.2% of their total expenditures.[14]

It is against this geopolitical, economic, and social backdrop that the Fathers of Confederation worked on the resolutions that would culminate in the BNA Act and the birth of Canada. It is no secret that many Fathers of Confederation wanted a unitary state rather than a federation—and certainly not a true confederation. This preference was to be clearly affirmed in the new country's division of powers.

Under the BNA Act, the governments of the colonies that would become the provinces of Ontario, Quebec, New Brunswick, and Nova Scotia were mainly left with local and private matters, including property and civil rights, which did not mean much financially back then. For its part, the federal government was granted the big responsibilities, including the construction of the Intercolonial Railway, navigation and shipping, defence, and western settlement. It was also granted residual power, that is, the power to legislate in areas not explicitly listed in the BNA Act.

As was the case with legislative powers, the division of fiscal powers under the BNA Act was heavily skewed in favour of the central government. Before Confederation, colonial governments relied almost exclusively on indirect taxation—mainly customs duties and excise taxes—to raise revenues. The BNA Act gave the monopoly over indirect taxation to the federal government, along with the authority to "raise money by any mode or system of taxation." For their part, provinces had to make do with direct taxation.[15] At the time, the only major form of direct taxation acceptable to residents was the property taxes levied by municipalities. Recognizing the impracticability of direct taxation for provinces, the Fathers of Confederation agreed that Ottawa would provide them with fixed subsidies (unadjusted for inflation). With this move, federal transfers to provinces were born. The inadequacy of such transfers—real or perceived—would become a permanent object of debate between Ottawa and the provinces.

While the Fathers of Confederation at least attempted to deal with the vertical imbalance resulting from the BNA Act, they chose not to do anything about the horizontal imbalance. Just before Confederation, municipal taxes represented roughly one-third of the revenues raised in the Province of Canada. In Nova Scotia and New Brunswick, where municipal governments were almost non-existent outside Halifax and Saint John, municipal revenues amounted to around only 10% of colonial revenues. This meant provincial governments in the Maritimes had to shoulder a larger burden to finance roads, education, and public welfare than in the Province of Canada. While the Fathers of Confederation were well aware of the situation, they chose not to take it into account, allocating federal subsidies

to provinces largely on a per capita basis. The result, as a royal commission report would eventually make clear,[16] was that Quebec and
Ontario received subsidies greater than their needs, while the positions of New Brunswick and, even more so, of Nova Scotia soon
became "intolerable."[17]

Over the next few years, adjustments were made to address the
most egregious cases of inadequacy of provincial revenues. The first
of these came two years after Confederation, in 1869, in the form of
the "better terms" agreement under which Nova Scotia received an
increased subsidy. Then, in 1870 and 1871, the inadequacy of the
per capita formula was made more evident when sparsely populated
Manitoba and British Columbia joined the federation.[18] Neither of
them received a subsidy that reflected its population as the amount
each would have received was acknowledged to be insufficient. Still,
despite these initial side-agreements, by the late 1880s all provinces except Ontario—whose municipal system was most developed—were calling for higher subsidies, but to no avail.[19] As a result,
provinces had to rely increasingly on deeply unpopular direct taxes
(chiefly corporation taxes and succession duties) as well as licences,
permits, and various other fees and penalties, to grow their revenues.
In 1874 federal subsidies represented 58% of total provincial revenues; by 1913 this proportion stood at 28%.[20]

While provinces managed to grow their revenues considerably,
their responsibilities were growing faster. As Canada industrialized
and urbanized rapidly toward the turn of the century, society became
more and more complex, requiring growing investments in areas such
as public education, public health, municipal infrastructure, and relief
for the poor. Soon after World War One, pressures would multiply
for putting in place the various costly social insurance programs that
make up today's welfare state. And, under the Constitution, dealing
with this was a provincial responsibility.

Building the Modern Welfare State:
A Painfully Slow Process

By international standards, Canada was late in the game in developing a modern welfare state. By the turn of the century, many countries

in continental Europe had made significant progress on this front. Germany, for instance, established the world's first "sickness" insurance program in 1883, followed by a workers' compensation program the next year, and an old-age pension regime in 1889.[21] By contrast, Canada made no progress to speak of in developing such programs until shortly before the outbreak of World War One.[22] As Dennis Guest notes in his seminal history of social security in Canada, the BNA Act was no stranger to this situation:

> [W]hile the need for health and welfare provisions on a nationwide basis grew with Canada's increasing industrialization, the responsibility for initiating and paying for these services was, by judicial interpretation, left firmly in the care of the provinces who lacked the necessary finances to carry out the responsibility. The impasse that developed because of the incongruity between legislative responsibility and financial capability was one reason for the delay in the establishment of vital programmes of social security in Canada. Insofar as the constitutional dilemma was concerned, advances in social welfare legislation had to wait upon three developments: a provincial government's willingness and ability to finance needed measures; an amendment to the B.N.A. Act to permit federal entry into an area of jurisdiction otherwise assigned to the provinces; or the development of stratagems to secure financial help without appearing to violate the provisions of the B.N.A. Act.[23]

All three developments would unfold, eventually. World War One provided a first major impetus for change. The emergency of raising much greater revenues to fight the war and organize the wartime economy enabled the federal government to enter a new tax field: personal income. This tax field, which eventually became the federal government's main source of revenues, would prove critical in funding future social security programs. The Great War also allowed Canadians to discover the power of the state as a force for improving their daily lives. Just prior to the war, the Canadian economy was in a sharp cyclical downturn, "throwing thousands of Canadians out of work and exposing them to the haphazard mixture of grudging municipal relief and private charity."[24] The war effort led by the federal government brought back full employment and boosted the country's productive capacity. This, along with the intervention of the federal government in supporting disabled soldiers and the widows and orphans of men killed on the battlefield, led Canadians to begin to realize that government could do more than simply maintain law and order.[25] The first cracks in the edifice of the *laissez-faire* doctrine were showing.

Not coincidentally, the end of World War One marked the beginning of the days when federal parties started competing with one another to define the national interest in social policy. By that time, it was firmly established that social policy was first and foremost—if not exclusively—a provincial jurisdiction. But citizens voting in federal elections had no time for constitutional niceties; they directed their demands for greater social protection to provincial and federal governments alike. The first major federal party to articulate a vision for the national interest in social policy was the Liberal Party at its 1919 convention in Ottawa. There, under its new leader, William Lyon Mackenzie King, the party made the following statement:

> So far as may be practicable having regard for Canada's financial position, an adequate system of social insurance against unemployment, sickness, dependence in old age, and other disability which would include old-age pensions, widow's pensions, and maternity benefits, should be instituted by the Federal Government in conjunction with the Governments of the several provinces.[26]

This vision would take nearly a half century to fully come to fruition. There were many obstacles, not the least of which was the division of powers between Ottawa and the provinces. An even greater obstacle at first was a concern to which King had alluded in his book *Industry and Humanity*, published in 1918: "the possible adverse effects of social security protection on the habits of thrift and industry."[27] And he was far from the only one with that concern. While progress had been achieved during the Great War, it would take time for the concept of social insurance to prevail over that of individual and family responsibility for dealing with the vicissitudes of economic life in an increasingly industrialized and urbanized society.

The Old Age Pensions Act of 1927

King's concern cast a long shadow over the federal government after the Great War. A prudent man worried about not getting too far ahead of the electorate,[28] King made little inroads on his party's vision following his election in 1921. King was the prime minister of Canada for all but five of the eighteen years from 1921 to the outbreak of World War Two; yet, his only major achievement in the area of social security was the adoption of old-age pensions in 1927. And even then, this measure was taken less out of principle than political necessity. From the end of the war until 1924, the priority of the federal government was to restore public finances—in those pre-Keynesian days, deficit-spending was not popular. In 1924, with financial circumstances improving, the House of Commons, under pressure notably from the Trades and Labour Congress of Canada, appointed a special committee to investigate old-age pensions. In its report, the committee recommended a means-tested pension of $20 per month for persons aged seventy years and older to be cost-shared equally between the federal government and the provinces. While such a measure was in line with its vision for social security, the government dragged its feet at first. As Dennis Guest notes:

> Despite the recommendations of the parliamentary committee in 1925, there was no mention of old age pension legislation in the Speech from the Throne on 8 January 1926. Nor was there any indication that the subject had been considered by the government. The only province that showed real interest was British Columbia. The spokesmen for other provinces expressed perfunctory interest or were hostile to what they considered federal interference in a provincial concern.
>
> But the issue was raised with determination by two Labour members from Winnipeg, J. S. Woodsworth and A. A. Heaps, at a time when King was desperately trying to hang on to power following the 1925 federal election which left the Liberals with only 99 seats in a 245 seat Commons. King had to count on the support of 24 Progressives, which could not always be relied upon, 4 Independents, and the 2 Labour members to counter the 116 Conservatives. Woodsworth and Heaps sent identical letters to King and the Conservative Leader

Arthur Meighen asking whether they had plans for the current session with respect to provision for the unemployed and old age pensions. Meighen's reply was non-committal, but King, anxious for legislative allies, arranged to draft an old age pensions bill immediately.[29]

The bill passed in the House of Commons, but the unelected Senate turned it back, arguing that pensions were a provincial responsibility and expressing concern about the "solidarity of family ties" if government took the responsibility of elderly care. Interestingly, the Upper Chamber had made no such objection two decades earlier in 1908, when the federal government introduced the Government Annuities Act, a retirement savings scheme. While both initiatives pertained to old-age pensions, the Government Annuities Act, which benefited only those who had contributed to the regime, did not affect the "habits of thrift and industry."

In the end, the bill was reintroduced the next year and became law. The Old Age Pensions Act was Canada's first major cost-shared social insurance program. It would become the main model for Ottawa's involvement in social policy, and in provincial affairs more generally, for many decades to come.

Unemployment: No Longer an Individual Problem

While strong pressures were also exerted on the federal government to develop a social insurance program in the area of unemployment, very little happened in the 1920s. In what had already become a familiar refrain, the federal government took refuge behind jurisdictional issues, asserting firmly that "unemployment relief always has been, and must necessarily continue to be, primarily a municipal responsibility, and in the second instance the responsibility of the province."[30] History would prove this wrong: ironically, unemployment insurance is one of only two areas of social policy for which the Constitution would be amended to transfer responsibility from provinces to the federal government. (The other is contributory pensions.)

If the Roaring Twenties put the problem of unemployment on the back burner, the Great Depression of the 1930s brought it right back to the fore. With close to one-quarter of the labour force unemployed nationally at the bottom of the Depression in 1933, recognition grew that unemployment was a social, not an individual, problem. In 1935 the Conservative government of R. B. Bennett introduced the Employment and Social Insurance Act, a bill to move away from "emergency relief measures" toward a "sound and scientific insurance against unemployment."[31] The bill was adopted by Parliament in that year; however, two years later, the Privy Council in London—which still had the ultimate say in interpreting Canada's Constitution—ruled the legislation beyond the powers of the federal government as it dealt with matters of "property and civil rights," a provincial jurisdiction. King had suspected all along that the courts and the Privy Council would consider the legislation as ultra vires; he had in fact accused Bennett of fuelling false hope among the electorate with his bill.[32] Returning to power in October 1935, after a five-year hiatus, King spent the remainder of the decade enjoining provinces to amend the Constitution to transfer the responsibility over unemployment insurance explicitly to the federal government. The last remaining holdout, Alberta, gave its consent in early 1940. The Constitution was amended on July 10, 1940, paving the way for the introduction of the Unemployment Insurance Act, which received royal assent less than a month later, on August 7, 1940.[33]

The Rowell-Sirois Commission

The constitutional impasse over unemployment insurance and the extreme strain the Great Depression exerted on provincial public finances—particularly in the drought-stricken Prairies—led to much talk about the adequacy of the existing division of powers between Ottawa and the provinces. Even the Bank of Canada weighed in on the issue, calling for a comprehensive inquiry.[34] This suggestion did not fall on deaf ears. King, seeing a way to lower the political temperature, jumped at the opportunity. In 1937 he created the Royal Commission on Dominion-Provincial Relations, which was asked to examine the distribution of legislative and fiscal powers and make recommendations to enable both levels of government to function effectively and efficiently.

The commission took three years to carry out its work, submitting its report to the government in 1940. The document, known as the Rowell-Sirois report after the names of its two presidents,[35] was a milestone in the history of federalism in Canada. A work of exceptional erudition, it provided the most comprehensive account of Canada's economic and fiscal history since Confederation. Moreover, according to Donald V. Smiley, one of Canada's most eminent scholars of federalism, the report was "the most comprehensive investigation of a working federal system that has ever been made."[36] Even more importantly, the commission's report was prescient about much of the future course of fiscal federalism in Canada, although it was far ahead of its time.

The Rowell-Sirois report anticipated the postwar explosion in spending needed to build Canada's welfare state. It also acknowledged that provinces did not have access to the necessary resources to shoulder the burden of their growing responsibilities in areas such as income support, health care, and education. The solution, however, did not lay in a wholesale transfer of responsibilities to the federal government. While the commission identified two areas where responsibility should be transferred to the federal government—unemployment insurance and contributory old-age pensions—it stressed the paramount importance of respecting and strengthening provincial autonomy in other areas. The commission did not accept the idea that the federal government should intervene directly in areas of provincial jurisdiction simply because of their supposed importance to the national interest: "Mere importance of a service does not justify its assumption by the Dominion."[37] Furthermore, the commission believed that real provincial autonomy could not be achieved without adequate financial means:

> No allocation of jurisdiction, over education and social services, for example, would be satisfactory which did not take full account of the strong existing loyalties to provincial traditions and institutions. The Commission's Plan seeks to ensure to every province a real and not an illusory autonomy by guaranteeing to it, free from conditions or control, the revenues necessary to perform those functions which relate closely to its social and cultural development.[38]

In short, for the commission, the genius of Canadian federalism required Ottawa to respect the "political, social and cultural individuality" of provinces.[39] Rather than encroaching on provincial jurisdictions in the name of a self-declared "national interest," Ottawa's role was to enable real provincial autonomy by ensuring all provinces, rich and poor alike, had access to adequate resources—a national standard—to carry out their responsibilities. This, the commission believed, could be achieved through federal grants with no strings attached to poorer provinces. Thus was born the principle of equalization. It would take nearly two decades to find its full expression in the Equalization program of 1957.

Unsurprisingly, the Rowell-Sirois Commission was critical of federal-provincial cost-sharing agreements that allowed Ottawa to legislate through the back door in areas of provincial jurisdiction.[40] In its view, such arrangements ran counter not only to the principle of provincial autonomy but also to that of accountability. Provincial governments must be accountable to their respective electorates for the priorities they set and how they spend money to deliver on them. When the federal government spends in a targeted manner on provincial matters, the priorities of provinces are affected. Poorer provinces may end up spending more on lower priority areas to the detriment of those of higher priority that are not the object of federal support. Richer provinces, for their part, may choose to spend less than they would otherwise in federally supported areas and use the money to spend more in areas not federally supported; alternatively, they may hold taxes lower than in poorer provinces. The end result is not only do cost-shared programs encroach on the autonomy and dilute the accountability of provinces, but also they exacerbate the fiscal imbalance between richer and poorer provinces.

A final point about the Rowell-Sirois Commission is that it saw the concepts of equity and efficiency as going hand-in-hand. Back then, the Canadian economy was much more integrated on an east-west basis than it is today. Accordingly, financial hardship in poorer regions that consumed the goods produced in richer regions would have major implications on the health of the national economy. Addressing the horizontal fiscal imbalance was, therefore, in the national interest not only from the perspectives of equity and fiscal federalism but also from an economic standpoint.

World War Two

World War Two was a critical juncture in the history of fiscal federalism and social security in Canada. As was the case during the Great War, the federal government took the lead in steering Canada's wartime economy. The complex needs of modern warfare required massive investments in upgrading Canada's manufacturing capacity for a wide array of goods. To meet the spending needs of the wartime economy, the federal government borrowed heavily. It also raised significantly more in taxes. In 1941, probably the bleakest year of the war for the Allies, the provinces consented to temporarily withdraw from the fields of personal and corporate income taxation in exchange for subsidies to replace lost revenues.[41] With Ottawa doing most of the spending and controlling the major tax bases, Canada looked more like a unitary state than a federation. This wartime centralization would have a profound effect on the balance of power between Ottawa and the provinces and the development of the welfare state in the decades that followed.

The war also brought back growth and full employment. Canadians once again had the opportunity to witness the powerful role the federal government could play in improving economic conditions. This, along with the still-fresh memory of the Great Depression, provided a prime environment for the teachings of Keynes to leave the classroom and make their way onto Main Street. By the end of the war, there was a general consensus on the need for Ottawa to play a leading role in ensuring full employment and a stable economy. Having built a modern bureaucracy to organize the war effort, it was in a good position to assume this role.

World War Two also accelerated planning on social security. The war exacted a great human toll, which came on top of years of deprivation during the Great Depression. In this context, dreaming of a better world was not just an abstract exercise but rather a morale-boosting one—"peace aims are war weapons," as the saying went.[42] This planning effort produced many reports, including the *Report on Social Security for Canada* published in 1943, also known as the Marsh report after the social scientist who penned it. The effect of this frenzy of activity over postwar planning was to initiate Canadians to the idea of a comprehensive social security system.[43]

The Postwar Years: The Apex of Joint Federalism

As the war neared its end, it first seemed the federal government was genuinely committed to improving social security in Canada. On August 6, 1945, the very same day the first atomic bomb was dropped on Hiroshima, first ministers met in Ottawa to discuss postwar plans. At this conference (known as the Dominion-Provincial Conference on Reconstruction), the federal government laid out substantial proposals for social security. The package, though not comprehensive, included a universal old-age pension system, assistance for the unemployed who were not protected by the unemployment insurance system, as well as a major cost-shared plan for a comprehensive public medical care system. In exchange, Ottawa was asking provinces to permanently vacate the major tax fields of corporate and personal income as well as succession duties, with compensation for the lost revenues.[44] Quebec and Ontario objected, seeing the proposal as involving a net transfer of resources to other provinces. The talks collapsed.[45]

In the aftermath of that failed conference, the federal government retreated and was never again to advance any comprehensive plan for social security. Progress from then on would be achieved in a step-by-step or piecemeal manner. It would also prove painfully slow. For the rest of the decade, while the British were busy implementing their National Health Service, nothing of substance came out of Ottawa. Some have suggested the government was not as interested in making progress on social security at the conference as much as in securing the tax fields it wanted in exchange. Such an interpretation is only reasonable given the priorities Ottawa articulated shortly after the conference:

> The government's intentions and priorities [on social security] were made clear in April, 1946, ten months after the federal election, when the two labour congresses presented their annual list of legislative demands to the federal cabinet. The Trades and Labour Congress, which had assisted the Liberals to victory by failing to endorse the CCF, was sharply rebuked by Finance Minister Ilsley for its "costly" demands. (Labour had requested that the government carry out its

social security promises.) Ilsley's reply was that the government's priorities were for reducing taxes, balancing the budget, and retrenchment. This prompted the Montreal Star to comment that this reckless expenditure over and above Canada's already colossal commitments for social security schemes should be set aside as outside the range of practical politics.[46]

While Ottawa pulled back, the public did not relent. Canada was rapidly industrializing and urbanizing, with more and more women entering the workforce. The "solidarity of family ties" was no longer deemed sufficient for dealing with the challenge of social security. Pressures on governments for better protection continued to mount. Unable to shoulder the burden of new programs on their own, municipalities and provinces turned to Ottawa for help. As its finances improved amid the rising affluence of the postwar years, and as it realized the importance that citizens attached to new social programs, Ottawa eventually responded.

Again, this happened in a piecemeal manner; there was no such thing as a federal master plan for social security. The fact remains, however, that Ottawa played a leading role in virtually every major social security initiative of the 1950s and 1960s. The milestones of this postwar federal involvement in provincial affairs include the Old Age Security Act and the Old Age Assistance Act (1951), allowances for those with blindness and disabilities (1951 and 1954), social assistance (1956), hospital care insurance (1957), youth allowances (1964), the Canada Pension Plan (1965), the Guaranteed Income Supplement (1966), and the Medical Care Act (1966). With the exceptions of the Old Age Security Act and the Canada Pension Plan (which were enabled through constitutional amendments in 1951 and 1964), Ottawa's tool of choice for intervening in provincial jurisdictions was the conditional grant. In exchange for meeting national standards, Ottawa would share with the provinces, usually on a fifty-fifty basis, the costs of various new initiatives. This tool was used extensively not only in social security but also in many other provincial areas, including infrastructure and post-secondary education.

In total, no fewer than fifty-six conditional grant programs were put in place between 1945 and 1962.[47] Underpinning these cost-sharing agreements was a complex apparatus of federal-provincial collaboration. At its heart were first ministers' and ministers' conferences, for which the preparatory work was carried out by committees of federal and provincial officials. As Smiley notes, in 1957, sixty-four such committees were in existence, ranging in scope from the Continuing Committee on Federal-Provincial Fiscal and Economic Matters to the Co-Ordinating Agency on Diseases of the Beaver.[48]

Historians of federalism have called the years from the end of World War Two to the late 1960s by various names that emphasize federal-provincial collaboration: joint federalism, collaborative federalism, executive federalism. Unsurprisingly, many have hailed this era of collaboration as epitomizing the flexibility and adaptability of Canadian federalism. It demonstrated, they argued, that the Constitution was not a straitjacket; on the contrary, with pragmatism and openness, much could be achieved through collaboration.

Conditions were certainly ripe for such extensive collaboration. As discussed, Ottawa came out of the war with a much more modern bureaucracy than its provincial counterparts, which provided it with the human capital to lead the development of Canada's welfare state, at least in the early stages. The war had also brought the country closer together, fostering a greater sense of solidarity. Social policy was a natural conduit for the expression of this solidarity, giving Ottawa considerable political legitimacy to intervene in provincial affairs. Furthermore, with the notable exception of Quebec, there was general consensus during much of that period about how to proceed in building the welfare state, which helped greatly in the establishment of "national standards."[49]

However, to borrow from Stephen Harper, this era was not all rainbows and unicorns either. Those who extol the brand of federalism on display during this era tend to omit an inconvenient truth, which is that provinces had little choice but to collaborate. Faced with growing responsibilities and baited with fifty-cent dollars from Ottawa, they had few options other than to be "flexible." The federation was then plagued by a sharp vertical imbalance, with Ottawa firmly holding the big end of the fiscal stick. Having centralized fiscal powers and raised federal taxes considerably during the war, the federal government had a very large footprint in the major tax fields. Ottawa could have decided to lower its fiscal burden to allow provinces to raise theirs as social policy gained prominence in the postwar years. Instead, it kept its taxes at levels that made continual provincial dependence on federal grants unavoidable.[50]

Ottawa invoked many reasons to keep its firm grip over the country's fiscal levers, first among which was its new responsibilities toward ensuring full employment and a stable economy. Another key reason, however, was Ottawa quickly realized the nation-building and political rewards that came with being perceived as leading the development of popular social programs. That the federal government came to be given much of the credit for Canada's welfare state should not come as a surprise. With the final say over the initiatives it would and would not support, Ottawa determined "national" priorities. And as it had final say in establishing "national standards," Ottawa significantly influenced how programs were formulated from coast to coast.

The vertical fiscal imbalance was not the only force that made collaboration a necessity. The horizontal fiscal imbalance had a similar effect on poorer provinces. We have seen that cost-shared agreements can distort the priorities of provinces and dilute their accountability. There is little doubt the governments of poorer provinces would have preferred to receive unconditional subsidies to spend as they saw fit based on the priorities they defended before their electorates. But the federal government offered no such grants, at least not in the beginning. As beggars cannot be choosers, poorer provinces preferred federal money with strings attached to no money at all. In due time, however, the burden on poorer provinces of coming up with matching funding to participate in federal programs would prove too much to bear. The federal government recognized this in 1957, when it put in place its first Equalization program, just in time for the coming of a costly universal hospital care insurance scheme.

An Alternative Scenario

It may be tempting to conclude that Canada's welfare state would be much less uniform today had Ottawa not played such a hands-on role in developing the various social programs that compose it. We should avoid rushing to such a conclusion. Had it decided to follow the Rowell-Sirois recommendation of enabling real provincial autonomy instead of intervening in provincial jurisdictions in the name of self-declared national interest, Ottawa would likely not have received as much political credit for building Canada's welfare state. Social policy might also play a lesser role in Canada's national identity today—though it would likely remain a distinct marker given the bastion of individualism and free markets south of the border. It is not clear, however, that social programs would be much less uniform across the land. As Smiley observed in 1962:

[T]he devising of explicit standards of provincial performance by the federal authorities, in consultation with the provinces or otherwise, and the enforcement of these by the federal government in connection with conditional grant programmes is only one of the possible procedures for attaining adequate performance by the provincial or local government in respect to particular functions. Assuming that a government has the financial resources permitting the provision of a particular service at adequate levels, the level at which the service will actually be provided will be determined in the long run by popular views about acceptable performance in respect to that activity. These views will in turn be determined by a complex and little-understood interaction between the public and the standards evolved by groups professionally involved in the provision of particular services—roads, education, welfare, hospitalization and so on. Thus, where there are large numbers of people who change their residences from province to province, where there are relatively easy means of communication, and where there are close and constructive relations among persons professionally engaged in public functions, we can expect that popular expectations will tend to become uniform as time goes on.[51]

Smiley wrote this at a time when transportation and communications, while improving, were not as inexpensive and easy as they are today. What has happened since suggests he may have been on to something. As we will see further on, the days are long gone when the federal government routinely attempted to dictate social policy. Today, Ottawa shoulders a much lower share of the cost of social programs than when they were created from the late 1920s to the 1960s. It also imposes dramatically fewer conditions in exchange for its funding. Yet, social programs across the country are as comparable as they have ever been.

What Smiley seems to have grasped more than fifty years ago is a powerful logic of emulation at work in Canadian federalism. Indeed, the previous chapter delineates examples of this logic of emulation in class-size reduction initiatives and wage-setting for public sector professionals, for instance. Our most iconic national symbol, Canada's health-care system, was also born from this logic. Ottawa did not take the lead in developing medicare—the greatest Canadian, according to CBC viewers, was not a federal prime minister but rather a provincial premier. Public health care spread from Saskatchewan to the rest of the country because it worked and other Canadians wanted the same. And by the time health-care programs were rolling out across the land, Canada had adopted an Equalization program that enabled poorer provinces to afford them. In short, they finally had meaningful autonomy.

From Conditional Grants to Block Funding

The era of collaborative federalism went with a bang, not a whimper. Indeed, the last major shared-cost agreement was none other than the Medical Care Act of 1966. By that time, however, collaborative federalism had run out of steam. In retrospect, it is easy to see why. The Rowell-Sirois report stressed the critical importance of preserving provincial autonomy for a number of reasons, not the least of which was the "political, social and cultural individuality" of provinces. By the middle of the 1960s, an increasingly nationalist Quebec announced it would "opt out" of any future cost-shared initiative with Ottawa. (It is difficult to see how a province can truly "opt out" of its own constitutional jurisdiction; while this expression is commonly used, it would be more appropriate to say other provinces have "opted into" programs proposed by the federal government.) Quebec's announcement was not shocking; it had opted out of many such initiatives in the past, usually with compensation. The province's habit had by then become problematic to political leaders in other provincial capitals and in Ottawa, who had grown quite concerned with "pushing Quebec into a 'special status' by virtue of its having already opted out of most of the national shared-cost social programs."[52] But political leaders in other provinces had grown uneasy with cost-sharing agreements for another reason: the costs of their social programs were escalating fast, and the nature of cost-sharing agreements was a major part of the problem. Provincial governments had little incentive to find efficiencies and control costs when their savings were "rewarded" with a corresponding loss in federal revenues.

In the 1970s, as Ottawa's fiscal situation deteriorated, the federal government grew increasingly sensitive to provincial calls for more flexibility. As Canada's economy stagnated, the fiscal eggs laid earlier were coming home to roost "as full-grown, angry chickens."[53] Pressures from cost-shared programs were adding up, notably to the rise in Equalization spending that followed the 1973 energy crisis.

Ottawa's response was what provinces had feared all along: retrenchment. Shortly after the energy crisis, Ottawa amended the Equalization formula to lower its overall outlays. In 1977 the federal government moved away from the long-standing model of conditional, fifty-fifty cost-shared agreements to a new "block funding" approach for health care and higher education. Under this new approach called Established Programs Financing (EPF), the federal government offered provinces a combination of cash and tax points that reflected the per capita federal program contributions in the base year of 1975–76 (a tax point transfer is an arrangement by which the federal government agrees to lower its tax rate so that provincial governments can raise theirs). These transfers were to be increased annually based on a three-year moving average of annual gross national product (GNP) growth. To appeal to provinces, funding came with many fewer strings attached. While Ottawa notionally allocated 68% of its funding to health care and the remaining 32% to higher education, provinces did not have to respect this allocation, nor were they required to match annual federal funding growth.

With this new formula, Ottawa had set in motion the process of disengaging from provincial social programs. From more than two-fifths in the late 1970s, Ottawa's share of funding for provincial health, higher education, and social programs is down to around one-fifth today. It worth noting that Ottawa's share of provincial spending on social programs was never fully 50% because cost-sharing agreements only applied to eligible expenses. For instance, in the health-care arena, Ottawa cost-shared only what would become known as Canada Health Act services (essentially, hospital and physician services). The federal share of overall provincial and territorial health expenditures (cash plus tax points) peaked at 43% in 1979–80.[54]

Leaving the Baby at the Doorstep: Federal Retrenchment, 1980s and 1990s

After the stagflation of the 1970s and the Thatcher and Reagan revolution, a conservative tide swept over Canada and much of the Western world. The ideological winds that accompanied this tide were not the only reason for Ottawa's retrenchment, which would continue for the remainder of the century; the reality of dealing with chronic deficits stretching back to the mid-1970s was also a powerful force for action. In 1986 the federal government announced that, beginning in 1986–87, EPF growth would be reduced by two percentage points. Beginning in 1989–90, a further cut of one percentage point would take effect. Then in 1990 a two-year freeze was announced, which would be extended until 1994–95.

The biggest blow for provinces came in 1995. In the early 1990s, the Canadian economy was grappling with a major recession, the longest since the Great Depression. Ottawa's already strained finances were hit hard, posting the largest deficit in its history in 1992–93. Two years later, in January 1995, a *Wall Street Journal* editorial dubbed Canada "an honorary member of the Third World," referring to the Canadian dollar as the "northern peso."[55] It was in this sombre context that finance Minister Paul Martin Jr. tabled his historic 1995 budget. A transformative document in many ways, it announced a major restructuring of the federal government, with more than forty-five thousand federal positions to be eliminated. Iconic Crown corporations such as CN were to be divested and the government's remaining shares in Petro-Canada were to be sold. Many taxes were raised and new user fees put in place. And last but not least, transfers to provinces would be cut back severely.

As in 1977, Ottawa's retrenchment from provincial social programs in the 1995 budget was enabled by reform in funding delivery. The 1977 EPF reform applied only to health care and higher education.

In the area of social assistance, where programs had been regrouped since 1966 under a single administrative framework called the Canada Assistance Plan (CAP), costs had continued to be shared on a fifty-fifty basis after 1977. CAP spending kept escalating in the 1980s; from 1985 to 1990, it grew on average by 6.5% annually. In 1990–91, a ceiling of 5% on funding growth (a "cap on CAP") was put in place for the three "have" provinces (Alberta, Ontario, and British Columbia). This cap remained until 1994–95. The 1995 budget completed the block funding reform started in 1977: It announced that funding for CAP and EPF would be wrapped into a single transfer, the Canada Health and Social Transfer (CHST). Ottawa would slash CHST funding over the second half of the 1990s. In 1994–95, cash transfers under EPF and CAP amounted to $17.4 billion. By 2000–01, CHST payments stood at $13.5 billion, a 23% decline. By comparison, elderly benefits—a federal responsibility—grew 18%, from $20.1 to $23.7 billion.[56] What is good for the goose is apparently not always good for the gander.

From the Fiscal Dividend to the "Fix for a Generation"

By the time Paul Martin Jr. delivered his 1995 budget, the dark clouds hanging over Canada's economy had started to dissipate. For nearly fifteen years starting in 1993, the Canadian economy grew robustly, riding on the coattails of a strong United States economy and, starting toward the turn of the millennium, steadily rising commodity prices. And as discussed, Canada's impressive performance was buttressed by labour force conditions: all baby boomers were still of working age and the number of women joining the workforce was still catching up with that of men.

With the return of prosperity and federal spending on a slower growth track, it did not take long for Ottawa to start producing substantial surpluses, and the national conversation quickly turned from eliminating the deficit to divvying up a growing "fiscal dividend." Unsurprisingly, surveys revealed Canadians' top priority for reinvestment was health care. The severe financial restraint of the 1990s had had many consequences on public health care in Canada, including more restricted access to specialists, longer wait times for non-emergency surgeries, and the loss of beds from hospital closures. As a result, Canadians' confidence in their provincial health-care systems had eroded.[57]

The federal government was quick to respond, despite health care being a provincial jurisdiction. Between 2000 and 2004, no fewer than three federal-provincial "agreements" were reached on health care, though there was not much to agree on: Ottawa boosted funding levels significantly but received very little in return. Having cut funding drastically just a few years earlier, it did not have much political legitimacy to ask for anything. Even funds that were "targeted" for specific uses (for instance, medical equipment or wait times reduction) came with no strings attached other than the obligation of provinces to report publicly on outcomes.

Perhaps the best known of these three "agreements" is the last one, the 10-Year Plan to Strengthen Health Care, announced in September 2004. This plan, which Prime Minister Paul Martin Jr. dubbed a "Fix for a Generation," called for $41 billion in new money over a decade. Of this amount, three-quarters went to a 6% annual increase in the Canada Health Transfer (CHT)—the CHST had been divided into the Canada Social Transfer (CST) and the Canada Health Transfer (CHT), thus making health-care funding increases appear larger than if they had remained buried inside the CHST. The remainder went for "targeted" initiatives, for which funds would be disbursed on a per capita basis.

The Harper Years: More Continuity than Rupture

Much has been written about how the Harper years marked a profound rupture from prior governments. Some analysts have even gone so far as accusing Harper of systematically dismantling the country.[58] But when it comes to how Ottawa shares wealth with provinces, Harper's record is one more of continuity than rupture. This is not to say that federal transfers remained the same under Harper. There were in fact important changes, all of which benefited western provinces most. However, with one substantive exception, Harper did not fundamentally alter the course of Canadian fiscal federalism. His take-it-or-leave-it style may have differed from many of his predecessors, but we should not confuse style with substance.

Perhaps the most visible sign of continuity was Harper's approach to health care. Whatever his reasons, Harper kept Paul Martin Jr.'s promise to grow the CHT by 6% annually for ten years and even extended it a few more years. He may not have held any first ministers' meetings to "negotiate" such an impressive rate of federal funding growth, but the money kept pouring in nevertheless. And like his predecessors, Harper did not impose any new meaningful requirements on provinces as to how new federal dollars should be spent.

Another legacy of the Harper government was to make major federal transfers to provinces less redistributive. In the 2007 budget, the government announced the CST would no longer provide more money to poorer than to richer provinces; all would be treated equally. As for the CHT, to respect the 10-Year Plan to Strengthen Health Care, the shift to per capita funding would start in 2014–15.

Here also, Harper was walking in the footsteps of his predecessors. Indeed, Harper was far from the first prime minister to treat as synonymous the values-laden concept of *equity* and the more easily measurable notion of *equality* in dispensing federal funding to provinces. This practice is as old as Confederation itself, as we have seen. More recently, the many new billions the Chrétien and Martin governments spent on targeted initiatives in health care did not take into account the uneven means of provincial governments; they, too, were allocated on a per capita basis. In fact, except for the CHT and the CST, this was the default approach of both Chrétien and Martin for providing extra cash to provinces. The Gas Tax Fund transfer is a case in point.

Certainly, Harper's decision to shift to a per capita formula for the CST and the CHT was much more consequential than similar actions taken previously by Chrétien or Martin. Still, all these moves had in common that they were politically attractive in the provinces where most voters live, starting with Ontario. For more than a decade now, Ontario has become increasingly vocal in wanting its "fair share" from the federal government. Whatever the reasons—a poorly performing economy or a growing realization that the province depends much less on consumers from poorer regions of the country than in the past—Ontario's resurgent provincialism was paid heed by Harper's Liberal predecessors and by Harper himself. In fact, for the Conservatives, shifting to a per capita allocation was even more politically attractive than for the Liberals. The Conservatives have never been popular east of the Ottawa River, having never managed to secure more than twenty seats.[59] It is the richer, faster-growing lands west of the Ottawa River that the Conservatives had in sight with their move to a per capita funding basis—the very lands that received twenty-seven of the thirty new seats added to the electoral map in time for the 2015 election.

The last major decision of the Harper government with regard to transfers to provinces was announced right before Christmas in 2011. On December 19, Minister Flaherty surprised his provincial colleagues at a ministers' meeting by declaring unilaterally that CHT funding would continue to escalate by 6% annually until 2016–17 and would then follow nominal GDP growth, with a floor of 3%. Naturally, many provinces decried this move by the federal government, claiming Ottawa was balancing its books on their backs. Yet Harper was not the first prime minister to act in this manner. In fact, the Trudeau government adopted a nearly identical approach in 1977 with its EPF reform.

Equalization is the only major area where it can be said Harper broke with past practice. Even on this file, however, he was not the true trailblazer—that honour belongs to Paul Martin Jr. In 2007 the Equalization program turned fifty. For almost its entire history, the program had the same fundamental architecture: its aim was to raise the ability of "poorer" provinces to spend on public services to a given "national" standard. The Equalization formula compared a province's fiscal capacity (its ability to generate revenues from various tax bases such as income taxes, sales taxes, natural resources, etc.) to that of a representative set of provinces (the national standard). If its fiscal capacity was below the standard, the province received Equalization payments. A logical consequence of this formula was that the total amount spent on Equalization was not determined in advance; it was a variable sum whose level depended upon disparities in fiscal capacity among provinces.

While the Equalization formula was amended many times over the years, these changes typically dealt with one or both of the two elements used to establish the national standard: the representative set of provinces and the tax bases used to compute fiscal capacity. Incidentally, the many important changes that have been brought to the national standard over the years are a major reason why the Equalization program does not offer a good basis for separating have from have-less provinces. The original standard for Equalization included only Canada's two richest provinces, which at the time were Ontario and British Columbia. By definition, such a standard implied the remaining eight provinces were have-less. But this was a high standard in the sense that a province could have a fiscal capacity above the national average, yet still receive Equalization payments. Later on, the standard would be changed to include a larger number of provinces. As the standard was brought down, the number of have provinces typically went up. For instance, under the current ten-province standard, four provinces do not receive Equalization.[60]

In 2004 then prime minister Martin announced changes that radically altered the architecture of the Equalization program. His government introduced a fixed framework under which overall Equalization funding was guaranteed to grow annually and recipient provinces would not see any declines in their payments. In other words, the overall amount spent in Equalization would no longer be determined solely by the gaps in fiscal capacities among provinces. While Martin's intention was to enhance Equalization for recipient provinces, it created a dangerous precedent that Harper would exploit shortly thereafter.

Harper reformed the Equalization program twice. In 2007 he renewed with the past, returning to the pre-2004 architecture under which Equalization payments were not set in advance but rather determined by fiscal capacity gaps among provinces. His reform included conventional changes such as returning to a ten-province standard, streamlining the number of tax bases that went into the calculation of provincial fiscal capacity from thirty-three to five, and introducing an element of flexibility that provided an incentive for provinces to develop their natural resources by lowering the Equalization "clawback" (the extent to which higher natural resources revenues resulted in lower Equalization payments).

Harper's second, more radical reform was announced in 2009. Not for the first time in the program's history, it was the perspective of Ontario receiving Equalization payments that prompted reform.[61] Given its size, Ontario's entry amid the ranks of Equalization recipients threatened to produce a dramatic escalation in the costs of the program, which had already grown considerably in previous years. To shield itself from this escalation, the federal government announced in Budget 2009 that it would cap the growth of total payments under the program to Canadian nominal GDP growth. With this change, Equalization became like a pie, which grows at best along with the national economy, to be shared among recipient provinces.[62] The rub, though, was that these provinces now include a new recipient, Ontario, whose sheer size is greater than the five other recipients combined. Making room for this new recipient negatively affected the payments of other provinces. In 2015–16, Ontario's Equalization payments stood at $2.4 billion or 14% of total payments. The impact of Harper's reforms on traditional recipients such as the Maritimes is clear. Take, for example, New Brunswick. From 2000–01 to 2009–10, the province's Equalization receipts grew from $1.151 billion to $1.689 billion, an annual growth rate of 4.4%. From 2009–10 to 2015–16, payments actually *declined*. This was not because the province's economy performed better than the rest of the country—it did much worse, in fact.

Summing Up

Successful federations adapt to evolving circumstances. The growing importance of social policy as Canada began to industrialize and urbanize rapidly toward the turn of the twentieth century profoundly reshaped Canadian fiscal federalism. At first, the division of powers under the BNA Act slowed the progress of Canada's welfare state. Judicial interpretation had made clear that social policy was first and foremost—if not exclusively—the responsibility of provinces, yet the latter lacked the financial clout to assume this responsibility effectively. The continued progress of industrialization, along with two world wars and the worst depression in the history of modern capitalism would eventually provide the necessary impetus for rolling out Canada's welfare state. Following World War Two, against the advice of the Rowell-Sirois Commission—put in place to advise Ottawa on this very matter—the federal government decided to invade the jurisdictions of provinces, baiting them with fifty-cent dollars in exchange for meeting "national standards" in areas as diverse as social assistance, health care, and higher education. Thus began the golden age of postwar "collaborative federalism," which lasted well into the 1960s.

Then, as program costs soared and political leaders realized the pitfalls of excessive centralization—including strengthening the distinct status of Quebec—the slow and steady process of federal retrenchment from funding and shaping social policy was set in motion. Until well into the 1970s, the federal government bore upwards of 40% of the cost of most provincial social programs and played a central role in formulating national standards of performance. Today, Ottawa funds only about 20% of their costs and imposes few meaningful conditions beyond the requirements of the Canada Health Act.[63] Despite Ottawa's sharp retrenchment, social programs across provinces are as comparable as ever.

Ottawa's role in redistributing wealth from richer to poorer provinces, while it remains very important, has diminished somewhat in recent years, at least in relation to the size of the national economy. Part of this shift is a matter of scale: Since the turn of the millennium, the federal government's fiscal burden (taxes as a percentage of GDP) is down by almost one-fifth, a decline that happened in almost identical proportions under the Liberals' and Conservatives' watch. The other reason is federal transfers to provinces have become less redistributive. Liberals initiated the change in shifting toward per capita funding—treating equity and equality as synonymous—for non-Equalization federal dollars provided to provinces; the Conservatives completed the shift. As for Equalization, it is no longer as effective as it was in the past in part because the Harper government capped overall spending under the program, thus limiting its effectiveness when provincial disparities are growing. But more fundamentally, Equalization deals only with provincial revenues. The Great Demographic Imbalance is widening the gap in spending needs between richer and poorer provinces. The CHT, the CST, and Equalization do not adequately address this gap. We turn to this issue in the next chapter.

Chapter 7

STAYING TOGETHER

Former United States defense secretary Donald Rumsfeld was no Yogi Berra, but he did produce more than one memorable quote in his long public career. By far the most famous is the one about "knowns and unknowns": "Reports that say something hasn't happened are always interesting to me because as we know, there are known knowns: there are things we know we know. We also know there are known unknowns: that is to say we know there are some things [we know] we do not know. But there are also unknown unknowns—the ones we don't know we don't know."[1]

There is little point discussing unknown unknowns, except to acknowledge they can upend our lives in totally unforeseeable ways. For instance, any attempt to predict Europe's demographic trajectory right before the Black Death wiped out around half of its population in the fourteenth century would have proven wildly off the mark.[2] The projections in this book are certainly not immune to such unknown unknowns; however, anyone who ventures into making long-term projections has little choice but to accept such contingencies may occur and move on assuming they will not—unless one's job is to plan for them.

Separating the known knowns from the known unknowns is more within our reach. Hopefully, this book has made a compelling case about one critical known known, which is Canada's Great Demographic Imbalance is not going away any time soon. Indeed, barring dramatic unknown unknowns, Canada will be aging at a fast and highly uneven pace over at least the next quarter century. This book has also made the case that, left unchecked, the Great Demographic Imbalance will create two classes of citizens: those who live in provinces that can likely afford the status quo and those who do not. What we don't know is how Canadians will respond to the consequences. Indeed, only time will tell whether Canadians will decide to share more of their wealth to prevent the balkanization of the country's welfare state—the fundamental known unknown of this book.

That said, while we may not know how the story of the Great Demographic Imbalance will end, we do know there are measures that can be taken to improve the odds it will not transform the country beyond recognition. This chapter explores these measures in greater detail, pointing out potential pitfalls and dead ends.

Helping Oneself First

My province, New Brunswick, will be among the most severely affected by the Great Demographic Imbalance. Yet if I were asked whether I am in favour of reforming Canada's federal transfer system to take into account the uneven aging of provinces, the answer would be, "No, not now," because poorer provinces must help themselves first before turning to Ottawa for more help. This is not as much a moral argument as a pragmatic concern: Canadians living in richer provinces will understandably balk at the idea of providing more support to poorer provinces that have not done what they could to address their challenges. And there is, indeed, still much that poorer provinces can do to improve their public finances without jeopardizing the integrity of their social programs.

Raising More Taxes

As discussed, Canadians living in poorer provinces already pay significantly more in taxes than those living in richer ones. In 2014–15, provincial fiscal burdens (own source revenues as a percentage of GDP) were 50% higher east than west of the Ottawa River.[3] This proportion has grown slightly larger since.

As of early May 2016, all provinces save Saskatchewan and Manitoba had tabled their budgets for fiscal year 2016–17. Four of them put forward major tax changes: Alberta, New Brunswick, Newfoundland and Labrador, and Prince Edward Island. Alberta

announced a new carbon tax but did not increase its fiscal burden—it claims its carbon tax will be revenue-neutral. With very little
debt and the country's youngest population, Alberta decided it could
afford to ride out the slump in oil prices by going deep in the red: the
projected deficit for 2016–17 is upwards of $10 billion (nearly $2,500
per person) and a return to fiscal balance is not expected before the
middle of the next decade.

Newfoundland and Labrador's reaction to the oil price shock was
entirely different. It had to be: As Canada's oldest, fastest-aging and
most heavily indebted province, Newfoundland and Labrador could
not afford Alberta's do-nothing approach. Closely watched by credit
rating agencies, Dwight Ball's government had to come up with a
credible plan for putting the province on a sustainable fiscal trajectory.

Newfoundland and Labrador is in a deep fiscal mess of its own
making. The government's books have been in deficit since 2012–
13, when oil was still trading at around $100 per barrel. The annual
deficit worsened dramatically as offshore royalties plummeted:
from $195 million in 2012–13, it shot up to $0.9 billion in 2014–15
and to a staggering $2.2 billion in 2015–16. In her 2016–17 Budget
speech, Finance Minister Cathy Bennett indicated that, had the government done nothing, the deficit would have reached a colossal
$2.7 billion (around 40% of program spending) in that fiscal year.
And not included in this figure is the government's borrowing of
an extra $1.3 billion to "invest" in the Muskrat Falls hydroelectric
generating station, a project plagued with delays and cost overruns
whose economics almost guarantees massive electricity rate hikes for
Newfoundlanders and Labradoreans for many years to come.

Given this dramatic fiscal deterioration, bold action was needed
to reassure credit markets. In Budget 2016–17, most of it came in
the form of countless tax and fee hikes. Among them was the government's decision to backtrack on a promise not to raise the HST (it
raised it from 13 to 15%).[4] The host of measures in Budget 2016–17
will translate into a sizeable increase in the province's fiscal burden. It
is projected they will generate $0.9 billion annually and bump up the
province's own source revenues by approximately 20%. Yet, despite
this sizeable increase, the government projects a $1.8 billion deficit
for 2016–17, or roughly $3,400 per person. At this pace, the province

would double its net debt in less than seven years, from around $12 to 24 billion.

Tax increases in Prince Edward Island and New Brunswick were far less dramatic. In both provinces, the main change was to raise the HST to 15%. Given that Nova Scotia and Quebec have already raised their sales taxes, all provinces east of the Ottawa River have now moved to fully occupy the tax room vacated by the Harper government when it lowered the GST to 6% in 2006 and to 5% in 2008.[5] This stands in stark contrast with the situation west of the river, where no province has yet done so.[6]

Following the eventful 2016-17 budget season in Atlantic Canada, fiscal burdens in all four provinces are now quite comparable, with own source revenues representing approximately 16% of GDP.[7] This level is high when compared to the average of provinces west of the Ottawa River, which stands at around 13%. However, it remains significantly below that in Quebec, Canada's most heavily taxed province, where own source revenues represent around 20% of its GDP. This last observation suggests that, however painful and unpopular such a prospect may be, taxes can likely be raised further in Atlantic Canada without unduly affecting economic growth.

Not everyone will agree with this statement, to be sure. There is much oversimplification and sloganeering in public debates about the relationship between taxes and economic growth. In the late 1990s, as the hype over globalization reached its zenith, many prominent analysts were insisting that for their economies to thrive, governments had to put on a "golden straitjacket" of balanced finances and competitive taxes. Many economists were also concerned that governments around the world would be engulfed in a race to the bottom that would considerably erode their ability to raise taxes without producing dire economic consequences, such as job-destroying capital flight.

Now that the dust has settled on this debate, the consensus is that these concerns were overblown. Tax revenues as a percentage of GDP remain at a peacetime high across the developed world. Tax competition has not had the steamroller effect that many anticipated. In fact, taxes on capital—the most mobile production factor—remain at generally similar levels across developed countries compared to where they were twenty-five years ago. There is no indication they are converging.[8] Yet we should not assume taxes do not matter. Empirical evidence suggests they do, up to a point. Fiscally induced migration is not just a theoretical possibility that can be safely ignored by policy-makers, nor is it the only consideration they need to keep in mind.[9] Still, their decisions about tax policy should be informed by empirical evidence, not ideology.

Of course, given their relatively high fiscal burdens, older, faster-aging provinces must tread carefully. In fact, Quebec, probably North America's most heavily taxed jurisdiction, may currently have little flexibility to raise its fiscal burden much further without counterproductive consequences.[10] It is no coincidence that Quebec's current efforts to balance its books are focused on the spending side. But other poorer provinces are not in the same position as *la belle province*, as we just saw.

Sooner or later, younger and slower-aging provinces will also have to raise their tax burdens to deal with the challenges of an aging population. As this happens, older, faster-aging provinces—the four Atlantic provinces in particular—will have more room to gradually raise their tax burdens. The word *gradually* is paramount. Provincial governments should be guided by empirical evidence. Moving gradually will allow them to take stock of the effects of their actions and to adjust accordingly.

However, higher taxes will not solve all the problems of Atlantic Canada, far from it. Provincial fiscal burdens in the region hover around 16% of GDP. We saw in chapter 5 that spending on health care alone would need to grow by around 10% of GDP over the next quarter century to maintain the status quo under the baseline scenario. Raising provincial fiscal burdens by half or more to meet extra spending pressures is simply not going to happen: taxpayers will likely revolt long before. Furthermore, such a dramatic increase would almost certainly cripple the region's economy as people, starting with the rich and well-educated, would leave the region in droves. Still, raising taxes moderately and prudently will demonstrate that Atlantic Canadians have asked more from themselves before asking for more from the rest of the country.

Fostering Economic Growth

Chapter 2 illustrates that population aging is not kind to the economies of older, faster-aging provinces. This is particularly so in Atlantic Canada, where its impact is devastating. And chapter 3 shows that poorer provinces cannot realistically hope to bridge the wide growth gap separating them from their richer counterparts. Yet poorer provinces are not powerless in their struggle to strengthen their economies.

Delving here into the details of the various strategies that all levels of government pursue to enhance productive potential, from investments in R&D and venture capital to tax policy and measures to foster greater participation in the labour force is beyond the scope of this book. The formulation of such strategies is an ongoing process, involving considerable learning and iteration. Having spent the better part of my career in Ottawa's economic development policy circles, I know first-hand that successful policy requires getting things right on a broad variety of fronts. I assume these efforts to get things right will continue in the years ahead, informed by empirical evidence rather than magical thinking.

That said, while governments must continue to improve their policy frameworks, we should not set our hopes too high regarding their outcomes. As discussed, the dynamics of productivity growth are very complex, involving many variables that are mostly beyond the control of governments. It's also worth keeping in mind that Canada's productivity growth gap with the United States has remained relatively intact despite major policy efforts over the years (NAFTA, the GST, record investments in knowledge creation, etc.).

Similarly, it is unrealistic to assume that a poorer region such as the Maritimes needs merely pull itself up by its bootstraps and overcome what Stephen Harper called its "culture of defeatism." If the remedy were that easy, the problem of regional economic development would have been solved long ago. The region has had many talented political and business leaders who tried their best to change its economic reality—Frank McKenna is just one who comes to mind. Despite their efforts and an alphabet soup of regional economic development initiatives by federal and provincial governments alike, the Maritimes remains today a less prosperous and dynamic place than the rest of

the country. The objective of self-sufficiency touted by many provincial and federal politicians remains as elusive as ever.

In short, the Maritimes' challenging position within the federation
goes back a long way, and economic geography continues to shape
the region's fortunes. This is not only the reality of the Maritimes but
also of small provinces without major metropolitan centres more
generally. Saskatchewan and Newfoundland and Labrador did not
wean themselves off Equalization because they suddenly found a way
to remove the straitjacket of economic geography. Abundant natural
resources in high demand rather than innovation were behind their
recent spectacular growth. Unfortunately, the Maritimes has not
been so lucky. That is not to say Maritimers can't do more to take
advantage of the resources they do have.

As discussed in chapter 3, while poorer provinces should not
bank on them to turn themselves into "have" provinces in the fore-
seeable future, natural resources can make a stronger contribution
to their economies. Natural resources are especially important for
Equalization-receiving provinces because of their economic geography and because of how the Equalization program works. Economic
growth and Equalization payments are closely linked and work in
opposite directions. A province's Equalization payments depend
directly on the gap between its fiscal capacity and the national standard (currently the average of all provinces). Economic growth raises
fiscal capacity. As such, the increase in own source revenues resulting
from economic growth will—all else being equal—largely be offset
by lower Equalization payments, thus having only a relatively small
net positive effect on total provincial revenues. This is particularly
the case for small provinces with little influence on the Equalization
standard. There is, however, one major exception to this rule: with
the changes to the Equalization formula in 2007, recipient provinces
now have much greater fiscal incentives to develop their natural
resources. These changes have considerably reduced the Equalization
clawback, which means that Equalization-receiving provinces stand
to make significantly larger fiscal gains from growth in this sector
than in others.

Drawing more from natural resources means taking a serious look at the potential of hydraulic fracturing of shale and other

tight geological formations to extract oil and/or natural gas. New Brunswick, Nova Scotia, and Quebec sit on sizeable natural gas deposits; Quebec also has shale oil deposits. Banning hydraulic fracturing while accepting oil sands and fracking dollars from richer provinces is not only hypocritical on the part of Equalization-receiving provinces, it also strains the case for asking for more in transfers from the have provinces. And the recent decline in prices is no excuse for inaction; rather, it presents an opportunity to lay the groundwork for exploiting shale oil and gas in the future.

Given how old the Maritimes already is and how fast the region is aging, it is hardly surprising to see local authorities pinning high hopes on immigration to address economic woes. In November 2015, my home city of Moncton (population approximately 140,000) announced it wants to welcome 1,000 immigrants annually by 2017.[11] Immigration is surely an important policy instrument for slowing down population aging and fostering growth, but for reasons outlined below and in the annex to this book, when it comes to the Great Demographic Imbalance, immigration is best viewed as a way to address its consequences than the phenomenon itself. In fact, increasing immigration levels, while necessary, will accelerate rather than slow down the Great Demographic Imbalance.

Just as it always has in the past, much of Canada's economic performance in the years ahead will depend on how many immigrants the country welcomes and how well they integrate into the labour force. Over the five years from 2010 to 2014, Canada has welcomed on average about 260,000 immigrants annually, or 0.73% of Canada's population. This rate has been fairly stable since the mid-1990s. If we look back further, Canada's immigration rate is now stronger than it was from the late 1970s to the late 1980s, but it is significantly lower than during the baby boom when is stood close to 1%.[12] It is almost impossible to determine how many immigrants Canadians will welcome in the years ahead. The country's "absorptive capacity" depends on the attitudes of Canadians toward immigration, which in turn depends on a broad range of economic, cultural, social, and even geopolitical factors.[13] It is reasonable to assume that as population aging tightens labour markets across the country, more Canadians will view higher immigration as key to economic prosperity. Conversely, fewer will likely view immigrants as taking jobs from existing workers.

In 2005, cognizant of a looming demographic crunch, the then Liberal Minister of Citizenship and Immigration Joe Volpe announced a long-term goal of increasing Canada's immigration rate to 1% of the population.[14] While this ambitious target has not yet been achieved, it remains realistic. If Canada managed to successfully integrate such a high flow of immigrants into its workforce, its long-term economic potential would improve. We are not talking here about returning to pre-2008 levels, but when it comes to economic growth, a few tenths of a percentage point add up in the long run.

Unfortunately, relatively little of this extra growth will occur in less dynamic economies lacking major metropolitan centres, such as those of Atlantic Canada. As the annex to this book makes clear, there is no easy way to grow a small, predominantly rural economy through immigration. It is possible to turn the immigration tap wide open in the short run, but for higher immigration flows to be sustainable, provinces must be able to offer an environment that will generate opportunities for newcomers. In small, more rural provinces, economic conditions drive immigration much more than the other way around.

I am not suggesting here that Atlantic Canada will not have more immigrants in the future. In ten or fifteen years, Atlantic Canadian communities, including rural ones, will most likely have significantly more foreign-born residents than they do now. With their fast-growing ranks of seniors and declining workforces, Atlantic provinces will need new workers in many industries, starting with nursing homes and other senior-care institutions. The rub, though, is that many Atlantic Canadian seniors will not have the resources to pay for the care services these new workers will provide.[15] The money will have to come from somewhere else, and not all of it can come from cash-strapped provincial governments. In that sense, just how many immigrants Atlantic Canadian communities will welcome will depend on how much money will come from Ottawa to care for their seniors.[16]

Transforming Public Spending

Public spending is the final area where older, faster-aging provinces need to do more before turning to Ottawa for more help. As the Great Demographic Imbalance worsens, poorer provinces will inevitably need to spend considerably more than their richer counterparts to maintain comparable services. But not all public spending is supposed to grow as population ages.

A good example is education, particularly the public school system. As Canada ages, its school population is declining. Naturally, this decline is most severe in faster-aging provinces. From 2001–02 to 2010–11, Quebec and Atlantic Canada lost 12% of their pupils, yet, as chapter 5 illustrates, rather than let educators go to reflect the decline, these provinces hired more of them. As a result, the student-educator ratio, a key indicator of resource intensity, dropped 14% from 14.8 to 12.7. West of the river, this ratio went from 16.4 to 14.4, a decline of 12%. Despite scant evidence that lower student-educator ratios lead to better educational outcomes, poorer provinces went from allocating significantly more resources to their public school system than richer provinces at the turn of the century to allocating even more a decade later.

I have said earlier that the great unknown of this book's discussion is whether richer provinces will be willing to share more of their wealth to prevent the balkanization of Canada's welfare state. They are much less likely to be willing do so as long as there are areas where programs are perceived to be "better" for reasons not directly related to aging.

While the issue of public schools concerns both Quebec and Atlantic Canada, the issue of health-care concerns Atlantic Canada more particularly. In 1992 governments in all four provinces spent roughly the same amount on health care, about $1,500 per person. This was $200 below the Canadian average. In 2012 average spending in Atlantic Canada had grown to slightly over $4,300, more than $450 above the Canadian average. If we consider only the three Maritime provinces, average spending was $4,100, or nearly $250 above the average of Canadian provinces. Only a fraction of the spending growth gap between Atlantic Canada and the Canadian average can be attributed to faster aging.

Many explanations have been offered to justify why it was normal for these four provinces to have grown their aging-adjusted health-care spending faster: a particularly popular one is that they are smaller, more rural provinces. While it does cost more to provide services to smaller populations dispersed over more rural landscapes, the population of the four Atlantic provinces was not much bigger twenty years ago. The region was also more, not less rural. These two factors can therefore hardly explain why spending *growth* has been stronger in Atlantic Canada than in the rest of the country. Clearly, something else was at play (including a "wealth effect" in the case of Newfoundland and Labrador[17]). Governments in Atlantic Canada must examine resource intensity in health-care services to find ways to provide more value-for-money.[18] Whether the solution lies in rationalizing provincial hospital networks (New Brunswick, for instance, has more than twenty hospitals for a population of around 750,000) or elsewhere is best left to experts in the field, but it is clear that vigorous efforts are necessary to improve performance.

Honouring the Constitution

Since 1982 Ottawa is constitutionally committed to the principle of doing what is necessary to avoid creating two classes of citizens based on the province of residence. Indeed, under section 36(2) of the Constitution Act, 1982, the Parliament of Canada and the federal government are "committed to the principle of making Equalization payments to ensure that provincial governments have sufficient revenues to provide reasonably comparable levels of public services at reasonably comparable levels of taxation."

Until recently, the Equalization program did a good job in delivering on this constitutionally enshrined principle. It is, however, no longer up to the task. Underlying the approach to the Equalization program's formula is the assumption that provinces have reasonably comparable needs. This is no longer the case. Population aging is becoming a key driver of health-care spending in older, faster-aging provinces, and its influence will only grow with time. Aging alone is projected to make real health-care spending in Atlantic Canada grow by more than 1.5% annually while the region's economy will remain stagnant. For Canada as a whole, aging-induced health spending should grow significantly slower than the economy.

That said, the principle of equalization may be enshrined in the Constitution, but poorer provinces will likely be disappointed if they try to leverage it to force Ottawa to bail them out from dire fiscal straits. There is a debate among constitutional scholars as to whether this principle is simply "aspirational" or is in fact "justiciable." In other words, it is unclear whether this is an empty promise or legally binding on the federal government.[19] Furthermore, even if section 36 were eventually determined to be justiciable and a court found in favour of one or more provinces, it would be unlikely to prescribe a particular solution, but would rather simply issue a declaration of unconstitutionality. Such a declaration would effectively return the issue to the political arena, requiring the federal government either to attempt to amend the Constitution or make the legislative and/or policy changes required to comply with constitutional norms.[20]

In short, the jury is still out on whether the equalization principle has any legal strength. Even if it could be leveraged successfully, redress would most likely have to come from political negotiations. The federal government would not likely provide faster-aging, have-less provinces with a better deal than it would otherwise, based on what it believes would make for good politics.

Good politics is the reason why I have argued that poorer provinces need to help themselves first before turning to Ottawa—the sequencing of events matters. But when they do turn to Ottawa with more political legitimacy, what should poorer provinces be asking for? Should they request CHT funding growth be put back at 6% as NDP leader Thomas Mulcair promised in the 2015 election? Should the CHT be modified to account for age, as Green Party leader Elizabeth May promised? The answer in both cases is no. For a number of reasons, Ottawa should keep CHT and CST growth at a minimum and focus on Equalization reform to ensure genuine provincial autonomy.

As we saw in chapter 6, Ottawa no longer plays a major role in shaping the direction of provincial social programs. For most of the past forty years, it has been retrenching from provincial social affairs, both funding-wise and policy-wise, yet provincial programs remain as comparable as they have ever been. To suggest that Ottawa must continue to grow its CHT and CST funding fast because it needs to maintain some sort of policy leverage is disingenuous. The reality is the federal government has probably lost the moral authority to do anything but try to enforce the conditions of the Canada Health Act. In the years ahead, richer provinces will likely have the means to maintain those conditions as they see fit; without further assistance, poorer provinces will not. The solution, however, will not be for Ottawa to hit them with the enforcement sledgehammer of the Canada Health Act, but rather to provide them with the resources necessary to deliver comparable services.

Given the above, the only remaining rationale for Ottawa to provide transfers such as the CHT and the CST to *all* provinces is to address the vertical fiscal imbalance. But, *provided Ottawa is committed to addressing the horizontal fiscal imbalance,* it is better to address the vertical imbalance by vacating tax room so that provinces can raise more taxes than to increase the CHT and CST. There are two related reasons for this recommendation. First, provinces are more likely to be good fiscal stewards if they are forced to ask for more money from taxpayers; they will have a greater incentive to control costs. The second reason for putting the CHT and the CST on a slower-growing or even lower path is to avoid fuelling growth in health-care costs. It is no coincidence that provincial health-care spending grew at breakneck speed in the 2000s when federal transfers were doing just the same. As mentioned, most of that new spending did not end up in better services but in higher pay for service providers. If Ottawa is powerless to prevent wage escalation for physicians and other health professionals, it should at least refrain from enabling it.

Again, putting CHT and CST transfers on a slower-growing track or even lowering them can only work if Ottawa is genuinely committed to honouring the Constitution in both letter and spirit, specifically the principle of ensuring provinces have sufficient revenues to provide reasonably comparable levels of public services at reasonably comparable levels of taxation. The Equalization program is no longer fit for the job, and this inadequacy will only worsen over time. Equalization needs to be amended to reflect the highly uneven pace of aging across the country.

Examining the intricate details of how best the Equalization formula could capture the impact of aging on provincial programs is a data-rich task best left to expert working groups led by the federal finance department. At a conceptual level, a major challenge will be identifying the provincial program areas that need to be equalized. Population aging has implications for provincial spending in a broad range of areas. As discussed, two of the most significant are health care and the public school system. The former exerts a pressure on spending, while the latter should theoretically lead to lower spending growth, particularly in older, faster-aging provinces.

Under a revised Equalization formula that would allow Ottawa to honour the Constitution, poorer provinces would receive Equalization payments to bring their total revenues in line with the national standard. The cap on growth in total Equalization outlays would be lifted (in an era of growing regional disparities, this by itself would likely translate into a significantly higher Equalization bill for Ottawa). In addition, poorer provinces would receive an extra payment reflecting the net extra costs of providing public services induced by population aging. To determine how large these payments should be, a national standard for services in program areas related to population aging would need to be established. Setting such a standard would preserve provincial autonomy. Quebec, for instance, may decide to provide subsidized daycare services—that is its prerogative in a well-functioning federation—but it would not necessarily receive more money because its additional Equalization payment would not be based on its own levels of services but rather on the national standard.

Inevitably, the idea of amending the Equalization program to take into account the uneven aging of provinces will fuel broader debate on the risks and challenges of moving toward a needs-based approach to Equalization. There are, of course, a variety of reasons besides population aging as to why spending may need to differ to provide reasonably comparable services. For instance, some have speculated that because wages are lower in Equalization-receiving provinces, the latter are in a position to provide more and better services with the same resources than those who are not Equalization recipients. I do not share this view—at least not for smaller, more rural provinces such as the Maritimes. While it is true that public sector wages are generally lower in Equalization-receiving provinces than in the rest of Canada, chapter 4 reveals that the two provinces that spend by far the least on public services have traditionally been considered richer provinces: Ontario and British Columbia. I have argued this is not because these two provinces offer less "generous" services than their counterparts. The more likely explanation is that as large provinces with major metropolitan centres, they benefit from significant economies of scale in the provision of their services.[21] With these economies of scale, a province such as Ontario can manage to provide similar services as the rest of the country at a lower cost while, at the same time, paying above-average wages to its public servants, teachers, and health professionals.[22]

Even if we set aside the issue of uneven aging for the moment, it is highly doubtful that amending the Equalization program to take into account both fiscal capacity and need would translate into lower payments to smaller, more rural provinces such as the Maritimes. Indeed, the opposite is more likely. That the Maritimes must spend more to provide similar services to the national average is not so hard to conceive. Take, for example, New Brunswick. The province has about the same population as Quebec City, yet it has four times as many hospitals. One can question whether New Brunswick can afford such an extensive hospital network (and without further federal assistance, it clearly cannot), but to say New Brunswick provides better health services than Quebec City just because it spends more on health care is simplistic. The bottom line is that operating a health-care system with many small, inefficient primary care facilities to serve a small, rural population costs more than concentrating services in a much smaller number of larger institutions.

While it would likely favour smaller provinces such as the Maritimes, I am not advocating for a move toward a full needs-based approach toward Equalization. This book has made clear that, until recently, the Equalization program has performed relatively well in achieving its objective of enabling poorer provinces to provide services that are reasonably comparable to the Canadian average. Amending the formula to reflect varying spending needs should focus on the one major trend changing the game: uneven regional aging. In itself, this will prove a highly complex task. There is no need to complicate it further by endlessly debating what else should be taken into account when looking at how costs compare across provinces. Too often in policy-making, the best is the enemy of the good. Perfection is not of this world.

A final issue in amending the Equalization program to reflect uneven population aging is what to do if a province has greater aging-induced needs and a greater fiscal capacity than the national standard, as is arguably still the case for Newfoundland and Labrador. Given that we have likely entered an era of great moderation in oil prices, it is not excluded that Newfoundland and Labrador could become an Equalization recipient again, even if the program is not amended to take into the account the effects of uneven population aging on spending needs.[23] However, should Newfoundland and Labrador or any other older province have a greater fiscal capacity than the national standard, it would only be logical to take this into account. A richer yet older province should only receive Equalization if its additional aging-related needs exceed its additional fiscal capacity relative to the national standard.

A Tale of Two Countries?

As we saw, the Great Demographic Imbalance is producing two Canadas, one that can likely afford to sustain the status quo for itself, despite feeling the pinch of demographics, and another in which several provinces could well be stuck between a financial abyss and the politically suicidal prospect of scaling back social programs, to the point of turning its residents into second-class citizens. It is in this context that poorer provinces will be asking for more money from richer ones to maintain their social programs.

Ultimately, the fate of poorer provinces is in the hands of their richer counterparts. The centre of gravity of Canadian politics sits firmly in the lands west of the Ottawa River and will only move further west as time passes. The richer provinces, where the great majority of people live, will decide whether or not Canada's welfare state will tell a tale of two countries.

This does not mean that all the poorer provinces can do is pray the richer ones come to their rescue. There are measures they can and must take to make it easier for Ottawa to provide them with more assistance on behalf of all Canadians. All poorer provinces must help themselves first. Ottawa may, at some point in the future, prove willing to amend its system of transfer payments to take age into account, but that does not mean it would be generous in bailing out a province that has been spending profligately while others have done everything they could to avoid falling over the cliff.

As the Roman poet Horace put it two millennia ago, "Adversity reveals genius, prosperity conceals it." Canada's Great Demographic Imbalance will once again offer a window into the genius of our country. Let us hope it will live up to the dreams of those who built medicare and the other progressive symbols that make up the Canadian social citizenship.

THE CASE OF PRINCE EDWARD ISLAND

hapter 1 outlines Statistics Canada's demographic projections for the 2013–38 period. The agency projects that Prince Edward Island's population growth will far exceed that of other Atlantic provinces and even Quebec. In fact, it suggests the island's population will grow slightly faster than Ontario's. This is an unlikely scenario, and this annex explains why.

Of course, Statistics Canada did not pull its population growth numbers for Prince Edward Island out of thin air. As is the case for all projections based on past trends, the agency's scenarios do have a historical footing. In recent years, Prince Edward Island has witnessed much stronger population growth than the other two Maritime provinces. Over the 2002–12 period, the island's population grew by 0.6% annually, six times faster than in Nova Scotia and New Brunswick.[1]

For the most part, Prince Edward Island's impressive performance was due to a single phenomenon, unprecedented in its modern history: booming immigration. Few people think of Prince Edward Island as an immigration hotspot, and for good reason. Before the middle of the last decade, immigration played a marginal role in the province's demographics. Until then, Prince Edward Island's inflows of immigrants, at about 150 to 200 each year, were very small, even for a province with a population of only 130,000.[2] The island's immigration record was roughly in line with Nova Scotia's and only slightly better than New Brunswick's. And all three provinces were vastly underperforming Canada as a whole.

Things started to change in the mid-2000s, when Prince Edward Island's immigration numbers escalated spectacularly. From a low of

89 in 2002–03, immigration grew to 738 in 2006–07. It kept going from there, reaching an all-time high of 2,609 in 2010–11. In that last year, Prince Edward Island took in more immigrants than Nova Scotia, whose population is nearly seven times greater.[3]

What happened? Did Prince Edward Island suddenly become a much more attractive place for prospective immigrants? The answer is no: Charlottetown did not become a better place overnight than, say, Halifax, to find a job or launch a business. Rather, the province took advantage of a new federal-provincial initiative to turn the immigration tap wide open with little regard for its actual immigration needs. Even worse, the events that unfolded in Prince Edward Island are a sorry tale of a government-sponsored cash-for-residency scheme that allowed relatively well-off would-be immigrants to jump the queue in exchange for cold, hard currency.

Here's the gist of how this scheme was set up: Under the Constitution, immigration is a shared federal-provincial responsibility. Until the turn of the millennium, with the exception of Quebec, immigration was managed almost exclusively by Ottawa. In 1998 an initiative called the Provincial Nominee Program (PNP) was put in place to improve the ability of provinces to select, attract, and retain immigrants to meet specific labour market needs and to otherwise contribute to economic development. This program was of mutual interest to Ottawa and most provinces: the federal government was seeking ways to ensure a more even distribution of immigration across the country while many provinces wanted a greater say in selecting immigrants to better meet specific local economic development needs.

Under the Canadian Charter of Rights and Freedoms, neither Ottawa nor the provinces can force immigrants to settle in a particular province. As permanent residents, immigrants have a constitutional right to live wherever they like in the country. One of the key objectives of the PNP, therefore, was to select prospective immigrants who would have a strong attachment to the province that would nominate them.[4]

In 2001 the Government of Prince Edward Island entered into a collaborative agreement with the Government of Canada that gave birth to the province's own PNP, setting out four distinct streams or categories under which its provincial government could nominate immigrants. In practice, however, one stream—the so-called "Immigrant Partner" category—accounted for nearly all (87%) of the province's nominees over the last decade.[5] Under this stream, prospective immigrants could obtain Canadian permanent residency in exchange for investing $200,000 in an existing Prince Edward Island company and taking an "active" role in it. The popularity of the Immigrant Partner category in Prince Edward Island stood in sharp contrast with the experience of other provinces, where skilled or semi-skilled workers, most of whom were required to have a job offer in the province where they wished to land as immigrants, represented around 70% of nominees. In Prince Edward Island, this category represented only 8%.[6]

On paper, the clear intent behind the Immigrant Partner stream was for the new immigrants to develop strong ties to Prince Edward Island. After all, it is hard to imagine how immigrant partners can play an active role in the management of a local restaurant, hotel, or convenience store if they live in Toronto or Vancouver. In practice, however, it turned out that prospective immigrants could easily buy their Canadian permanent residency without ever having to set foot in Prince Edward Island or meeting anyone involved in the company in which they had "invested" because the Government of Prince Edward Island had converted—"perverted" is perhaps a better word—its PNP program into a cash-for-residency scheme. It did so through two deliberate moves. First, it decided that all that was required to fulfill the definition of active involvement in a company was to sit on its board. Second, it allowed local companies to treat investments from immigrant partners essentially as gifts: in most instances, all companies had to do in exchange for the funds was issue preferred shares that usually precluded the immigrants' partners from redeeming them or being paid dividends. In other words, immigrant partners were treated as passive investors, or more accurately perhaps, passive donors.[7]

With this promise of free money for local businesses, it is no surprise that demand for immigrant partner investment skyrocketed. Soon enough, the boards of directors of hundreds and hundreds of local companies were populated with Asian names. In fact, many corporations were specifically set up to receive such investments, including non-profit entities. The demand for immigrant partners was such that when an insufficient number of prospective nominees with $200,000 to spare could be found, an ingenuous mechanism was put in place to lower the actual amount invested by would-be immigrants while still pretending they had come up with the required $200,000.[8]

In 2008, concerned that Prince Edward Island's behaviour was a threat to the integrity of the country's immigration system, the federal government decided to exercise its regulatory powers in order to shut down the province's Immigrant Partner stream of its PNP (it rewrote regulations to rule out passive investments). An investigative report in the *Huffington Post* eloquently summed up what happened next:

> [Ottawa's decision to shut down the program] led to a showdown in the spring of 2008 as P.E.I. raced to nominate as many immigrants as it could before the new regulations took effect, while federal officials became increasingly alarmed at what the sudden surge would mean for processing times, due diligence in selecting applicants and the possibility of fraud.
>
> In the program's last days, P.E.I. was nominating so many immigrants from China that they accounted for 88 per cent of all provincial nominees—from all provinces—applying through Canada's mission in Hong Kong.[9]

Many local businesses benefited from the hundreds of millions in free money that washed up on the island's shores while the program lasted. Those who benefited the most, however, were the intermediaries: the immigration lawyers and other consultants whose various fees counted toward the immigrant partners' investment.[10]

In 2011 the province introduced a new model for its PNP. While it is too early to draw any conclusions about its success, it is noteworthy that immigration flows are down considerably from their peaks reached just a few years earlier.[11]

So, how did Prince Edward Island's opportunistic and ethically questionable immigration boom affect the province's demographic trajectory? Here, a clear distinction between short- and long-term impact is important. Prince Edward Island's PNP has had an undeniable impact on its population growth in recent years. From 2002 to 2012, the province's population grew by 8,400 or about 6%, while New Brunswick's and Nova Scotia's stagnated.[12] But we need to look at the numbers in greater detail to understand to what extent the province's immigration boom has changed its demographic dynamics. Over that same period, an estimated total of more than 18,000 immigrants claimed Prince Edward Island as their province of landing (i.e., the province they declared as the one where they intended to reside). Of that number, close to 40%, or a little less than 7,000, likely never set foot on the island. In the province's peak immigration years (toward the end of the last decade), this proportion was closer to 50%.[13]

Furthermore, of the approximately 11,400 immigrants who did land in Prince Edward Island, a large proportion of them did not stay long.[14] According to data from Citizenship and Immigration, of those who landed over the seven years from 2001 to 2009, a little more than half (55%) were still in the province three years later. For a small province like Prince Edward Island, this seems a reasonable retention rate. However, closer scrutiny of the numbers reveals a marked deterioration in retention rates over time. For immigrants who arrived over the three years from 2001 to 2003, more than eight out of ten (84%) remained on the island three years later. For those who arrived between 2007 and 2009, this proportion was down to less than half (47%).

Another way to look at deteriorating rates that provides a better indication of the evolution of long-term residency patterns is to consider how long it took for retention rates to fall below 50% for each annual cohort of immigrants. For immigrants who arrived in the early half of the last decade, prior to the PNP-induced immigration boom, this threshold of below 50% was never reached: more than half of them still reside in Prince Edward Island today. For the years 2006 to 2007, when immigration was ramping up, more than half had left the island after four years. For the high immigrations years of 2008 to 2010, it took only two years for more than half to leave. No such rapid deterioration in retention rates has occurred in neighbouring New Brunswick and Nova Scotia, neither of which used their PNPs to fuel similar immigration booms as in Prince Edward Island.[15]

In summary, there are declining returns to immigration when a province turns to it without any regard for its ability to absorb the immigrants. Those who arrived earlier on Prince Edward Island had the opportunity to acquire or open up new local businesses, such as restaurants and other small retail businesses. But the island is a small market. In order to keep sustainably growing a population through immigration, newcomers must be in a position to earn a living locally. As the flow of new opportunities open to immigrants on the island slowed down, retention rates eventually nosedived.

This brings us to the crux of why Statistics Canada's population projection for Prince Edward Island is not likely to pan out. The agency makes two inappropriate assumptions about the fundamental drivers of the province's population growth. The first is to assume that immigrants will continue to rush in at more or less the same pace as in recent years, which is more than three times faster than in New Brunswick and Nova Scotia. If the province's long-term prospects are indeed limited by its absorptive capacity, then it is unreasonable to assume it will continue to outperform its neighbours to such an extent over the long run. Secondly, while the agency's model does capture Prince Edward Island's strong immigration growth of recent years, it fails to adequately take into account the flip side of this coin, which is that more and more immigrants leave soon after they arrive.

Indeed, under all scenarios, the agency assumes Prince Edward Island will do better than Nova Scotia and New Brunswick on the interprovincial migration front, meaning it will either gain relatively more or lose fewer people to other provinces than its two neighbouring provinces. In reality, quite the contrary is happening. As a result of its higher immigration flows, Prince Edward Island's interprovincial migration record has deteriorated sharply, relative to Nova Scotia and New Brunswick. Until the middle of the last decade, Prince Edward Island was generally doing better than Nova Scotia and New Brunswick in terms of interprovincial migration. From 1998–99 to 2003–04, Nova Scotia and New Brunswick lost a combined 10,084 people, while Prince Edward Island gained 833. In other words, interprovincial migration added on average 0.12% to the island's population annually while it subtracted 0.12% from that of its two sister provinces. In contrast, over the 2006–07 to 2013–14 period, all three provinces lost people to the rest of the country. But the rate for Prince Edward Island (-0.39% on average annually) was nearly twice as high as the combined rate of Nova Scotia and New Brunswick (-0.20%).[16]

To sum up, Prince Edward Island may well grow marginally faster than the rest of the Maritimes in the decades ahead. But to achieve considerably faster population growth in the long run, it must be able to offer an environment that generates many more opportunities for newcomers than its neighbouring provinces. A quick-money, cash-for-residency scheme will not cut it.

NOTES

Epigraph

1   Quoted in Ferguson, *Kissinger*, 268. Kissinger and Stolzenbach both worked at the US Army's Operations Research Center, an institution that was formally part of John Hopkins University based at Fort McNair in Washington, DC.

Introduction

1   See the seven-part series *Canada's Aging Population and Public Policy* prepared by the Library of Parliament Research Staff, 2012; Office of the Parliamentary Budget Officer, *Fiscal Sustainability Report*, February 18, 2010; and Duckett and Peetoom, *Canadian Medicare*. I am referring here only to the impact of aging. There are other challenges to the sustainability of Canada's social programs—medicare in particular. Some are discussed later, in chapters 4 and 5.

2   According to Donald J. Savoie, the ink was barely dry on the Quebec Conference in 1864, which produced the seventy-two resolutions laying the framework for the Canadian Constitution, before Nova Scotia and New Brunswick were having serious second thoughts. Those resolutions were never presented to the New Brunswick and Nova Scotia legislatures. The pro-Confederation party in New Brunswick suffered a harsh defeat in 1865. Savoie quotes W. S. MacNutt, who remarks, New Brunswick entered Confederation with "very little grace and no gratitude," under the strong influence of British authority, "not forced but strongly asserted," and the "adroit persuasions of Macdonald and his colleagues in Canada." Savoie adds that although Premier Tupper managed to bring Nova Scotia into Confederation without an election, his pro-Confederation party was soundly defeated in both the provincial and federal elections in fall 1867. Savoie, *Visiting Grandchildren*, 24.

3   "And the Greatest Canadian of All Time Is...," CBC Digital Archives.

4   In polls conducted by Environics, a polling and market research firm, from 1997 to 2012, among more than a dozen symbols of national identity (e.g., the Canadian Charter of Rights and Freedoms, the Canadian flag, hockey, the Queen), the health-care system consistently topped the list as the symbol most likely to be considered "very important" by the largest number of Canadians. I am not aware of any other country where this is the case. Environics Institute, *Focus Canada 2012*.

5   Finance Canada, *Fiscal Reference Tables*, September 2015.

6   Milne, *Tug of War*, 172.

7   There are many other reasons why spending across provinces may differ. This topic is treated in further detail in chapters 4, 5, and 7.

8   I refer here to own-source revenues as a percentage of GDP. Data on GDP from Statistics Canada, Canadian Socio-Economic Information Management System (CANSIM), table 384-0038 and own source revenues from Finance Canada, *Fiscal Reference Tables*, September 2015.

9   From fiscal year 2000–01 to 2014–15, federal revenues as a percentage of GDP declined from 17.7% to 14.3%. Finance Canada, *Fiscal Reference Tables*, September 2015; and Statistics Canada, CANSIM, table 384-0038.

Chapter 1

1   British Columbia is older than its western counterparts, in part because it is a long-standing destination of choice for retirees. We will also see later that the province has one of the country's lowest fertility rates.

2   It can be said that British Columbia is the same age as Quebec, at least when one considers only median age and the share of seniors, two key indicators of a population's age structure. However, we will see later in this chapter and the next that British Columbia's aging dynamics differ on other counts and that population aging is expected to have significantly lesser economic consequences in that province than in Quebec.

3   The age distribution of women of childbearing age also matters as women are more likely to have babies at some points than others over the course of their reproductive lives.

4   This indicator takes into account the age structure of the population (mortality rates are lower when the overall population is younger, and vice versa). Canada's age-standardized mortality rate has declined from 615.5 per 100,000 in 2000 to 492 in 2011. Statistics Canada, CANSIM, table 102-0552.

5   The median age in Canada in 2015 stood at 40.5. Statistics Canada, CANSIM, table 051-0001, and "Median Age Canada, 1901–2011."

6   Statistics Canada, data provided to author.

7   Migration, the third factor that determines population aging, had less of a clear-cut role during the baby boom than it does today. At the time, immigrants were typically older than the median Canadian; their immediate impact was thus to make Canada's population older. However, as the lion's share of immigrants were of childbearing age, immigration eventually contributed to making Canada's population younger through the highly favourable impact it had on the country's birth rates.

8   This is the gap between Quebec and the rest of the country. The gap between Quebec and the Canadian average (including Quebec) is 1.5 years—see table 1.1; numbers do not add up due to rounding.

9   Strictly speaking, no two provinces have the same age. For this to be the case, their age structures would have to be identical. Unless otherwise noted, all age

comparisons across provinces in this chapter refer to median age.

10   See for instance Boesveld, "Canada's Latest Baby Boom Caught Experts by Surprise."

11   I am referring to the total fertility rate (TFR), which can be viewed as the number of children that a typical woman would have over her lifetime, based on the age-specific birth rates in any given year. Technically, the TFR is defined as "the average number of children who would be born to a synthetic cohort of women whose age-specific birth rates were the same as those actually observed in the year in question." Organisation for Economic Co-operation and Development, (OECD), *Society at a Glance 2001*, 24.

12   Statistics Canada, *Canada Year Book 1970–1971*.

13   Statistics Canada, CANSIM, table 102-4505.

14   *Canada Year Book 1970–1971*.

15   Sleebos, *Low Fertility Rates in OECD Countries*.

16   Henripin, *Tendances et facteurs de la fécondité au Canada*.

17   Lachapelle and Henripin, *The Demolinguistic Situation in Canada*.

18   *Canada Year Book 1970–1971*.

19   Foot with Stoffman, *Boom, Bust & Echo*, 19.

20   *Canada Year Book 1969*.

21   *Canada Year Book 1956* and *Canada Year Book 1969*.

22   More precisely, because Eastern Canada generally had higher birth rates during the baby boom, its share of young people (aged zero to fourteen) was larger and faster-growing than in the rest of the country. This compensated for the region's smaller and faster-declining share of working-age adults (fifteen to sixty-four) brought about by its poorer migration record. As a result, while Eastern Canada's share of seniors (sixty-five and over) grew—due in no small part to sustained improvements in life expectancy—it did not do so significantly faster than in the rest of the country.

23   We will see later that when one considers only median age and share of seniors, Quebec is now aging at roughly the same pace as British Columbia and Ontario. However, this does not affect the overall conclusion that eastern provinces are aging faster than their western counterparts.

24   Data on fertility rates in this section are from Statistics Canada, *Canada Year Book 1970–1971*; *Report on the Demographic Situation in Canada 2002*; and CANSIM, table 102-4505.

25   In addition to Sleebos, *Low Fertility Rates in OECD Countries*, cited above, see for instance Health Canada, "Changing Fertility Patterns"; Duclos, Lefebvre, and Merrigan, "A 'Natural Experiment' on the Economics of Storks"; and Milligan, "Subsidizing the Stork."

26   Data on child-bearing age women from Statistics Canada, CANSIM, table 051-0001.

27   Statistics Canada, CANSIM, table 102-4505.

28   Statistics Canada, "Estimated population of Canada, 1605 to present."

29　Statistics Canada, CANSIM, table 051-0001.

30　Statistics Canada, CANSIM, table 051-0004.

31　Statistics Canada, "Population, Urban and Rural, by Province and Territory."

32　Okonny-Myers, "The Interprovincial Mobility of Immigrants in Canada."

33　Except in 2009 when the Great Recession led to a significant decline in the price of oil and a slowdown in oil sands activity. Statistics Canada, CANSIM, table 051-0004.

34　Statistics Canada, CANSIM, tables 051-0004 and 384-0038.

35　These assumptions relate to fertility rates, life expectancy, immigration and emigration rates, returning immigrant rates, net temporary emigration, non-permanent residents, and interprovincial migration. While three assumptions are made for most of these factors (low, medium, high), for interprovincial migration, five assumptions are presented based on five historical periods: 1991–92 to 2010–11 (M1 scenario); 1991–92 to 1999–2000 (M2); 1999–2000 to 2002–03 (M3); 2004–05 to 2007–08 (M4); and 2009–10 to 2010–11 (M5). Our baseline projection uses Statistics Canada's "M1" scenario. Because it is more volatile than other components of population growth, interprovincial migration tends to play a key role in explaining changes in provincial population growth over time. This is particularly so for smaller provinces. While the five assumptions about interprovincial migration listed above do materially affect the population growth projections of several smaller provinces—Saskatchewan and Newfoundland and Labrador in particular—they do not fundamentally alter the conclusions of this chapter: regardless of the assumption one adopts, Newfoundland and Labrador is projected to remain the oldest province in the country followed by the Maritimes, while the Prairies are projected to remain the youngest. The same pattern applies to the shares of senior residents. Statistics Canada, "Population Projections for Canada (2013 to 2063), Provinces and Territories (2013 to 2038)."

Chapter 2

1　Under neoclassical theory, such convergence would occur over the long run in a world with perfect competition, without externalities.

2　See for instance, Inwood and Irwin, "Land, Income and Regional Inequality: New Estimates of Provincial Incomes and Growth in Canada, 1871–1891." Despite its title, the paper contains data on regional disparities over a much longer period.

3　Keynes, *A Tract on Monetary Reform*, 80.

4　Fourastié, *Les Trente Glorieuses*. Although Fourastié coined this expression to describe the postwar growth experience in France, it is also often used to refer to the broader postwar experience in western countries.

5　Savoie, *Visiting Grandchildren*, 85.

6　Ibid., 81–83.

7　The topic of regional economic convergence was in vogue in the late 1990s. Serge Coulombe from the University of Ottawa was its leading researcher in Canada. His many papers (see bibliography) extensively document the convergence process. The evidence suggests Canadian provinces have been diverging on some key indicators in recent years, mainly as a result of high oil prices—see for instance Capeluck, 2014.

8   Statistics Canada, CANSIM, table 051-0001.

9   See Coulombe, *Economic Growth and Provincial Disparity*; and Coulombe and Tremblay, "Human Capital and Regional Convergence in Canada."

10   Statistics Canada, CANSIM, tables 051-0001 and 282-0002, *Canada Year Book 1967*, and "Estimated Population of Canada, 1605 to Present."

11   Strictly speaking, I should add that an economy also grows when the average number of hours worked per worker increases. However, as this number has declined slightly in recent decades, labour force growth was the sole driver of growth in the number of hours worked.

12   Statistics Canada, *Labour Force Survey Estimates (LFS), Retirement Age by Class of Worker and Sex*, 2013.

13   I refer here only to the economic impact of labour force growth resulting from the baby boom generation reaching working age. I do not take into account at this point the relationship between age and productivity growth. This is covered later in the chapter.

14   Statistics Canada, CANSIM, table 282-0002.

15   Costa, "From Mill Town to Board Room", 101.

16   "Women Outnumber Men at Most Medical Schools," *Maclean's*; Brown, "McLachlin Challenges Profession to Question Status Quo on Women in Law and Business"; *The State of Women in Academic Medicine*, Association of American Medical Colleges; and *A Current Glance at Women in the Law*, American Bar Association.

17   Allum and Okahana, *Graduate Enrollment and Degrees: 2004 to 2014*; and Statistics Canada, CANSIM, table 477-0019.

18   Growth in the fifteen to twenty-four age category was more modest, given the importance of, and the growth in, the number of students in this category. Women's participation rate in this category did, however, converge with that of their male counterparts. Statistics Canada, CANSIM, table 282-0002.

19   Another phenomenon that made a lesser but not insignificant contribution to labour force growth was larger cohorts of younger workers in the 1990s and early 2000s—most of them children of baby boomers—replacing smaller cohorts of workers born during the Great Depression and the Second World War. A similar phenomenon will not reoccur over at least the next two decades, as the cohorts exiting the labour force (from the baby boom generation) will be much larger than those that will be entering.

20   Data on population growth and labour force in this section are from Statistics Canada, CANSIM, tables 051-0001 and 282-0002. The last year in these series at the time of writing was 2014.

21   OECD, "Labour Productivity Levels in the Total Economy."

22   Statistics Canada, CANSIM, table 383-0029.

23   Resource-rich Alberta was among the slowest-growing provinces in terms of

labour productivity, mainly because oil sands exploitation is generally much more labour intensive than offshore and other forms of conventional oil production. From 2000 to 2010, the number of hours worked in Alberta's business sector grew three times faster than in Newfoundland and Labrador. In short, while economic growth was robust in both provinces, labour productivity growth was much weaker in Alberta than in Newfoundland and Labrador.

24   Statistics Canada, CANSIM, table 383-0029.

25   Ibid.

26   See Maestas, Mullen, and Powell, "The Effect of Population Aging on Economic Growth."

27   Technological change plays a critical role in long-term productivity growth. The standards of living we enjoy are built on numerous innovations, from electricity to the internal combustion engine, mass manufacturing, and the Internet. Predicting how technology will evolve and affect long-term productivity and growth, particularly in smaller economies, is nearly impossible.

28   For instance, when one considers all ten-year periods from 1983 to 2013, the average labour productivity growth of the Canadian economy ranges from 0.8% to 1.8%. When one looks at all fifteen-year periods, the range is reduced by half (1.1% to 1.6%). In fact, in all but two of the fifteen such periods, productivity growth ranged from 1.1% to 1.4%. Similar results apply for most provinces. Statistics Canada, CANSIM, tables 282-0018 and 384-0038.

29   Statistics Canada, CANSIM, table 383-0029. The projections use real value added per hour worked rather than real GDP per hour worked as the measure of labour productivity. This measure, which adjusts GDP data to avoid any double-counting in the production of goods, is the most widely used in productivity studies.

30   The shift in Newfoundland and Labrador's industrial structure is clearly visible in GDP data. From 1998 to 2013 GDP in extractive industries (mining, quarrying, and oil and gas extraction) grew by nearly 200% from $3.0 to $8.9 billion. Meanwhile, GDP in the rest of the provincial economy only grew by 25%. In 2013 GDP in extractive industries was thirty-seven times larger than that of fishing, hunting, and trapping. For labour productivity to continue to grow at the pace witnessed over the 1998–2013 period (and the period from 1998 to 2008 more particularly), GDP in extractive industries would have to continue to post similar explosive growth as during this period. This is an unlikely scenario in a world of double-digit oil, even if oil production increases considerably. Statistics Canada, CANSIM, table 379-0030.

31   Statistics Canada, CANSIM, table 282-0018. All data for the remainder of this section are from this table.

32   Statistics Canada, CANSIM, table 384-0038.

33   GDP per capita in the Maritimes grew on average by 1.9% annually, while the Canadian average was 1.5%. Statistics Canada, CANSIM, tables 051-0001 and 384-0038.

34   There are many ways to look at regional disparities, but here the focus is on

whether the provinces that are significantly poorer than the Canadian average will pull closer to it from now until 2038. The answer is no. In 2013 GDP per capita in the Maritimes, Canada's poorest region, stood at a bit over 77% of the national average. Quebec came next, at about 84%. From 2013 to 2038, all four provinces are expected to grow slower than the national average. This is a significant change from the previous quarter century. In 1988 the poorest four provinces were the Atlantic provinces, with a GDP per capita of about 73% of the national average. From 1988 to 2013, all four provinces grew faster than the national average.

35   The Equalization program is discussed in chapters 6 and 7. At this point, it suffices to indicate that the Harper government capped growth in total Equalization outlays at Canada's nominal GDP growth in the 2000s. As we will see, this significantly affects the ability of the Equalization program to adequately address growing regional economic disparities.

Chapter 3

1   Discussion in chapter 1 notes that eastern provinces exited the baby boom younger than all their western counterparts, except for Alberta. It is only toward the end of the baby boom that they started aging faster, as their poorer migration records were no longer offset by higher birth rates.

2   Statistics Canada, CANSIM, tables 051-0001, 051-0004, and 384-0038.

3   See for instance Centre for Population, Aging and Health, "Quebec's Family Policies Benefit Childbearing and Work."

4   Statistics Canada, CANSIM, tables 051-0001 and 102-4505.

5   Immigration is also an increasingly popular elixir. This topic is addressed in chapter 7 and the annex of this book.

6   There are many good books and reports on innovation and its impact on Canada. A classic is Kristian Palda's *Innovation Policy and Canada's Competitiveness*. Another primer on innovation is provided by Yves Bourgeois and Samuel LeBlanc in *Innovation in Atlantic Canada*. A more recent source is the report from the Expert Panel on Business Innovation, *Innovation and Business Strategy*.

7   "Planet of the Phones," *The Economist*, February 28, 2015.

8   See Saunders, *The Economic History of the Maritime Provinces*, 20–23.

9   See for instance the Expert Panel on the State of Industrial R&D in Canada, *The State of Industrial R&D in Canada*.

10   Poitras, "Tories Challenge Liberals on Natural Resource Development"; and "Alward Says He Wants to Do It Like Saskatchewan," Acadia Broadcasting.

11   See Rubin, *The Carbon Bubble*.

12   Statistics Canada, CANSIM, table 379-0030. I define the natural resource economy as comprising agriculture, forestry, fishing and hunting, mining and quarrying, and oil and gas extraction. In 2012 New Brunswick's GDP stood at $29 billion, while Saskatchewan's natural resources sector represented $24.4 billion of its $74.9 billion GDP (at basic prices).

13   See Campbell, "Natural Gas from Shale in New Brunswick," in Saillant and

Campbell (eds.), *Shale Gas in New Brunswick.*

14   Statistics Canada, CANSIM, table 379-0030, current dollars (basic prices).

15   Data on commodity prices for Canada are drawn from Bank of Canada, "Commodity Price Index."

16   Another source of supply growth are projects in development. This is notably the case for oil sands production in Alberta. In spring 2015, the National Energy Board noted that despite the recent dramatic drop in oil prices, it expected bitumen production from recently completed and nearly completed projects to raise production by nearly 50% from 2014 to 2018. (National Energy Board, "Market Snapshot.")

17   See for instance Erten and Ocampo, "Super-Cycles of Commodity Prices Since the Mid-Nineteenth Century."

18   Federal Reserve Board, "Testimony of Chairman Alan Greenspan before the Committee on Financial Services, U.S. House of Representatives."

19   "Sheikhs v. Shale: The New Economics of Oil," *The Economist.*

20   *Tight oil* is a general term for oil contained in petroleum-bearing formations of low permeability, including shale and other formations such as tight sandstone.

21   See Webster, "Going Global: Tight Oil Production."

22   "OPEC Expects Oil Prices to Be about $76 a Barrel in 2025—WSJ," Reuters.

23   Organization of the Petroleum Exporting Countries (OPEC), *2015 World Oil Outlook,* 45.

Chapter 4

1   U.S. Department of the Treasury, "Historical Debt Outstanding: Annual 2002–2012."

2   The expression, "We're all Keynesians now," is often attributed to Richard Nixon, who used similar language to reflect his changing views on the role of government in times of financial crisis when the United States abandoned the gold standard in 1971. It was first coined, however, by Milton Friedman, one of the leading economists of the twentieth century, known for his strong beliefs in free markets ("The Economy: We're All Keynesians Now," *Time*).

3   I am not suggesting the Canadian economy has not been affected by slow global growth since the end of the Great Recession. It is quite likely that Canada would have fared better under more favourable global economic conditions. Short-term economic growth can diverge considerably from that of economic potential, particularly when there is considerable slack in the economy. However, in the long run, Canada's economic growth is constrained by the growth of its economic potential.

4   Finance Canada, *Fiscal Reference Tables,* September 2015; and Statistics Canada, CANSIM, table 384-0038. This analysis does not take into account the potential stimulative impact of a lower fiscal burden on GDP.

5   Finance Canada, *Fiscal Reference Tables,* September 2015; and Statistics Canada, CANSIM, table 384-0038.

6   Data for 1960 are from Tanzi and Schuknecht, *Public Spending in the 20th Century.*

They cover Australia, Austria, Canada, France, Germany, Ireland, Italy, Japan, New Zealand, Norway, Sweden, Switzerland, United Kingdom, and the United States. Data for 2011 are for all OECD countries, OECD, *National Accounts at a Glance 2013*.

7   Section 36(2) of the Constitution Act, 1982, states the Parliament of Canada and the federal government are "committed to the principle of making equalization payments to ensure that provincial governments have sufficient revenues to provide reasonably comparable levels of public services at reasonably comparable levels of taxation."

8   This table and the conclusions derived from it differ in some aspects from what I wrote in *Over the Cliff? Acting Now to Avoid New Brunswick's Bankruptcy*. In *Over the Cliff?*, I used a weighted average for computing the Canadian average for provincial program spending. This was appropriate as my aim was to compare New Brunswick to Canada as a whole, rather than to other provinces. It is more appropriate in comparing spending per person across provinces to give equal weight to all provinces regardless of their size. Another difference relates to the data for Quebec. I noted in *Over the Cliff?* that public account data on program spending are not strictly comparable across provinces but that the latter increasingly use similar reporting methods. Until last year, however, Quebec's data on program spending were significantly underreported in Finance Canada's *Fiscal Reference Tables*. Since the October 2014 edition of the *Tables*, Quebec no longer sits at the bottom of provinces for its spending per capita but is instead more or less in line with the national average. Finally, data for Nova Scotia has been adjusted to include supplementary in-year appropriations, which are not adequately reflected in the *Fiscal Reference Tables*.

9   There are many misconceptions regarding the "generosity" of Quebec's welfare state and who pays for it. In some cases, claims that Quebec is more generous than other provinces are not well founded. For instance, many commentators point to the province's much lower tuition fees (more than 50% lower than the average for the rest of Canada) as an example of a more generous policy that other provinces consider unaffordable. Yet, in reality, Quebec does not provide significantly more funding to its universities than other provinces. Rather than drawing larger government subsidies to offset lower tuition revenues, Quebec universities have to make do with fewer resources. They do so notably by paying lower wages. In turn, the issue of wages leads to a second set of misconceptions about how Quebec's welfare state is funded. In 2011 employees from the broader public sector (which includes public institutions in health, education, and social services) earned 17% less in Quebec than elsewhere in the country. If Quebec salaries were the same as the rest of Canada, the province would have had to spend an extra $6 billion annually—10% of its program expenditures—to deliver existing services. By comparison, Quebec has received on average from 2009–10 to 2011–12 roughly $7.5 billion in annual Equalization payments from Ottawa. Lower wages are thus almost as important as Equalization in explaining how Quebec can afford its public services. Of course, Quebec can avoid paying higher wages in part because

its distinct cultural and linguistic setting makes it less vulnerable than other provinces to outmigration (more on this in chapter 5). *Sources:* Statistics Canada, catalogue 81-582-X, and CANSIM, tables 477-0021 to 0024 and 0058, as well as 183-0002; Finance Canada, *Fiscal Reference Tables*, September 2015; and Finances Québec, *Comptes publics du Quebec 2013–14*, vol. 2.

10   Tuition fees in the Maritimes are among the highest in the country. We will see in chapters 5 and 7, on an aging-adjusted basis, health-care spending is in line with the Canadian average despite the fact that the region is much more rural. The same applies to social assistance (see data from the now-defunct National Council of Welfare, "Statistical Tables," 2012). Finally, as we will see later, resource intensity in the education sector is higher in the Maritimes, but this has more to do with the region's challenge in scaling down its school system to reflect new demographic realities than a deliberate attempt to provide more generous services.

11   Finance Canada, *Fiscal Reference Tables*, September 2015; and Statistics Canada, CANSIM, table 384-0038. Data for fiscal year 2013-14.

12   National Energy Board, "Canadian Energy Overview 2014."

13   Provincial liquor monopolies in Canada are highly profitable businesses. This, however, is not because they are particularly good at what they do, but rather because as monopolies, they can charge prices for their products that far exceed the cost of acquiring and selling them. The monopoly's profit—a hidden tax on alcohol—is simply transferred to the government. In some cases, a provincial government could collect the same if not more revenues by allowing private businesses to sell alcohol products and taxing the latter so that average prices stayed more or less the same. In the end, whether the dismantling of a liquor monopoly would be beneficial to a government's coffers is an empirical question whose answer may differ from province to province. For more details, see Tankou Kamela, *Que faire avec Alcools N.-B.?*

14   This is the case in the sense that the vast majority of revenues will typically come from the pockets of local residents. Strictly speaking, user fees are not taxes, but they add to the overall burden that residents must bear.

Chapter 5

1   For a primer on the Canada Health Act, see *The Canada Health Act*, Library of Parliament.

2   Grant and Hurley, "Unhealthy Pressure."

3   See for instance the comparative study of the Commonwealth Fund, which ranks the health-care systems of eleven advanced economies, including France, Australia, the United Kingdom, and the United States, on such aspects as the quality of care, access (cost and timeliness), efficiency, and equity. On this ranking, Canada comes in tenth position, ahead of only the United States (Commonwealth Fund, *Mirror, Mirror on the Wall*). Other surveys do not provide much better results (see Simpson, *Chronic Condition*).

4   OECD, "Health Expenditure and Financing."

5   Simpson, *Chronic Condition*, 7.

6   Chronic wait times are a form of rationing. As hospital and physician services are universally accessible at no charge, there is no price mechanism to balance supply and demand. Demand in excess of supply simply translates into longer waiting lists. Chronic wait times breed unfairness as Canadians who are more fortunate can jump the queue if they so wish by flying to, say, Boston or a more exotic destination, such as Cuba, to get their treatment.

7   Picard, "Who's Fighting for Private Health Insurance in Canada?"; and Chaoulli v. Quebec (Attorney General), [2005].

8   The federal government alone has instituted six commissions on health care. See Health Canada, "Federal Commissions on Health Care."

9   Canadian Institute for Health Information (CIHI), *National Health Expenditure Trends, 1975 to 2014*.

10   To estimate aging-related spending growth over 2002–12, aging-adjusted spending for 2002 is computed using 2012 age-specific spending and the age structure of the population for 2002. This methodology assumes an unchanged distribution of age-specific spending over time. While this assumption does not hold for all provinces and time periods, no clear relationship could be identified between population aging and the per capita age-specific distribution of spending.

11   CIHI, *National Health Expenditure Trends, 1975 to 2015*.

12   Statistics Canada, CANSIM, table 051-0001; and CIHI, *Canada's Health Care Providers*, 2012 and 2013.

13   Statistics Canada, CANSIM, table 281-0027 and 326-0021. Data include overtime.

14   Total clinical payments are the sum of physicians' clinical payments from fee-for-service and alternative payments. Fee-for-service is by far the most widespread form of compensation. Alternative payments include salaries and other compensation approaches beyond fee-for-service such as capitation (payment per patient rather than service). Total clinical payments depend on two factors: the average payment per service and the overall number of services performed. Average gross compensation is simply the product of average payment per service and the number of services performed. Over the 2002–12 period, the average fee was up sharply, while the number of services per physician (called "utilization per physician") was down modestly. CIHI, *National Health Expenditure Trends, 1975 to 2014*, and *National Physician Database, 2011–12* and *2012–13*.

15   CIHI, *Supply, Distribution and Migration of Canadian Physicians*, 2003 and 2013.

16   CIHI, *National Physician Database, 2012–13*; and *National Grouping System Categories Report, 2002–03*. I say this is a rough proxy because it does not take into account changes in the mix of medical services provided by physicians—physicians' fees depend on the nature of the medical visits, consultations, and procedures. It's also worth noting that I refer to wage growth rather than compensation growth because for most physicians, compensation is not only determined by the fees they receive for their services, but also by the number of services they perform.

17 Grant and Hurley, "Unhealthy Pressure." The authors reconciled data from a variety of sources to build a consistent time series of the average income of physicians—see annex of their paper.

18 Finance Canada, *Fiscal Reference Tables*, September 2015; and CIHI, *National Health Expenditure Trends, 1975 to 2015*.

19 It is the fastest-growing extended period (ten or more years) on record in CIHI's database, which goes back to 1975 (CIHI, *National Health Expenditure Trends, 1975 to 2015*).

20 The CHST was put in place in the 1996–97 fiscal year, replacing two previous federal transfers, the Established Programs Financing (for health care and education) and the Canada Assistance Plan (for social assistance). The CHST, which was split into the Canada Health Transfer and the Canada Social Transfer in 2004–05, contained both a cash and tax point transfer component. The cash portions of the CHST and then the combined CHT and CST increased from $21.1 billion in 2002–3 to $40.8 billion in 2012–13. More details in chapter 6.

21 "Some Doctors Overbilling Medicare without Penalty," CBC *News New Brunswick*.

22 Grant and Hurley, "Unhealthy Pressure." The authors' quote is from Katz, Charles, Lomas, and Welch, "Physician Relations in Canada."

23 Ibid. The authors' quote is from Barer, Evans, and Labelle, *The Frozen North*.

24 CIHI, *National Health Expenditure Trends, 1975 to 2014*.

25 Morgan, "The Incoming Rise of Prescription Drug Spending."

26 More formally, growth is calculated as the annual change (compound annual growth rate) in age-adjusted provincial health spending. Age-adjusted provincial health spending in a given year is calculated as follows: $HSt = \Sigma HSi,2012 \times PSi,t$, where $HSi,2012$ represents health spending per person for age category i in the year 2012 and PSi,t is the share of the total population of age category i at time t. This equation assumes a stable distribution of age-specific spending over time. CIHI data on spending by age category is available for the 1998 to 2012 period. Over that period, the variance in the age distribution of spending has declined mildly, which suggests that using 2012 as the reference point may slightly underestimate the actual historical impact of aging on health spending. It is impossible to determine how this variance will evolve in the future. As discussed previously in this chapter, the age distribution of spending will be shaped notably by technological developments—for instance, new drugs for cancer may add pressure to spending for the older age category, while a less hospital-centric approach to treating older patients could lead to savings. I use 2012 as the reference point to project the future impact of aging, as it is most reflective of recent trends and thus the current breakdown of spending by age category.

27 Grant and Hurley, "Unhealthy Pressure."

28 Ibid.

29 Evidence of this can be found in the fact that differences in earnings across provinces are relatively modest and smaller than they were thirty years ago. The coefficient of variation of physicians' earnings across provinces in 2011 was 0.14.

This was computed using data from Grant and Hurley in "Unhealthy Pressure" based on gross average earnings of physicians. Differences in real incomes may in fact be even smaller as Grant and Hurley do not control for such factors as the cost of maintaining a practice, which is higher in Ontario and western provinces than in Quebec and Atlantic Canada. They do not control either for differences in the cost of living across regions.

30 Data on physician earnings from Cutler and Ly, "The (Paper)Work of Medicine." For more on physician migration, see CIHI, *Supply, Distribution and Migration of Canadian Physicians*; and Canadian Health Services Research Foundation (CHSRF), "Myth: Canadian Doctors are Leaving for the United States in Droves."

31 Archambault, "Le revenu des médecins de famille bondit de 12% en un an."

32 As of writing (winter 2016). CIHI, *National Health Expenditure Trends, 1975 to 2015.*

33 Newfoundland and Labrador outspent the rest of the country by a wide margin from 1987 to 2012. The province's aging-adjusted health-care spending grew by 2.6% annually, considerably above the ten-province average of 1.8%. Newfoundland and Labrador's experience, along with the fact that the Prairies also outspent the rest of the country (albeit by a smaller margin), point to the presence of a "wealth effect" in health-care spending—the regions with the fastest growth in incomes tend to witness the fastest growth in non-aging related health-care spending. I have decided not to incorporate this effect—which amplifies spending pressures in faster growing provinces and moderates them in slower growing ones—in my projections for a number of reasons, the most important being that given population aging and slower economic growth, all provinces will face some pressures to contain health-care costs. Another reason is the case of Quebec. From 1987 to 2012, Quebec had managed to contain non-aging spending growth to 1.0% annually. For reasons outlined earlier in this chapter, it is doubtful it will be able to contain spending growth to this extent in the future.

34 CIHI, *National Health Expenditure Trends, 1975 to 2014.*

35 Of course, health care affordability in poorer provinces also depends on federal transfers, particularly Equalization. But we should not exaggerate its impact. Consider, for instance, the Maritimes: Assuming 40% of Equalization receipts are spent by the provinces on health care, then the share of health care spending financed by Equalization in the region amounts to about 2% of its GDP. With total Equalization outlays capped at nominal GDP growth, it is not likely that this proportion will grow much in the years ahead. Meanwhile, provincial spending on health care as a percentage of GDP could double from around 10% to 20%.

36 The fiscal burden would, however, be high by historical standards, close to their highest levels over the past half century. Finance Canada, *Fiscal Reference Tables*, September 2015 and September 2000.

37 See table 4.1.

38 Statistics Canada, CANSIM, table 478-0014; and Finance Canada, *Fiscal Reference Tables*, September 2015.

39   Statistics Canada considers the children of baby boomers as those born between 1972 and 1992, "Generations in Canada."

40   Statistics Canada, "Full-Time Equivalent Enrolments in Public Elementary and Secondary Schools, Canada, Provinces and Territories, 2001/2002 to 2010/2011."

41   For a summary of the research on this issue, see Guillemette, "School Class Size: Smaller Isn't Better."

42   Statistics Canada, "Student-Educator Ratio in Public Elementary and Secondary Schools, Canada, Provinces and Territories, 2001/2002 to 2010/2011."

43   New Brunswick Department of Education and Early Childhood Development, *Annual Report, 2001–02* and *2010–11.*

44   Conference Board of Canada, *How Canada Performs.*

45   Includes subsidies to universities and colleges and student aid spending. Estimate based on Statistics Canada, CANSIM, table 477-0058; Finance Canada, *Fiscal Reference Tables,* September 2015; and provincial public accounts.

46   Statistics Canada, CANSIM, table 477-0019.

47   Statistics Canada, CANSIM, table 477-0013. Data are available only from 1992–93 to 2008–09, but show a robust growth path and a gain of close to 66% over that period alone.

48   Some studies suggest this could be the most important factor affecting enrolment in post-secondary institutions. See Finnie, Mueller, Sweetman, and Usher, eds., *Who Goes? Who Stays? What Matters?.*

49   Statistics Canada, CANSIM, table 477-0019.

50   Statistics Canada, CANSIM, table 477-0058.

51   Statistics Canada, "Number and Salary of Full-Time University Teaching Staff, by Academic Rank and Sex, Canada and Provinces, 2000/2001 and 2010/2011."

52   Statistics Canada, CANSIM, table 281-0027.

Chapter 6

1   I adopt here a broad definition of taxation that encompasses all government revenues.

2   As we saw earlier, while projections for median age and share of seniors suggest that Quebec and British Columbia will age at roughly the same pace, the consequences of population aging on economic growth will be more severe in Quebec; it is thus fair to say that aging will affect Quebec more than British Columbia.

3   Many individuals—seniors in particular—pay taxes although they are not employed. There are many more seniors in poorer provinces. However, they typically have significantly lower incomes than their counterparts living in richer provinces, which means they pay less in taxes. These two factors—greater share of seniors but lower average incomes in poorer than in richer provinces—thus cancel each other out to a significant extent.

4   There are few recent studies that examine the overall distributional aspects of taxation in Canada. The only one I am aware of dates back to 2007 and was

conducted by Marc Lee from the Canadian Centre for Policy Alternatives. Lee examines taxes in Canada over the 1990–2005 period to determine whether federal and provincial taxes have become more or less progressive. The study looks at all sources of income (including employment income, inheritances, employer-provided benefits, and capital gains) as well as all taxes (including on personal income, property, and corporate income). The results show that in 2005, federal taxes were progressive over the first 60% of the income distribution, with taxpayers in the bottom decile paying less than 10% of their income in federal taxes and those in the sixth decile paying a bit less than 20%. From the sixth up to the ninth decile, the federal tax system was proportional, meaning that federal taxes as a percentage of income remained stable at close to 20%. From the ninetieth to the ninety-fifth percentile, the federal tax system was progressive again and subsequently turned regressive for the remaining top 5%. Lee, *Eroding Tax Fairness.*

5   Finance Canada, "Your Tax Dollar."

6   Service Canada, "Canada Pension Plan and Old Age Security—Monthly Statistical Bulletins, July 2015."

7   In 2012–13, Atlantic Canadians paid a total of $1.4 billion in Employment Insurance premiums, while they received $2.6 billion in benefits. Data on benefits pertain to the fiscal year 2012–13, while those on premiums are for the year 2012. See Canada Employment Insurance Commission, *2013/14 EI Monitoring and Assessment Report.*

8   Ibid.

9   This excludes an amount of $3.5 billion under the Territorial Formula Financing to help territories deliver their programs and services. Finance Canada, "Federal Support to Provinces and Territories."

10   Statistics Canada, CANSIM, table 358-0001.

11   Receiver General for Canada, *Consolidated Financial Statements of the Government of Canada 2014–2015,* 19; and Receiver General for Canada, *Public Accounts of Canada 2014,* 2.

12   For instance, Saskatchewan and Newfoundland and Labrador, which both ranked in the top three on GDP per capita, took in a net benefit from federal tax-and-spend activities. The fact that Newfoundland and Labrador has the oldest population and a high unemployment rate largely explains why it continues to take in a sizeable net benefit. As for Saskatchewan, its high share of Aboriginal residents is a key reason for its (smaller) net benefit.

13   See Jeffery and Heald, "Money Matters: Territorial Finance in Decentralized States."

14   Goffman, *Some Fiscal Aspects of Public Welfare in Canada,* quoted in Guest, *The Emergence of Social Security in Canada,* 102. Public welfare included public health and relief for the poor.

15   The issue of indirect versus direct taxation refers to who pays and who ultimately bears the burden of a tax; a direct tax is one that is borne by those who pay it. For

example, a tax on personal income is a direct tax since the person who pays it is the same as the one who earned the income. A custom duty, an excise tax, or even a sales tax is an indirect tax insofar as the entity that pays it to the government (e.g., the importer or the merchant) is not the same as the one that ultimately bears its costs (the consumer). In Canada, courts have interpreted the concept of direct taxation broadly to the point of making the distinction between direct and indirect taxes almost irrelevant. This judicial interpretation of direct taxation means that in practice provinces now enjoy taxation powers that are almost as broad as those of the federal government. This, however, was not the case at the time of Confederation.

16   The Royal Commission on Dominion-Provincial Relations.

17   Government of Canada, *Report of the Royal Commission on Dominion-Provincial Relations*, vol. 1, *Canada: 1867–1939*, 45.

18   Ibid., 60–61.

19   Ibid., 61.

20   Ibid., 64–86.

21   United States Social Security Administration, "Social Security History: Otto von Bismarck."

22   At the federal level, the only noteworthy foray in social affairs was the Government Annuities Act of 1908, a retirement savings program. Such a program did very little to help the poor to save for retirement. It did not help existing seniors either. At the provincial level, the first initiatives were in the area of workmen's compensation; Quebec led the way in 1908 with legislation providing for non-compulsory insurance, and Ontario introduced a compulsory scheme six years later, in 1914. Guest, *The Emergence of Social Security in Canada*, 34–44.

23   Ibid., 7–8.

24   Ibid., 48.

25   Ibid.

26   MacGregor Dawson, *William Lyon Mackenzie King*, vol. 1, 300.

27   King, *Industry and Humanity*, 354.

28   MacMillan, *History's People*, 49–50.

29   Guest, *The Emergence of Social Security in Canada*, 75.

30   Grauer, *Public Assistance and Social Insurance*, 17.

31   Guest, *The Emergence of Social Security in Canada*, 88.

32   Ibid., 89.

33   Ibid., 106.

34   Ibid., 91.

35   The first president was Ontario chief justice Newton Wesley Rowell. Health concerns forced him to withdraw from the commission. He was replaced by Quebec notary and professor Joseph Sirois, who himself had replaced Judge Thibaudeau Rinfret, who also had to step down due to poor health.

36   Smiley, "The Rowell-Sirois Report, Provincial Autonomy, and Post-War Canadian Federalism." 54.

37   Government of Canada, *Report of the Royal Commission on Dominion-Provincial Relations*, vol. 2, *Recommendations*, 34.

38   Ibid., 80.

39   Ibid.

40   It has been, and continues to be, argued by many that the federal government's use of its spending power to create cost-shared programs meeting "national standards" is not an encroachment of provincial jurisdiction. Here is how Smiley viewed this issue:

> The exercise of spending power provides a means by which the federal government can by unilateral action involve itself in many matters which under traditional understandings of the constitution have been the exclusive concern of the provinces. Although it is not within my competence to judge the constitutionality of the various uses of this power, which have been justified as an exercise of an inherent prerogative power of the federal Crown to disburse its revenues as it chooses subject only to prior parliamentary authorization and as exercises of Parliament's jurisdiction over "The Public Debt and Property," it appears to a layman to be the most superficial sort of quibbling to assert that when Parliament appropriates funds in aid of say, vocational training or housing, and enacts in some detail the circumstances under which such moneys are to be available that Parliament is not in fact "legislating" in such fields.

Smiley, "The Rowell-Sirois Report, Provincial Autonomy, and Post-War Canadian Federalism," 61.

41   Guest, *The Emergence of Social Security in Canada*, 134.

42   "A Post-War Programme for the U.S.," *International Labour Review*, 47, quoted in Guest, *The Emergence of Social Security in Canada*, 126.

43   Guest, *The Emergence of Social Security in Canada*, 142.

44   Ibid., 134–35. Ottawa was also offering fixed subsidies to provinces on a per capita basis.

45   Ibid., 140.

46   Ibid., 137–38.

47   Ibid., 180.

48   Smiley, "The Rowell-Sirois Report, Provincial Autonomy, and Post-War Canadian Federalism," 60.

49   Milne, *Tug of War*, 173.

50   Ibid., 167.

51   Smiley, "The Rowell-Sirois Report, Provincial Autonomy, and Post-War Canadian Federalism," 68.

52   Milne, *Tug of War*, 172.

53   Dupré, "Reflections on the Fiscal and Economic Aspects of Government by Conference," 55, quoted in Ibid., 176.

54   Commission on the Future of Health Care in Canada, *Building on Values*, 2002, 66–67.

55   "Bankrupt Canada?," *Wall Street Journal.*

56   Finance Canada, *Fiscal Reference Tables,* September 2015.

57   Iglehart, "Revisiting the Canadian Health Care System."

58   Jeffrey Brooke from Concordia University wrote 417 pages buttressing this thesis. Brooke, *Dismantling Canada.*

59   I am referring to the Conservatives, not the Progressive Conservatives.

60   At the time of writing (winter 2016).

61   The Equalization formula was amended in the mid-1970s as fiscal gaps among provinces rose amidst sharply higher oil prices. The reform prevented Ontario from becoming a recipient province. Equalization is clearly an area where Ontario has not historically received its "fair share."

62   Of course, if gaps in fiscal capacity among provinces narrow sufficiently, overall Equalization payments can go down. When gaps widen, Ottawa's tab is limited to nominal GDP growth.

63   For more details, see Madore, "The Canada Health Act."

Chapter 7

1   Rumsfeld, "Known and Unknown."

2   The estimates vary on the number of casualties from the bubonic plague of fourteenth-century Europe, with some claiming it could have reached around 50 million or 60% of Europe's entire population. See Benedictow, "The Black Death."

3   This observation is based on comparing the weighted average for the five eastern with the five western provinces. On a non-weighted basis, the gap between East and West is narrowed by half. Finance Canada, *Fiscal Reference Tables,* September 2015; and Statistics Canada, CANSIM, table 384-0038.

4   The previous government had adopted an increase in the HST to 15% which was to take effect on January 1, 2016, but Dwight Ball's new government cancelled it shortly after being elected on November 20, 2015.

5   Since July 1, 2016, the HST in the four Atlantic provinces is set at 15%, except in Prince Edward Island, where this new rate only takes effect on October 1, 2016. In 2006, before the first cut in the GST was implemented, the HST stood at 15% in New Brunswick, Nova Scotia, and Newfoundland and Labrador. In Prince Edward Island, the HST was only adopted in 2013. Prior to that year, the PST in Prince Edward Island had stood at 10% since 1981. When the HST came into effect in 2013, it was set at 14%. While the provincial share of the HST (9%) was lower than the rate for the PST it replaced, the shift to the HST nevertheless allowed the province to reap greater revenues mainly because the PST applied to fewer goods and services than the HST. Finally, in Quebec, where the provincial sales tax (PST) is harmonized with the GST since 2013 but remains a separate tax, the effective rate of the two taxes combined is 14.975%. Prior to 2006, the combined rate of the PST and the GST was 14.875% (the PST was set at 7.5% but since it also applied to the GST, this translated into an effective PST rate of 7.875%). Source: Revenu Québec, *Tables of GST and QST Rates,* and Kenway, "PST, GST, HST Rates by Province."

6   Only Manitoba has raised its provincial sales tax (PST) since 2006, a one percentage point increase in 2013 that Brian Pallister's government elected in April 2016 has promised to reverse in its first mandate. British Columbia introduced the HST in 2010 but reverted to its PST following a referendum in 2011.

7   Estimates for 2016–17. If offshore oil royalties are excluded, Newfoundland and Labrador's fiscal burden remains slightly lower, at around 15%. Finance Canada, *Fiscal Reference Tables*, September 2015; Statistics Canada, CANSIM, table 384-0038; and RBC Economics, *Provincial Outlook*, March 2016; and budgets of the four Atlantic provinces for 2016-17.

8   The race to the bottom never happened because capital does not move from one location to another simply because taxes are lower. Businesses consider other important factors in deciding where to locate, such as high-quality local infrastructure, a good regulatory environment, easy access to markets, deep pools of talent and specialized services, strong educational institutions, and good quality of life. Similarly, workers consider many things before deciding to pack up and head to a lower tax province. For many of them, home is where their hearts are. The tens of thousands of Atlantic Canadians who regularly commuted until recently by plane to and from Alberta—a distance similar to that separating France from Siberia—are a striking reminder that roots, family, culture, and language matter. Sources: Friedman, *The Lexus and the Olive Tree*; OECD, *Harmful Tax Competition*; OECD, "Revenue Statistics"; Troeger, "Tax Competition and the Myth of the 'Race to the Bottom'"; as well as Day and Winer, *Interregional Migration and Public Policy in Canada*.

9   The impact of taxes on economic growth is a complex issue extending well beyond the scope of this book. It suffices to say here that policy-makers have to consider many other variables than the possibility of fiscally-induced migration, including the impact of taxes on decisions of firms and individuals to save and invest. The tax mix (consumption taxes, personal income and corporate income taxes, etc.) is just as important if not more important than the level of taxes.

10   In 2014 the government appointed an expert commission on Quebec's taxation. The commission called for a complex overhaul of the province's tax system but insisted it be done in a revenue-neutral way as it felt Quebec had no room to manoeuvre in increasing its fiscal burden.

11   Choi, "Moncton Sets New Targets for Attracting Immigrants."

12   Statistics Canada, CANSIM, tables 051-0001 and 051-0004; and *Canada Year Book*, various years.

13   See for instance "Absorptive Capacity," Metropolis Conversation Series.

14   Guillemette and Robson, "No Elixir of Youth."

15   A large proportion of seniors, particularly in poorer provinces, have relatively low incomes. In 2011 the median income of Atlantic Canadians aged sixty-five years and over was $20,800, 10% below the country as a whole. Of this $20,800, around 70% was made up of government transfers (CPP, OAS, GIS). Statistics Canada, CANSIM, table 202-0407.

16 Some of that money will come in the form of OAS and GIS benefits, but these can only realistically help shoulder a small fraction of escalating health and other elderly care costs.

17 See note 33 in chapter 5 for a discussion of the relationship between rising wealth and health care spending.

18 The concept of resource intensity refers to the amount of resources to perform a given service. Two provinces with similar resource intensities will not necessarily spend the same amounts on health care. For instance, two provinces may dedicate the same resources to treat a patient with diabetes (that is, they may have the same resource intensity), yet the province where diabetes is more prevalent will spend more.

19 In 2009 in Cape Breton (Regional Municipality) v. Nova Scotia (Attorney General), [2008] NSSC 111, the Nova Scotia Court of Appeal found that, in an "appropriate context," section 36 of the *Constitution Act* "might represent a justiciable commitment." At least two other appeal court decisions state reasonable arguments can be made that section 36 "could possibly have been intended to create enforceable rights" (Manitoba Keewatino Okimakanak v. Manitoba Hydro-Electric Board, [1992]). Peter Hogg, a constitutional law scholar, argues, "The constitutional obligation to make adequate equalization payments to the poorer provinces is probably too vague, and too political, to be justiciable." *Constitutional Law of Canada*, 156.

20 See Cape Breton (Regional Municipality) v. Nova Scotia (Attorney General), [2008] NSSC 111.

21 Some have argued that the greater importance of private schools in provinces such as Quebec, British Columbia, and Ontario are a major factor depressing the level of spending in these provinces. This is not the case. Spending on private schools in these provinces ranges between about $115 to $150 per person (Statistics Canada, table 478-0014). As chapter 4 shows, the public spending gaps between Ontario and British Columbia, on the one hand, and the average of Canadian provinces on the other are around $2,000 and $1,500 per person respectively.

22 We have focused on Ontario and British Columbia as examples of two provinces benefiting from greater economies of scale given their large populations and major metropolitan areas. Quebec and Alberta also likely benefit from important economies of scale. We have seen in chapter 4 that Quebec, the country's second largest province, spends slightly less than the average of Canadian provinces despite having more "generous" social programs than the rest of the country. Alberta also likely benefits from important economies of scale, although it spends more than the Canadian average on public services. This is because of the savings from economies of scale are likely offset by the "wealth effect" that strong growth has had on provincial public spending in that province.

23 The recent oil price collapse is not yet fully captured in Equalization numbers as fiscal capacity is calculated based on a three-year moving average with a two-year lag.

Annex

1   Statistics Canada, CANSIM, table 051-0001.

2   Statistics Canada, CANSIM, tables 051-0001 and 051-0004.

3   Statistics Canada, CANSIM, table 051-0004.

4   The term *nominate* recognizes the fact that neither Ottawa nor the provinces can force immigrants to settle in one particular province.

5   Grant Thornton, *Prince Edward Island Provincial Nominee Program Evaluation Results.*

6   Citizenship and Immigration Canada, *Evaluation of the Provincial Nominee Program.*

7   For a good summary of how the Immigrant Partner stream of the province's PNP was implemented—as well as the implications for those involved in it—see "Cashing In: Inside PEI's Controversial Immigrant Partner Program," *Huffington Post.* This investigative report was part of a series on this topic from students in the journalism program at Halifax-based University of King's College, which was nominated for a National Newspaper Award.

8   Ibid.

9   "Cashing In: Behind Ottawa's Tense Showdown with PEI Over its Immigrant Partner Program," *Huffington Post.*

10   See "Cashing In: Inside PEI's Controversial Immigration Partner Program" and other reports from students of the University of King's College at immigrate. kingsjournalism.com.

11   Statistics Canada, CANSIM, table 051-0004.

12   Statistics Canada, CANSIM, table 051-0001.

13   It's worth noting that Prince Edward Island's attraction ratio (the percentage of immigrants who actually settled in their province of landing) went down significantly with the introduction of its PNP. Things were not supposed to go that way since the very purpose of provincial nominee programs was to select nominees who had a stronger attachment to their province of landing. In neighbouring New Brunswick and Nova Scotia, the introduction of nominee programs worked as intended, with attraction ratios hovering around the mid-80%. This shows to what extent Prince Edward Island's PNP was used by immigrants to fast-track their way into Canada. Data on immigration in each province from Statistics Canada, CANSIM, table 051-0004. Data on the approximate number of people who designated a given province as their province of landing (but may not actually have landed there) derived using the actual number who did land (CANSIM, table 051-0004) and the approximate proportion of immigrants who designated the province as their province of landing but chose to settle elsewhere. This proportion was obtained from Citizenship and Immigration's longitudinal immigration database (IMDB), which tracks the mobility of immigrants from their time of entry into Canada through tax filing data (Statistics Canada, CANSIM, table 054-0003).

14   The calculation is performed as follows: A= B*(1/1-C), where A is the number of immigrants who designated Prince Edward Island as their province of landing, B is the number of immigrants who actually landed in the province (11,400), and C is the proportion of individuals who designated the province as their province of landing but did not land there (40%).

15   Data on retention rates from Statistics Canada, CANSIM, table 054-0003.

16   Statistics Canada, CANSIM, table 051-0004.

BIBLIOGRAPHY

"Absorptive Capacity." Metropolis Conversation Series, November
1999. www.canada.metropolis.net/research-policy/conversation/
conversation_1.html.

Advisory Panel on Healthcare Innovation. *Unleashing Innovation: Excellent
Healthcare for Canada*. Ottawa: Health Canada, 2015.

Allum, Jeff and Okahana, Hironao. *Graduate Enrollment and Degrees: 2004
to 2014*. Washington, DC: Council of Graduate Schools, 2015.

"Alward Says He Wants to Do It Like Saskatchewan." Acadia Broadcasting,
September 18, 2014. www.country94.ca/news/1162155611/
alward-says-he-wants-do-it-saskatchewan.

American Bar Association. *A Current Glance at Women in the Law*. Chicago:
American Bar Association, 2014.

"And the Greatest Canadian of All Time Is...." CBC Digital Archives.
November 29, 2004. www.cbc.ca/archives/categories/arts-
entertainment/media/media-general/and-the-greatest-canadian-of-
all-times-is.html.

"A Post-War Programme for the U.S." *International Labour Review*, 47
(1943): 450–65.

Archambault, Héloïse. "Le revenu des médecins de famille
bondit de 12% en un an." *Journal de Montréal*, September
27, 2014. www.journaldemontreal.com/2014/09/27/
le-revenu-des-medecins-de-famille-bondit-de-12-en-un-an.

Association of American Medical Colleges. *The State of Women in
Academic Medicine: The Pipeline and Pathways to Leadership*, 2014.
www.members.aamc.org/eweb/upload/The%20State%20Of%20
Women%20in%20Academic%20Medicine%202013-2014%20final.
pdf.

Bank of Canada."Commodity Price Index–Annual." www.bankofcanada.
ca/rates/price-indexes/bcpi/commodity-price-index-annual/.

"Bankrupt Canada?" *Wall Street Journal*, January 12, 2015.

Barer, M. L., R. G. Evans, and R. Labelle. *The Frozen North: Controlling*

Physicians Costs through Controlling Fees—The Canadian Experience. U. S. Office of Technology Assessment, 1985.

Benedictow, Ole J. "The Black Death: The Greatest Catastrophe Ever." *History Today* 55, no. 3 (March 2005). www.historytoday.com/ ole-j-benedictow/black-death-greatest-catastrophe-ever.

BMO Wealth Institute. "Where Do Canadians Plan to Retire, and Why?" BMO Financial Group. August 2013. www.bmo.com/pdf/mf/ prospectus/en/BMO_Retirement_Institute%20Report_En.pdf.

Boesveld, Sarah. "Canada's Latest Baby Boom Caught Experts by Surprise—In Part Because Our Birth Rate Is Declining," *National Post*, January 4, 2014. www.news.nationalpost.com/news/canada/ canadas-latest-baby-boom-caught-experts-by-surprise-in-part-because-our-birth-rate-is-declining.

Bourgeois, Yves and Samuel LeBlanc. *Innovation in Atlantic Canada.* Moncton: Canadian Institute for Research on Regional Development, 2002.

Brooke, Jeffrey. *Dismantling Canada: Stephen Harper's New Conservative Agenda.* Montreal: McGill-Queen's University Press, 2015.

Brown, Jennifer. "McLachlin Challenges Profession to Question Status Quo on Women in Law and Business." www.canadianlawyermag.com/ legalfeeds/2026/mclachlin-challenges-profession-to-question-status-quo-on-women-in-law-and-business.html.

Brown, Mark and Ryan Macdonald. "Provincial Convergence and Divergence in Canada, 1926 to 2011." Statistics Canada: Economic Analysis (EA) Research Paper Series, February 2015.

Canada Employment Insurance Commission. *2013/14 EI Monitoring and Assessment Report.* www.esdc.gc.ca/en/reports/ei/monitoring2014/ index.page.

Canadian Bar Association v. HMTQ et al., [2006] BCSC 1342.

Canadian Health Services Research Foundation (CHSRF). "Myth: Canadian Doctors Are Leaving for the United States in Droves." March 2008. www.cfhi-fcass.ca/sf-docs/default-source/mythbusters/ Myth_Drs_are_leaving_for_the_US_EN_FINAL.pdf?sfvrsn=0.

Canadian Institute for Health Information (CIHI). *Canada's Health Care Providers: Provincial Profiles 2012* and *Provincial Profiles 2013.* secure. cihi.ca/estore/productSeries.htm?locale=fr&pc=PCC314.

———. *National Health Expenditure Trends, 1975 to 2014* and *1975 to 2015.* secure.cihi.ca/estore/productSeries.htm?locale=en&pc=PCC52.

———. *National Physician Database, 2011-12* and *2012-13.* secure.cihi.ca/ estore/productSeries.htm?pc=PCC476.

———. *National Grouping System Categories Report, Canada, 2002-03.* secure.cihi.ca/estore/productSeries.htm?locale=en&pc=PCC38.

———. *Reciprocal Billing Report, Canada, 2002-03.* secure.cihi.ca/estore/ productSeries.htm?pc=PCC39.

————. *Supply, Distribution and Migration of Canadian Physicians*, 2003 and 2013. secure.cihi.ca/estore/productSeries.htm?pc=PCC34.

Cape Breton (Regional Municipality) v. Nova Scotia (Attorney General), [2008] NSSC 111.

Capeluck, Evan. "Convergence Across Provincial Economies in Canada: Trends, Drivers, and Implications." Ottawa: Centre for the Study of Living Standards, 2014.

"Cashing In: Behind Ottawa's Tense Showdown with PEI Over its Immigrant Partner Program," and "Cashing In: Inside PEI's Controversial Immigrant Partner Program," *Huffington Post*, September 5, 2012. Part of series of reports available at immigrate. kingsjournalism.com.

Centre for Population, Aging and Health, Western University. "Quebec's Family Policies Benefit Childbearing and Work." Policy brief no. 12. August 2013. sociology.uwo.ca/cluster/en/publications/docs/ policy_briefs/PolicyBrief12.pdf.

Chaoulli v. Quebec (Attorney General), [2005]. 1 S.C.R. 791, 2005 SCC 35. scc-csc.lexum.com/decisia-scc-csc/scc-csc/scc-csc/en/ item/2237/index.do.

Choi, Jennifer. "Moncton Sets New Targets for Attracting Immigrants." *CBC News New Brunswick*, November 9, 2015. www.cbc.ca/news/ canada/new-brunswick/immigration-moncton-economy-1.3308329.

Citizenship and Immigration Canada. *Evaluation of the Provincial Nominee Program*. September 2011. www.cic.gc.ca/english/pdf/research-stats/ evaluation-pnp2011.pdf.

Commission on the Future of Health Care in Canada. *Building on Values: The Future of Health Care in Canada—Final Report*, 2002. publications.gc.ca/collections/Collection/CP32-85-2002E.pdf.

Commonwealth Fund. *Mirror, Mirror on the Wall: How the Performance of the U.S. Health Care System Compares Internationally*. June 2014. www.commonwealthfund.org/publications/fund-reports/2014/jun/ mirror-mirror.

Conference Board of Canada. *How Canada Performs*. www. conferenceboard.ca/hcp/provincial/education.aspx.

Constitution Act, 1982. www.laws-lois.justice.gc.ca/eng/const/.

Costa, Dora L. "From Mill Town to Board Room: The Rise of Women's Paid Labor." *Journal of Economic Perspectives* 14, no. 4 (Autumn 2000): 101–22.

Coulombe, Serge. *Economic Growth and Provincial Disparity: A New View of an Old Canadian Problem*. Commentary 122. Toronto: C. D. Howe Institute, March 1999.

———— and Jean-François Tremblay. "Human Capital and Regional Convergence in Canada." *Journal of Economic Studies* 28, no. 3 (2001): 154–80.

Cutler, David M. and Dan P. Ly. "The (Paper)Work of Medicine: Understanding International Medical Costs." *Journal of Economic Perspectives* 25, no. 2 (Spring 2011).

Day, Kathleen and Stanley L. Winer. *Interregional Migration and Public Policy in Canada*. Montreal and Kingston: McGill-Queen's University Press, 2012.

Dominion Bureau of Statistics. *Canada Year Book*, 1956, 1969, 1970-1971, and 1973 editions. Ottawa: 1957, 1969, 1971, and 1973.

Duckett, Stephen and Adrian Peetoom. *Canadian Medicare: We Need It and We Can Keep It*. Montreal: McGill-Queen's University Press, 2013.

Duclos, Édith, Pierre Lefebvre, and Philip Merrigan. "A 'Natural Experiment' on the Economics of Storks: Evidence on the Impact of Differential Family Policy on Fertility Rates in Canada." Working Paper no. 136, Center for Research on Economic Fluctuation and Employment. Montreal: Université du Québec à Montréal, May 2001.

Dupré, Stefan. "Reflections on the Fiscal and Economic Aspects of Government by Conference." *Canadian Public Administration*, no. 23 (Spring 1980): 55.

Environics Institute. *Focus Canada 2012*. www.environicsinstitute.org/ uploads/institute-projects/environics%20institute%20-%20focus%20 canada%202012%20final%20report.pdf.

Erten, Bilge and José Antonio Ocampo. "Super-Cycles of Commodity Prices Since the Mid-Nineteenth Century." DESA Working Paper No. 110. United Nations Department of Economic and Social Affairs, February 2012.

Expert Panel on Business Innovation. *Innovation and Business Strategy: Why Canada Falls Short*. Ottawa: Council of Canadian Academies, June 2009.

Expert Panel on the State of Industrial R&D in Canada. *The State of Industrial R&D in Canada*. Ottawa: Council of Canadian Academies, 2013.

Federal Reserve Board. "Testimony of Chairman Alan Greenspan before the Committee on Financial Services, U.S. House of Representatives, July 20, 2005." Washington, Federal Reserve Board. www. federalreserve.gov/boarddocs/hh/2005/july/testimony.htm.

Feehan, Jim. "Canada's Equalization Formula: Peering Inside the Black Box…and Beyond." SPP Research Papers, University of Calgary School of Public Policy, 7, no. 24, September 2014.

Ferguson, Niall. *Kissinger, 1923-1968: The Idealist*. Vol. 1. New York: Penguin Press, 2015.

Finance Canada. "Federal Support to Provinces and Territories," 2015. www.fin.gc.ca/fedprov/mtp-eng.asp.

———. *Fiscal Reference Tables*, 2000, 2014, and 2015. www.fin.gc.ca/pub/ frt-trf/index-eng.asp.

————. "Your Tax Dollar." www.fin.gc.ca/tax-impot/2014/2013-14-e.pdf.

Finances Québec. *Comptes publics 2013-2014.* Vols. 1–2. Québec, November 2014.

Finnie, R., R. Mueller, A. Sweetman, and A. Usher (eds.). *Who Goes? Who Stays? What Matters? Accessing and Persisting in Post-secondary Education in Canada.* Kingston: Queen's University School of Policy Studies Series, 2008.

Foot, David with Daniel Stoffman. *Boom, Bust & Echo: How to Profit from the Coming Demographic Shift.* Toronto: Macfarlane Walter & Ross, 1996.

Fourastié, Jean. *Les Trente Glorieuses ou La révolution invisible de 1946 à 1975.* Paris: Fayard, 1979.

Friedman, Thomas. *The Lexus and the Olive Tree.* New York, NY: Farrar, Straus and Giroux, 2000.

Gauvreau, Danielle, Diane Gervais, and Peter Gossage. *La fécondité des Québécoises 1870–1970 : d'une exception à l'autre.* Montréal: Boréal, 2007.

Goffman, Irving J. *Some Fiscal Aspects of Public Welfare in Canada.* Toronto: Canadian Tax Foundation, 1965.

Government of Canada. *Report of the Royal Commission on Dominion-Provincial Relations.* Vols. 1–2, *Canada: 1867–1939.* Ottawa, 1940.

Grant, Hugh M. and Jeremiah Hurley. "Unhealthy Pressure: How Physician Pay Demands Put the Squeeze on Provincial Health Care Budgets." University of Calgary School of Public Policy Research Papers. Vol. 6, no. 2, July 2014.

Grant Thornton. *Prince Edward Island Provincial Nominee Program Evaluation Results.* Report commissioned by the Government of Prince Edward Island, December 31, 2012.

Grauer, A. E. *Public Assistance and Social Insurance: A Study Performed for the Royal Commission on Dominion-Provincial Relations.* Ottawa: J. O. Patenaude, Printer to the King, 1939.

Guest, Dennis. *The Emergence of Social Security in Canada.* 1st ed. Vancouver: University of British Columbia Press, 1980.

Guillemette, Yvan. "School Class Size: Smaller Isn't Better." *Commentary* 215, C. D. Howe Institute, August 2005.

———— and William B. P. Robson. "No Elixir of Youth: Immigration Cannot Keep Canada Young." *C. D. Howe Institute Backgrounder* 96, September 2006.

Guly, Christopher. "Apprenticeship to Academe: The History of Law Schools in Canada." *Lawyers Weekly*, 24 September 2010. lawyersweekly.ca/index.php?section=article&articleid=1255.

Gusen, Peter. "Expenditure Need: Equalization's Other Half." Mowat Centre for Policy Innovation, University of Toronto School of Public Policy and Governance, February 2012.

Health Canada. "Changing Fertility Patterns: Trends and Implications." *Health Policy Research Bulletin 10*, May 2005.

———. "Federal Commissions on Health Care." 2009. www.hc-sc.gc.ca/ hcs-sss/com/fed/index-eng.php.

Henripin, Jacques. *Tendances et facteurs de la fécondité au Canada*. Ottawa: Bureau fédéral de la statistique, 1968.

Hogg, Peter. *Constitutional Law of Canada*. Student ed. Toronto: Carswell, 2000.

Iglehart, John K. "Revisiting the Canadian Health Care System." *New England Journal of Medicine* 342 (June 29, 2000): 2007–2012.

Institut de la statistique du Québec. *Le bilan démographique du Québec, Édition 2013*. Québec, 2013.

Inwood, K. and Jim Irwin. "Land, Income and Regional Inequality: New Estimates of Provincial Incomes and Growth in Canada, 1871–1891." *Acadiensis* 31, no. 2, (Spring 2002): 157–84.

Jeffery, Charlie and David Heald. "Money Matters: Territorial Finance in Decentralized States." Special issue of *Regional and Federal Studies* 13, no. 4 (2003).

Katz, Stephen J., Cathy Charles, Jonathan Lomas, and H. Gilbert Welch. "Physician Relations in Canada: Shooting Inward as the Circle Closes." *Journal of Health Politics Policy and Law* 22, no. 6 (December 1997): 1413–31.

Kenway, L. "PST, GST, HST Rates by Province: Current and Historical Sales Tax Rates." www.bookkeeping-essentials.com/GST-HST-rate.html.

Keynes, John Maynard. *A Tract on Monetary Reform*. London: MacMillan and Co., 1924.

King, William Lyon Mackenzie. *Industry and Humanity*. Toronto: Thomas Allen, 1918.

Lachapelle, Réjean and Jacques Henripin. *The Demolinguistic Situation in Canada: Past Trends and Future Prospects*. Montréal: l'Institut de recherches politiques, 1980.

Lee, Marc. "Eroding Tax Fairness: Tax Incidence in Canada, 1990 to 2005." Toronto: Canadian Centre for Policy Alternatives, November 2007.

Library of Parliament. *Canada's Aging Population and Public Policy*. Ottawa, 2012. www.lop.parl.gc.ca/content/lop/ResearchPublications/2011-63-e.htm.

MacGregor Dawson, R. *William Lyon Mackenzie King*. Vol. 1. Toronto: University of Toronto Press, 1959.

MacMillan, Margaret. *History's People: Personalities and the Past*. Toronto: Anansi, 2015.

Madore, Odette. "The *Canada Health Act*: Overview and Options." Library of Parliament, *Current Issue Review*, no. 94-4E.

Maestas, Nicole, Kathleen J. Mullen, and David Powell. "The Effect of Population Aging on Economic Growth." Santa Monica: RAND Corporation Working Paper 1063, October 2014. www.rand.org/pubs/working_papers/WR1063.html.

Manitoba Keewatino Okimakanak v. Manitoba Hydro-Electric Board, [1992] Suit No. AI 92-30-00687.

Milligan, K. "Subsidizing the Stork: New Evidence on Tax Incentives and Fertility." National Bureau of Economic Research, Working Paper 8845, March 2002.

Milne, David. *Tug of War: Ottawa and the Provinces under Trudeau and Mulroney.* Toronto: James Lorimer, 1986.

Morgan, Steve. "The Incoming Rise of Prescription Drug Spending." *Huffington Post,* December 17, 2013. www.huffingtonpost.ca/steve-morgan/rise-of-prescription-drug-spending_b_4467272.html.

National Council of Welfare. "Statistical Tables," 2012. liveweb.archive.org/web/20120923172528 / www.ncw.gc.ca/l.3bd.2t.1ilshtml@-eng.jsp?lid=331&fid=32.

National Energy Board. "Canadian Energy Overview 2014—Energy Briefing Note." July 2015. www.neb-one.gc.ca/nrg/ntgrtd/mrkt/vrvw/2014/index-eng.html.

———. "Market Snapshot: Oil Sands Production Likely to Continue Growing in the Short Term." March 26, 2015. www.neb-one.gc.ca/nrg/ntgrtd/mrkt/snpsht/2015/03-04lsndprdctnl-eng.html.

New Brunswick Department of Education and Early Childhood Development. *Annual Report, 2001–02* and *2010–11.*

Nova Scotia Department of Finance and Treasury Board. *Public Accounts 2014.* Vol. 1. www.novascotia.ca/finance/site-finance/media/finance/PublicAccounts2014/2014_Vol1.pdf.

———. *Public Accounts 2004.* Vol. 1. www.novascotia.ca/finance/publish/paccts/04vol1.pdf.

Office of the Parliamentary Budget Officer. *Fiscal Sustainability Report.* February 28, 2010. www.parl.gc.ca/pbo-dpb/documents/FSR_2010.pdf.

Okonny-Myers, Ima. "The Interprovincial Mobility of Immigrants in Canada." Citizenship and Immigration Canada Research and Evaluation, June 2010.

"OPEC Expects Oil Prices to Be about $76 a Barrel in 2025—WSJ." Reuters, May 11, 2015. in.reuters.com/article/2015/05/11/oil-opec.

Organisation for Economic Co-operation and Development. *Society at a Glance 2001.* OECD Social Indicators. Paris: OECD Publishing, 2001.

———. *Harmful Tax Competition: An Emerging Issue.* Paris: OECD, 1998.

———. "Labour Productivity Levels in the Total Economy." 2013. stats.oecd.org/Index.aspx?DataSetCode=LEVEL.

————. *National Accounts at a Glance 2013*. Paris: OECD, 2013. dx.doi. org/10.1787/na_glance-2013-en.

————. "Health Expenditure and Financing." stats.oecd.org/index. aspx?DataSetCode=SHA.

————. "OECD Revenue Statistics: Comparative Tables." stats.oecd.org/ Index.aspx?DataSetCode=REV.

Organization of the Petroleum Exporting Countries (OPEC). *2015 World Oil Outlook*. Vienna: OPEC Secretariat, 2015.

Palda, Kristian. *Innovation Policy and Canada's Competitiveness*. Vancouver: The Fraser Institute, 1993.

Picard, André. "Who's Fighting for Private Health Insurance in Canada?" *Globe and Mail*, September 25, 2012.

"Planet of the Phones." *The Economist*, February 28, 2015. www.economist. com/news/leaders/21645180-smartphone-ubiquitous-addictive-and-transformative-planet-phones.

Poitras, Jacques. "Tories Challenge Liberals on Natural Resource Development." CBC *News New Brunswick*, August 14, 2004. www.cbc.ca/news/canada/new-brunswick/tories-challenge-liberals-on-natural-resource-development-1.2736181.

RBC Economics. *Provincial Outlook*. March 2016. www.rbc.com/economics/economic-reports/provincial-economic-forecasts.html.

Receiver General for Canada. *Consolidated Financial Statements of the Government of Canada and Report of the Auditor General of Canada 2014–2015*. www.tpsgc-pwgsc.gc.ca/recgen/cpc-pac/2015/pdf/v1s02-eng.pdf.

————. *Public Accounts of Canada 2014*. Vol. 2, section 15. www.tpsgc-pwgsc.gc.ca/recgen/cpc-pac/index-eng.html.

Revenu Québec. "Tables of GST and QST Rates." www.revenuquebec.ca/fr/entreprises/taxes/tpstvhtvq/reglesdebase/historiquetauxtpstvq. aspx.

Robson, William B. P. "Time and Money: The Challenge of Demographic Change and Government Finances in Canada." *C. D. Howe Institute Backgrounder* no. 109, December 2007.

Rubin, Jeff. *The Carbon Bubble: What Happens to Us When It Bursts*. Toronto: Knopf Random Vintage Canada, 2015.

————. *The End of Growth*. Toronto: Random House Canada, 2012.

Rumsfeld, Donald. "Author's Note," *Known and Unknown: A Memoir*. New York: Penguin Group, 2011: xiii–xvi. papers.rumsfeld.com/about/page/authors-note.

Saillant, Richard. *Over the Cliff? Acting Now to Avoid New Brunswick's Bankruptcy*. Moncton: Canadian Institute for Research on Public Policy and Public Administration, 2014.

───── and David Campbell (eds.). *Shale Gas in New Brunswick: Towards a Better Understanding*. Moncton: Canadian Institute for Research on Public Policy and Public Administration, 2014.

Saunders, S. A. *The Economic History of the Maritime Provinces*. Fredericton: Acadiensis Press, 1984.

Savoie, Donald J. *Visiting Grandchildren: Economic Development in the Maritimes*. Toronto: University of Toronto Press, 2006.

Service Canada. "Canada Pension Plan and Old Age Security—Monthly Statistical Bulletins—July 2015." www.servicecanada.gc.ca/eng/ services/pensions/statistics/bulletins/07-15.shtml#t3.

"Sheikhs v. Shale: The New Economics of Oil." *The Economist*, December 6, 2014. www.economist.com/news/leaders/21635472-economics-oil-have-changed-some-businesses-will-go-bust-market-will-be.

Simpson, Jeffrey. *Chronic Condition: Why Canada's Health Care System Needs to Be Dragged into the 21st Century*. Toronto: Penguin, 2012.

Sleebos, Joëlle E. *Low Fertility Rates in OECD Countries: Facts and Policy Responses*. Paris: OECD, 2003.

Smiley, Donald V. "The Rowell-Sirois Report, Provincial Autonomy, and Post-War Canadian Federalism." *The Canadian Journal of Economics and Political Science* 28, no. 1 (February 1962): 54–69.

"Some Doctors Overbilling Medicare without Penalty." CBC *News New Brunswick*, December 4, 2012. www.cbc.ca/news/canada/new-brunswick/ some-doctors-overbilling-medicare-without-penalty-1.1159570.

Statistics Canada. Canadian Socio-Economic Information Management System (CANSIM), various tables.

───── . "Education Indicators in Canada: Report of the Pan-Canadian Education Indicators Program." December 2012. www.statcan.gc.ca/ pub/81-582-x/2015003/tbl-eng.htm.

───── . "Estimated Population of Canada, 1605 to Present." www.statcan. gc.ca/pub/98-187-x/4151287-eng.htm.

───── . "Full-time Equivalent Enrolments in Public Elementary and Secondary Schools, Canada, Provinces and Territories, 2001/2002 to 2010/2011." www.statcan.gc.ca/pub/81-582-x/2013001/tbl/tblc2.1-eng.htm.

───── . "Generations in Canada." www12.statcan.gc.ca/census-recensement/2011/as-sa/98-311-x/98-311-x2011003_2-eng.cfm.

───── . *Labour Force Survey Estimates (LFS), Retirement Age by Class of Worker and Sex*, 2013. data.gc.ca/data/en/dataset/ f8a67b0a-28fb-4796-8e4e-89045f019e36.

───── . "Median Age Canada, 1901–2011." www12.statcan.ca/English/ census01/products/analytic/companion/age/cdamedaget.cfm.

———. Number and Salary of Full-Time University Teaching Staff, by Academic Rank and Sex, Canada and Provinces, 2000/2001 and 2010/2011." www.statcan.gc.ca/pub/81-582-x/2012002/tbl/tbld3.4-eng.htm.

———. "Population, Urban and Rural, by Province and Territory," 2011. www.statcan.gc.ca/tables-tableaux/sum-som/l01/cst01/demo62a-eng.htm.

———. "Provincial and Territorial Economic Accounts: Data Tables," catalogue 13-018-X. www5.statcan.gc.ca/olc-cel/olc.action?objId=13-018-X&objType=2&lang=en&limit=0.

———. Report on the Demographic Situation in Canada 2002. Ottawa: 2003.

———. "Student-Educator Ratio in Public Elementary and Secondary Schools, Canada, Provinces and Territories, 2001/2002 to 2010/2011." www.statcan.gc.ca/pub/81-582-x/2013001/tbl/tblc2.3-eng.htm.

Service Canada. "Canada Pension Plan and Old Age Security—Monthly Statistical Bulletins—July 2015." www.servicecanada.gc.ca/eng/services/pensions/statistics/bulletins/07-15.shtml#t3.

Tankou Kamela, Valery Martial. Que faire avec Alcool N.-B.? Moncton: Donald J. Savoie Institute, 2016.

Tanzi, Vito and Ludger Schuknecht. Public Spending in the 20th Century: A Global Perspective. Cambridge: Cambridge University Press, 2000.

TD Economics. "From a Longer-Term Growth Perspective, West Is Still the Best." Special Report, April 10, 2015. https://www.td.com/document/PDF/economics/special/LongtermGrowthPerspective.pdf.

"The Economy: We're All Keynesians Now." Time, December 31, 1965. http://content.time.com/time/magazine/article/0,9171,842353,00.html.

Troeger, Vera. "Tax Competition and the Myth of the 'Race to the Bottom': Why Governments Still Tax Capital." CAGE-Chatham House Series, no. 4, February 2013. www2.warwick.ac.uk/fac/soc/economics/research/centres/cage/onlinepublications/briefing/0213bp_troeger1.pdf.

U.S. Department of the Treasury. "Historical Debt Outstanding: Annual 2002–2015." www.treasurydirect.gov/govt/reports/pd/histdebt/histdebt_histo5.htm.

U.S. Social Security Administration. "Social Security History: Otto von Bismarck." www.ssa.gov/history/ottob.html.

Verma, Ravi B. P., Shirley Loh, S. Y. Dai, and David Ford. "Fertility
    Projections for Canada, Provinces and Territories, 1993–2016."
    Statistics Canada Research Paper, catalogue no. 91F0015MIE—No.
    001, June 1996.
Webster, Jamie. "Going Global: Tight Oil Production." July 2014. http://
    www.eia.gov/conference/2014/pdf/presentations/webster.pdf.
"Women Outnumber Men at Most Medical Schools." *Maclean's*, September
    16, 2010. www2.macleans.ca/2010/09/16/how-many-get-in.

INDEX